Contextualising Caste

A selection of previous *Sociological Review* Monographs

Life and Work History Analyses[†]
ed. Shirley Dex

The Sociology of Monsters[†]
ed. John Law

Sport, Leisure and Social Relations[†]
eds John Horne, David Jary and Alan Tomlinson

Gender and Bureaucracy[*]
eds Mike Savage and Anne Witz

The Sociology of Death: theory, culture, practice[*]
ed. David Clark

[†] Available from The Sociological Review Office, Keele University, Keele, Staffs ST5 5BG.
[*] Available from Marston Book Services, PO Box 87, Osney Mead, Oxford, OX2 0DT.

Contextualising Caste:
Post-Dumontian Approaches

Edited by Mary Searle-Chatterjee and Ursula Sharma

Blackwell Publishers/The Sociological Review

British Library Cataloguing in Publication Data

A CIP catalogue record for this book is available from the British Library

Library of Congress Cataloging-in-Publication Data

Contextualising caste: post-Dumontian approaches / edited by Mary
Searle-Chatterjee and Ursula Sharma.
    p.   cm.—(The Sociological review monograph series; 41)
1. Caste—India.   2. India—Social conditions.   3. India—Politics
and government.   4. Philosophy, Indic.   5. Dumont, Louis, 1911–
        I. Series: Sociological review monograph; 41.
    HT720.C66   1995   305.5'122'0954—dc20   94–31459

ISBN 0–631–19283–2

Printed in Great Britain by T.J. Press (Padstow) Ltd., Padstow, Cornwall.
This book is printed on acid-free paper.

Contents

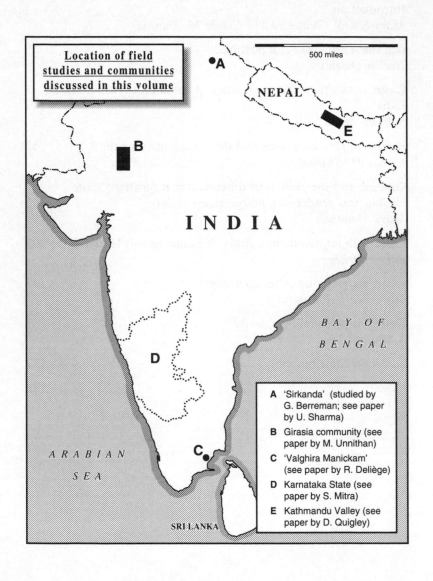

Location of field
studies and communities
discussed in this volume

500 miles

●A

NEPAL

E

B

INDIA

BAY OF
BENGAL

D

ARABIAN
SEA

C●

SRI LANKA

A 'Sirkanda' (studied by
  G. Berreman; see paper
  by U. Sharma)
B Girasia community (see
  paper by M. Unnithan)
C 'Valghira Manickam'
  (see paper by R. Deliège)
D Karnataka State (see
  paper by S. Mitra)
E Kathmandu Valley (see
  paper by D. Quigley)

Introduction

Mary Searle-Chatterjee and Ursula Sharma

The intention which motivated this collection was a desire to 'put caste in its place'. Western anthropological discourse about India has been dominated by discussions of caste, indeed anthropologists have 'epitomised' Indian society in terms of caste (Burghart, 1990:264). We can, with Béteille, see this as a privileging of the 'ritual' aspects of Indian society which follows from the recent stress on 'difference' and contrast in anthropology (Béteille, 1991:33).

By 'putting caste in its place' we do not mean denying its importance but rather trying to identify its importance relative to other aspects of social life which might also be considered axial to South Asian society, and subjecting the fascination it has had for western anthropologists to critical scrutiny.

Most of the chapters in this book are by social anthropologists. One chapter (by Subrata Mitra) is by a political scientist; we have been struck by the fact that some of the best commentaries on social processes in South Asia have come from political scientists. Another chapter (by A. Shukra) is in the nature of a personal testament. While not focusing on the experiential aspects of caste in this volume, we wished to remind readers (and ourselves) that a critical stance towards the 'epitomising' tradition does not deny the centrality of caste as lived experience for many people, especially those whose experience of caste is oppressive.

A subsidiary motive to this book is a hope that thereby the study of India may be recovered for the general sociologist. Many of the classical sociologists wrote about India. Most western sociological discourse about India has situated itself within the 'sociology of development' which has relatively few concerns in common with the anthropological literature referred to above.

In any case, sociology in Britain today is unashamedly 'western-centric' in its interests and has largely retreated from any broadly comparative project. This has been left to the anthropologists who themselves are less unanimous than before as to how and why one should compare and (as Sharma argues in this volume) in the case of 'Indianists' have tended to resist the project of comparison althogether.[1]

So much for the title of the collection. But what about the sub-title? The volume was not originally intended as a critique of Dumont's work. After all, many have been written already. But reading through the contributions, we were struck by their explicit or implicit reference to Dumont's theory about caste in Indian society. What can account for the enduring capacity of his agenda to dominate discussions of Indian society? No doubt Appadurai is correct in suggesting that the idea of Indian society as dominated by caste hierarchy fulfils the need for a single and powerful organising image which enables people in the west to think about a particular non-western society, an image which

> capture(s) internal realities in terms that serve the discursive
> needs of general theory in the metropolis. (Appadurai,
> 1992:45).

Certainly Dumont's ideas have exercised less hegemony among social scientists in India itself.

What western anthropologists have found attractive, or at any rate impossible to ignore, is Dumont's insistence that academics exorcise themselves of their own ethnocentric intellectual cate-gories in order to do justice to the ways of thinking of another civilisation. Caste, he argued, has tended to be seen through the filter of the individualistic mode of thought dominant in the west, in terms of which it becomes either unintelligible or pathological. To understand caste we have to

> leave the shelter of (our) own values that we may eventually
> arrive at an anthropological appreciation of those very values.
> (Dumont, 1972:36).

This provocative challenge accorded well with the mood of a generation who made the overland trek to the subcontinent in a similar search for something other than what they knew, and it continued to be taken seriously by anthropologists in a discipline dominated by ever more relativistic definitions of their project.

But perhaps we have learnt our lessons in the school of Indology and are ready to graduate and move on? The papers in this volume, though only representing a selection of the directions which a post-Dumontian sociology of South Asia might take, all suggest that while it is hard to write about caste without referring to Dumont, his theoretical assumption that hierarchy is indeed central to an understanding of the nature of South Asian society needs to be questioned.[2]

Dumont as a point of departure; a model of Indian society

Where most of the contributors to this volume agree with Dumont however is in the need for a *theoretical* understanding of the role of caste in South Asian society, such as will not be obtained by simply accumulating further ethnographic or historical material (see especially Quigley's chapter).

At the risk of repeating what several contributors have said in their individual summaries of Dumont's position, let us reiterate the main characteristics of his theory. In *Homo Hierarchicus* (of which an English language edition was first published in 1970) Dumont argued for a structural understanding of Hindu society, based on a serious consideration of indigenous ideology (using the term in a non-Marxist sense) with the opposition of the pure and the impure underlying the hierarchical organisation of castes. 'Hierarchy' here means much more than simply inequality or superordination but 'the superiority of the pure to the impure' which demands that the pure and the impure be kept apart. It is a hierarchy of value, in which the 'part' (eg the individual group or person) can only be seen in relation to the encompassing whole, the entire structure. What distinguishes Hindu caste from other structures which superficially resemble it is the subordination of power to status. The secular power of the king is subordinate in ideological terms to the ritual purity of the Brahman.

Dumont claimed that he was using Lévi-Straussian structuralist approaches to uncover the system of oppositions which gave meaning to the social order (Dumont, 1972:77–80). However whereas Lévi-Strauss used his method mainly only to illuminate texts, rituals or sequences of action, Dumont attempted to apply it to all, or at any rate to the central, aspects of a whole civilisation. He insisted that castes, or *jatis* (a term widely used in South Asia to refer to an identifiable caste group of any order of segmentation[3]) were to be seen not as isolated fixed or bounded entities, for that would be to fall into a European atomistic form of thinking, converting processes into things with essences. This insight was a valuable one in that it drew attention to the futility of agonising about the difference between a 'caste' and a 'sub-caste', or, in cases of status ambiguity, whether a particular group 'really' belonged to this or that caste. He then however proceeded to turn Hindu society itself into something with an essential nature. Dynamic processes were said to animate the whole, but they were self-generating and continuous over time, relatively insulated from outside forces. Dumont himself acknowledged the influence of Talcott Parsons and his functionalist model of society (Dumont, 1972:54). Indeed Dumont was later to make the extraordinarily revealing observation that Leibniz's conception of monads is a model which fits our needs for a metaphor for a culture or society (Dumont, 1986:210). The very aspect of Leibniz's model that has troubled later philosophers, the fact that no two monads can ever have any causal relationship to each other (Russell, 1961:565) did not trouble Dumont. Indeed he praised Leibniz for substituting difference for a supposed continuity (Dumont, 1986:215).

> Each culture (or society) expresses the universal in its own way, as does each of Leibniz's monads; and it is not impossible to conceive of a procedure – complicated and laborious it is true – which would enable one to pass from one monad or culture through the intermediary of the universal taken as a sum integral of all known cultures, the monad of all monads, present on everyone's horizon. (Dumont, 1986:210).

Ironically enough, in British social science holistic community studies of this kind were about to disappear, being replaced by a more historical sociology. But the appeal of Dumont's proposal that we focus on indigenous ideologies in order to develop a reflexive understanding of our own ways of thinking seems to have blinded western anthropologists to the fact that Dumont was also suggesting that there are only two basic ways of thinking, the holistic and the individualistic, the traditional and the modern (1972:44,36;1986:215–6).

From a novel starting point therefore Dumont came to a familiar conclusion; India represented a premodern mode of thinking and social organisation. This recalled the dichotomous ideal types, representations of 'self' and 'others' found in many societies. Nobuhiro Nagashima aptly described this tendency on his paper 'A reversed world – or is it?'

> At no time in Japanese history has there existed any mono-
> lithic totality of culture. Most Japanese however appear to
> believe that the western way of thinking is radically different
> from their own . . . an example of the tendency among various
> peoples to regard other cultures as a reversed world
> (Nagashima, 1973:92).

Nagashima lists the qualities which the Japanese generally attributed to themselves, and contrasts these with the obverse characteristics which they attribute to the West, noting however that the latter are equally applied to the Chinese. In a much better known work published in the same year, Said was to point out the self-serving nature of such dichotomous representations in Europe. The fact that Dumont wrote sympathetically about the 'reversed values' found in India does not make this aspect of his work less suspect. Said pointed out that despite its apparent contrast with other European attitudes to the Orient, romanticism shared the same assumption of different human essences and irresolvable contrasts (Said, 1978). In this sense it was what Inden called the 'loyal opposition' (Inden, 1986:401–46). Dumont's work then may function (quite contrary to his intentions) to legitimate the idea that the West represents a fundamentally different kind of society and hence its economic superiority and political 'modernity' do not require any special explanation. His thought is however but one example of the widespread human tendency to binary thinking in which the complexity of the historical processes is simplified through the construction of systems of oppositions. Dumont, then, rather than elucidating oppositions central to Indian culture, has revived the myth that there are but two basic kinds of human beings and two kinds of society. It may be for this reason that he has never had much appeal to social scientists in the subcontinent who have been generally more concerned with issues of social transformation.

Like most travellers, both Indian and Euro-American, Dumont confuses two separate ideas; distinctiveness (which is a logical concept) and typicality (which is a statistical or empirical concept). He regarded what was saliently different about Indian society from a western point of view (caste, purity and pollution concepts, etc) as equivalent to what was typical of or central to it. In much the same way, the 'typical' dishes of a region turn out often to be simply those that are saliently different from those of other regions rather than those which are eaten most often or which are central to the local diet. Debates among both Europeans and Indian logicians about the nature of classification have recognised that the attempt to characterise the nature or essence of any entity is affected both by the standpoint and the purpose of the classifier.[4] From the western point of view, caste is certainly distinctive, at least if we take seriously Dumont's strictures that we pay particular attention to the indigenous ideology of purity and pollution. But how could we be sure that it is 'typical' of Indian society in the sense of central to it? The problems are greater if we attempt to characterise the entire society rather than a particular region or institution.

Caste and the denial of agency

Dumont encouraged us to think of caste in terms of ideology rather than in terms of empirically observable groups of people having some kind of essential identity. Of course castes, if they are anything at all, must be groups of people, but the principles on which they constitute themselves should be the focus of our concern. If we concentrate on the groups rather than the principles we are liable to get distracted by the very questions which dominate local political conflicts. Are the Girasias (or the Kolis, or any of the various minor landowning castes which claim the status) 'really' Rajputs? (See Unnithan's chapter in this volume.) Are the Pallars 'really' superior to the Paraiyars? (See Deliège's chapter.)

This was a great advance. However there were weaknesses in his notion of ideology, especially the notion of encompassment. As Inden has pointed out, this and similar theories involve ideas of structure which admit of no agency on the part of the Hindus who have/belong to/talk in terms of castes. If we wish to bypass the language of agency of persons we might object to Dumont anyway on the grounds that all ideologies *attempt* to encompass other values, though they seldom succeed entirely. That is the characteristic of ideologies. Quigley (1993, and in this volume) builds on the Hocartian notion of the king (or the local politically dominant caste) rather than the Brahman acting as the fulcrum of the system, but this need not mean claiming that 'secular' political values encompass ritual hierarchical ones, which would be to fall back into the same trap. A sociological approach suggests that we should ask the sceptical question; who is advocating a particular ideology, and who is convinced by their claims? Brahmans will routinely claim superior ritual purity and some non-Brahmans will be convinced by their claims, while others regard them as polluted by the need to accept the sin offerings of those who hire their ritual services.

The language of Brahmanical purity and pollution therefore competes with other languages which promote different ways of viewing the relations between people who regard themselves as belonging to castes. In some local caste hierarchies, the aristocratic and military values of the Kshatriya were more often emulated than the ritual virtues of the Brahmans in the attempts of local groups to raise their profile and make claims to status (as discovered by sociologists pre-Dumont, eg Srinivas, 1966:22). These findings need not appear as empirical deviations from an ideal type, simply as evidence that the separation of power and status in Hindu society which Dumont recognised appears as a contested proposition rather than a central principle.

Most of the languages which people use to advance the claims of their caste involve reference to hierarchy in the loose, popular (non-Dumontian) sense but there are other languages available. The idea of territoriality for instance permits some groups to advance claims to local dominance or control of land on the grounds that they are the 'original inhabitants' of a particular area (see Deliège's comments on the Chettiars in his chapter in this volume). And even those who cannot expect to gain much local kudos from such a claim still refer to the idea of territoriality in their self-depiction (see Searle-Chatterjee 1994, forthcoming).

The distinction between 'tribes' and 'castes' in South Asia, which exercised social anthropologists for a long time, was made on the grounds that 'tribes' tended to be groups which were associated with a particular territory whereas castes were groups which arranged themselves hierarchically in relation to one another within the same territory. With hindsight we can see that this debate reified differences in the terms in which groups of people who regard themselves as sharing an identity and status speak about themselves in a way that was probably not very useful. Unnithan's chapter demonstrates the impossibility of sorting out some of these groups into 'tribes' on the one hand and 'castes' on the other in any empirical sense. The local reality appears so messy that even a straightforward empirical description of what is going on seems problematic enough, let alone a theory which comprehends these diverse claims and self-identifications.

Let us attempt the following mental experiment. Suppose we were to describe civil society in South Asia in terms of people attempting to group themselves into units to which individuals are ascribed by birth. These groups usually practise marriage restrictions of some kind, often complete endogamy. They often use the language of ritual hierarchy to order their relations at the local level (or some version thereof) but they may refer to other ideological frameworks as well as or instead of the language of hierarchy, such as the languages of hypergamy, territoriality (more often used by so called 'tribes') or descent (widely used both by Hindu castes and Muslim groups).

The value of the experiment is that it obliges us to see Indian society as very complex indeed, not integrated by a single systematic principle apart from that of differentiation. Caste is one, albeit a very important one, of many modes of differentiation, most of which have political implications of some kind. A theory of caste needs therefore to contribute to a more general theory which accounts for the apparently fissile nature of South Asian society.

The disadvantage of the experiment is that the use of the term 'languages' encourages the view that caste, and indeed the other frameworks we have mentioned, exist only as rhetoric and not as practice. This is certainly not the case, as Shukra's personal testament shows. Caste is undoubtedly also *performed* in a variety of ways (through exacting or offering deference, through forming caste associations, through formulating marriage requirements). To write of the 'language' of caste could suggest that it is 'merely' a matter of words rather than action. In any case, a Brahman might well question this idea that words and actions are opposed, such is the power of the *mantra*. Let us therefore write of groups 'invoking' the principles of caste and hierarchy – the term 'invocation' has performative as well as linguistic connotations.

Secondly, who are these 'groups' who attempt to constitute themselves, mobilise, invoke the principles of caste, tribe, etc? Have not the concrete groups which Dumont sought to deconstruct now come in by the back door? If, as Inden suggests, we wish to recover the notion of human agency from essentialising western discourse on India, we need to think about who or what mighty exercise agency (Inden, 1990:24). When people act in the name of caste they do not do so as individuals. Therefore the idea of castes as concrete groupings as opposed to Dumontian sets of relations cannot be dismissed entirely.

We can think therefore of caste in terms of a system of groups or as an ideological system of thought, but it is probably more useful to regard it in terms of a system of action (flexible and mutable – perhaps in reality a collection of modes of action). To look at caste as something which people 'do' rather than something which they 'are' appears to go against the grain of modern interest in identity, but the two perspectives are complementary if we regard identity as something which emerges in certain situations. Shukra's chapter presents caste identity as something inescapable (even in the diaspora) so far as the 'untouchable' is concerned; here caste is experienced not so much something which you 'do' as something which is 'done to you' by other (high caste) people. Yet this very oppression produces a 'Dalit' identity on the basis of which some Dalits act and organise. The relationship between 'doing' caste and 'being' a member of a particular caste needs to be discussed in the context of a political psychology which would also embrace the relationship between 'doing' and 'being' in the other contexts we have mentioned (tribe, religion, etc).

Periodisation and history; the 'traditional' and the modern again

Viewing caste in terms of action is not without its own problems but it does enable us to escape from fruitless debates about whether caste has changed its 'essential' character in the modern period.

It is certainly true that there are many interactional contexts, especially in urban India, in which caste identity has limited relevance (Berreman, 1979a. See also Kolenda, 1986 for a good general discussion of modern trends with regard to caste). Dumont, like many others, is incapable of analysing this modern situation in other than terms of the dualism we discussed above. In as much as they continue to enact 'traditional' hierarchy in some form South Asians are deprived of a history and are trapped in an eternal ethnographic present (Fabian, 1983) or rather an ethnographic past. The only alternative model available to him is that of individualistic western society which from the point of view of South Asia is an importation, an intrusion. There is nothing else in this schema that Dumont's India could turn into if it does not continue true to its essential hierarchical self.

On the other hand you could argue that in this respect Dumont only manifests in an extremely explicit form an opposition between traditional and modern which can be found in most sociological writing in some form or another. You could even defend Dumont in that for him the traditional is far from being a 'residual' category, as it is in much of this kind of discourse, but is presented as a form of society which has vigour and coherence in its own right.

Recent debates about post-modernism have given new life to the western interest in the contrast between the 'traditional' and the 'modern'. Defining the 'modern' (because unless you have defined modernity you cannot identify the post-modern as a radically new cultural or societal form) has again become a fashionable activity. The forms which characterise the modern often turn out to be very much the same as those identified in the more sophisticated participants in debates conducted in the '50s and '60s about 'modernisation' (eg Eisenstadt, 1966). In both debates, when it came to defining the nature of modernisation outside the West, the modern has too often been defined in such a way that there was no particular value in using this term rather than simply talking about 'westernisation';

> In the case of non-western societies modernization as an 'end state' has become synonymous with Westernization . . . The theory offers no alternative for understanding change in any way other than westernization and moving to that stage in the universal history of secularism and differentiation. (Baykan, 1990:138).

Institutions such as the various forms of fragmentation identified above and elsewhere in this volume (caste, tribe, religious group, etc) may be seen as a 'traditional' residue which Indian society must rid itself of if it wishes to transform itself into a democratic and economically successful nation. Or they can be seen as capable of taking on quite 'modern' forms in the context of the nation state. Thus Weiner showed that in what he called the 'politics of scarcity' there is a tension between (on the one hand) the notion of rational planning as a mode of economic development in conditions of scarcity and underdevelopment, and (on the other) a relatively liberal political system. In this context numerous pressure groups (many of them organised along 'traditional' lines of ethnicity, caste, language group, tribe, etc) attempt to influence the way in which resources are used (Weiner, 1962). The caste associations discussed by Mitra (this volume) are indeed therefore a peculiarly modern mode of 'performing caste' – not because they act out some essentialised form of 'modernism' but because they arise in response to modern political conditions. To use Giddens's concept, they 'disembed' a caste from specific and highly local hierarchies and give it a quasi universal meaning (Giddens, 1990). Caste solidarities are then used to consolidate political and cultural capital of various kinds for members.

This may be a local manifestation of a very general phenomenon. Baykan, in the context of a discussion of modernity and Islamic fundamentalism in the Middle East, notes that ties of clientage, family and faction are often the links which connect the village to the modern centres of political and economic power. As such they are far from being 'residues' and she describes this situation as (structural) modernisation without (cultural) modernism (Baykan, 1990:141–2). But if the culture which produces the Bharatiya Janta Party, caste associations, religious 'fundamentalisms' of various kinds such as we see in India as elsewhere, is not 'modern' then how are we to describe it? Possibly we may learn from Berreman's comparative work on caste and race that periodization of forms of caste as 'traditional' or 'modern' obscure common interactional modes of exacting deference and corresponding processes of resistance which take place in a wide range of societies at different periods. (See Berreman, 1979b, also Scott, 1990 for a cross-cultural discussion of such forms of resistance). Perhaps we do better and more wide-ranging social science when we not only abandon essentialism but also the project of periodization?

Equality, competition and secular ideologies of status; the comparison with peasant societies

One form of comparison which is now seldom favoured by anthropologists working on South Asia is the consideration of the region in terms of *peasant* society. Formerly this was not the case. Joyce Pettigrew, for instances, explicitly places her study of Punjabi Jat politics within the context of studies of peasant communities in Southern Europe and elsewhere (Pettigrew, 1975:16) even though much of the time she is asserting that Punjab is *not* like Sicily or Spain. Oscar Lewis conducted a more systematic comparison between the Delhi State village of Rampura and the Mexican village of Tepotzlan, again finding differences as well as similarities. But neither writer regards either the general features of South Asian society nor the specific presence of caste as an obstacle to comparison. Looking again at the literature on peasant societies dating from the '50s and '60s, especially what anthropologists and sociologists had to say about the moral and ideological dimensions of peasant society, we find as much that relates to our (ie the editors') own experience of local Indian community life as we do in the literature that deals with hierarchy. Banfield's work on the peasant ethos of the Italian village now seems dated in many respects, but some passages could as well be describing the Indian village of Ghanyari, where Sharma has conducted fieldwork, as the Italian commune of Montegrano.

As the Montegranesi see it, friends and neighbours are not only costly but potentially dangerous as well. No family, they think, can stand to see another prosper without feeling envy and wishing the other harm. Friends and neighbours are, of course, particularly liable to envy, both because they know one's business better than do others and because they feel themselves to be more directly in competition. (Banfield, 1958:115).

Along with family solidarity we find suspicion of non-family, a sense that if you do well, others will not applaud your success but seek to bring you down (Banfield, 1958:111). In Ghanyari certainly, cutting down the 'tall poppies' (to use an Australian phrase) is a feature of local rural life. If you cannot benefit directly from the success of another (through being related or by becoming their client in some sense) then everyone will understand if you seek to bring then down to your own level. This, at least is the case among caste equals or those who regard themselves as having equivalent standing.

The sociology of envy is fairly well documented in South Asia as elsewhere. Pocock write of *najar*, the evil eye, the magical harm that the envious or greedy are supposed to be able to work on the objects of their envy and greed. It tells us, he says, of

> status and equality. Najar is not to be feared among equals such as brothers, nor among people whose status is clearly different and defined. It is to be feared when those who should be equal are not so in fact. (Pocock, 1973:39).

Najar is therefore especially likely to be found where members of a large caste share ritual status but show many individual differences in terms of wealth and political standing. It would seem then that caste values, though they do not in themselves create this fear of the evil eye, may increase the incidence of it, since caste boundaries are very tough. Successful or upwardly mobile groups within a locally well-represented caste may be in a position to repudiate ties with an identifiable group of less prosperous caste fellows, but more often they are obliged to face the interpersonal consequences of status dissonance. At a macro level there is usually some kind of crude approximation between caste and class in that it is very unusual to find a locally dominant caste unable to wring practical acknowledgement of ritual superiority from those who are dependent upon them as clients or tenants even if, as is sometimes the case, they do not claim high status within the *varna* system. At the micro level everyone has experience of situations where ritual status and class do not coincide.

The lack of a perfect fit between caste cleavages and class divisions is well known and some have always maintained that caste is a device through which local class relations are masked and thus perpetuated.

> The caste system has functioned to prevent the formation of social classes with commonality of interests and purpose. In other words, caste derives its viability from its partial masking of extreme socio-economic differences. (Mencher 1991:109).

There may well be some truth in this fairly widely expressed idea, though it will hardly do as a general theory of caste (as opposed to a simple description of the effects that caste divisions may have). It seems strange that dominant groups should be happy to perpetuate an ideology which not only prevents the lower castes from uniting and realising their class interests but also ensures that the upper classes themselves are liable to be divided by caste cleavages (and those who dominate local systems of production constantly exposed more directly to the envy of their poorer caste fellows, to boot).

But the evil eye is not only found in caste society (eg see Janice Boddy's account of how the idea is used in a Sudan village, Boddy, 1989:145). It is an icon of the fear and suspicion that peasants entertain towards, or expect from, those who are their neighbours and competitors in a view of life that sees wealth, power and status as part of a 'limited good' (Foster, 1965). From this point of view caste appears as just a particular way of defining the local reference group, the pool of status equals who are eligible to see themselves in competition with each other.

Studies conducted after the impact of Dumont's thesis have sometimes recovered 'egalitarianism' as a contradictory or complementary value present in the caste system. Parry, for instance, notes the egalitarianism implicit in certain forms of Hindu land tenure. Hierarchy between castes or hypergamous segments of castes is countered by an internal stress on the equivalence of members of the same group (Parry, 1974). Deliège (this volume) also discovers egalitarianism among a low caste and sees this as the failure of hierarchical values to penetrate the 'system' fully.

The egalitarianism, however, that insists on cutting the 'tall poppies' down to size can also be seen as part of a bundle of values relating to competition and status, secular in as much as they have no particular link with notions of purity and pollution, nor any location within the ideology of Hinduism or any other religion. The concept of *izzat* (or honour) is little discussed in the literature on Hindu society, except in the literature in gender and sexual behaviour (see Mandelbaum, 1988:119ff). However, it clearly has wider references, in particular to power and consumption (see Pettigrew, 1975, Raheja, 1988:238). *Izzat* is about maintaining the reputation of the family for the capacity to sustain and defend its interests, by appropriate dispensation of gifts and hospitality in situations where they are due, by retaliation to threats and insults where possible. Such 'politics of reputation' (Bailey, 1971) will be perfectly familiar to students of agrarian communities in many societies, even if they are not always expressed through the vocabulary of *izzat* or 'honour and shame'. Indeed we found notions of *izzat* expressed both among rural Brahmans (in Ghanyari) and among urban sweepers (in Varanasi), so the phenomenon is by no means solely a rural one.

We note therefore two things which call our attention to the comparability of South Asian society, its lack of uniqueness. Firstly, as in other peasant societies, we find strongly expressed ideas about equality and competition for status, although obviously everyone is not equal to everyone else, nor will everyone be encouraged to see themselves as in promiscuous competition with all others. Secondly we find a set of well-elaborated ideological notions about status which are neither purely materialistic nor can be described as specifically ritual or religious. They inform the interaction of local families quite as much as considerations of purity and pollution and the politics of the local community can seldom be understood without reference to them.

The 'untouchables'; test case for social theory and for democracy

If inequality can be expressed and discussed in both ritual and secular terms, then the same is true of egalitarianism. Dumont and others have noted the assertion of the spiritual equality of all men in the *bhakti* (devotional) tradition of Hindu religiosity. In this tradition salvation is not to be found in ritual practice nor simply in good deeds or altruism, but through sincere devotion to God. In the congregation of devotees God heeds neither caste nor creed nor gender, but there is pure communitas (in theory at least) among the faithful. Not surprisingly, early *bhakti* movements were conspicuously popular with the middle and lower castes and seem to have provided a vocabulary for resistance to the hierarchical values of caste and Brahmanism, even if they did not lead to their dissolution as institutions.

But low castes seem also to be capable of developing a secular egalitarian consciousness which is more far-reaching than the simple assertion of equality among caste members discussed in the last section. Deliège (this volume) and Berreman (discussed by Sharma in this volume) both assert that 'untouchables' do not really believe that the high castes are better or purer than they, and Shukra (this volume) makes the same point forcibly from his own experience.

The matter of social ideologies among 'untouchables' has become something of a test case for holistic theories of Hindu culture. If the low castes can be shown to reject the notion of ritual hierarchy then the thesis of the centrality of hierarchy in

Hindu society takes a body blow. If however the 'untouchables' can be shown to accept hierarchy in some sense or other, then the coherence of Hindu society is vindicated. Those who have made a particular study of 'untouchable' communities have adduced much empirical evidence and do not agree among themselves (Deliège, 1992; Moffat, 1979. See also Freeman, 1986 for a summary and discussion of these debates). The fact that these debates have taken place at all perhaps reveals the naivety of anthropologists who ever imagined that members of a highly differentiated society would ever draw consistently upon one ideology alone. No one, after all, is surprised when working class British draw upon collectivist notions in one set of circumstances and the ideology of liberal individualism in another. It is the very nature of social life that a set of dominant values frequently *fails* to entirely encompass another set of values and the contradictory untidiness of ideological configurations is revealed.

Deschamps, in a study of the relation between identity and power in France, has argued that members of upper level groups see themselves as individuals rather than as members of groups. They are said to use the singular personal pronoun more often and to stress personal agency. This is contrasted with individuals in lower status categories among whom category or group membership is more salient. Racial identity was more important to black people, gender identity more important to women (Deschamps, 1982:85–97). We do not know if this is true of South Asia too, or whether, as Dumont's analysis might suggest, these findings may depend upon the greater individualism of western societies. But Deschamps's work does however suggest more interesting ways of asking the question 'do low castes think about caste differently from the high castes?'

Untouchability has also proved to be a test case for democracy in India in the sense that of all ritual divisions it is the most resistant. Liberals contemplating untouchability in India are faced with the same dilemma as western liberals contemplating the realities of racism, desiring to resist racism yet finding that positive discrimination or similar policies run counter to an ideological notion of individualism and individual achievement. Liberal political values deny the relevance of ascriptive divisions as basis for discrimination of any kind in the public sphere, which then appears as injustice against a fellow citizen. Yet faced with the very pervasiveness of such discrimination, in practice the only way to deal with it appears to be to recognise the disadvan-

16

taged or oppressed caste/race as a particular category of citizenry whose members need special protection, thus inscribing into the law or constitution the very principles which are being denied. Sheth (1991) has referred to the response of some sociologists to the Mandal Commission Report (which recommended the further extension of what in western countries would be terms positive discrimination policies in favour of the 'untouchable' and other 'scheduled' castes) and the general uncertainty among Indian intellectuals as to whether the Indian polity is best seen as a collection of *individual persons*, having diverse class standings and economic needs, or an assemblage of *collectivities* constituted on largely ascriptive and ritual principles. It can of course legitimately be seen in either light, but that does not solve the problem as to which view should inform policy makers.

Caste, class and family

A widespread interpretation of the modern role of caste is that it is only a significant determinant of behaviour at the point of marriage. Restrictions on eating and drinking with, let alone touching, people of low caste are certainly rendered meaningless in many urban contexts by the close proximity of anonymous strangers in buses, city streets, office canteens. A quick glance at the matrimonial advertisements in any newspaper reveals that even in marriage, caste is only one consideration among many (such as occupation, age, appearance, educational status). For a minority of advertisers caste may even be less important than these other considerations, and a union with a spouse from a different caste is acceptable provided the status gap is not too conspicuous and other requirements are fulfilled.

Béteille would go further and points to the existence of a group who have virtually withdrawn their commitment to caste altogether. These are found mainly among the 'managerial, administrative and related occupations' (Béteille, 1992:15). Béteille concludes from this, not that caste has disappeared or is disappearing from Indian society, but that the family rather than caste is the institution which reproduces inequality. The particular form of the family is changing but it seems to be a wider unit than the 'nuclear family household'. In the middle class strata to which Béteille refers, promoting the interest of one's own family (even at the expense of others, whether they belong to one's own caste or not) is regarded as in no way immoral (Banfield's 'amoral familism' in urban guise?). Indeed it is the duty of parents to accumulate whatever forms of capital they can – social, cultural or economic – to pass on to their children, whereas to promote the interests of one's caste is regarded as contrary to a notion of public citizenship and national unity. Certainly if there is an ideological language which everyone understands and approves of today it is the ideology of the family. Indian films make constant reference to this ideology; could they maintain their wide appeal if they gave similar attention to notions of hierarchy?

We could say of course that the development which Béteille refers to reveals one of the areas of Indian life in which pure class interest is neither complicated nor veiled by local caste or other 'primordial' ties. But as we have already argued, the notion of caste as 'false consciousness' is rather a clumsy one if it is made to do more than simply describe. (If the veil of caste is apparently capable of suddenly falling away, why did this not occur earlier for dominant groups?). A better way of accounting for the behaviour of the group Béteille refers to would be to say that they see the cultural and social capital to be generated through appeal to caste and similar 'primordial' solidarities (see Searle-Chatterjee's chapter) as less valuable than those which can be accumulated by other means (education, professional solidarities, links with groups outside India, etc). They appear as an emergent class group. Whereas in the western context the study of class has been very largely the study of class 'cultures', class seems to have been treated as a culturally 'empty' category in the Indian context. Nonetheless, a middle class culture is now beginning to emerge.[5]

From the point of view of much work on rural society, family and caste cannot be opposed. In Ghanyari, at the time of Sharma's first fieldwork in 1966, a person's practical experience of caste identity was their experience of kinship and affinity, in the sense that the vast majority of the members of their own caste with whom they were acquainted and with whom they would interact in the normal course of affairs would be people with whom they could trace some linkage of either kinship or marriage. Their knowledge of corporate caste identity was effectively awareness of belonging to a network of families related by marriage, spread over a limited geographical area. Nowadays the Brahmans of Ghanyari acknowledge a broader sense of identity as Brahmans by routinely using the caste surname 'Sharma' widely used by Brahmans in North West India. They identify themselves thereby with Brahmans who may not be related, and who may not even live in the same state, and whom they would be unable to locate by simple reference to village of origin and father's name (more disembedding!). However this identity is still hypothetical for most people for whom, in practical terms, caste is still experienced most directly and concretely via kinship and marriage.

This is not universally the case. In some areas we find locally juxtaposed groups who are defined as belonging to the same caste but who cannot intermarry and who therefore cannot be kin to each other (Deliège, this volume). Shah has drawn attention to vertical divisions of castes into endogamous sections, separate but not always hierarchically arranged, as well as the better documented hypergamous/hierarchical divisions (Shah, 1982). In some documented cases a break in connubium is precipitated when one section of a caste, by taking advantage of some new economic opportunity, makes substantial gains and seeks to slough off its identification with other less successful members. (Notwithstanding what was said about the toughness of caste coherence in the last section, there is a sociology of 'ditching' as well as a sociology of envy). The internal dynamics of the groups we call castes are extremely diverse. If there is any lesson to be learned it is that the caste system has no essence. *Pace* Shah we would not use the existence of vertical endogamous divisions as evidence that caste divisions are not 'essentially' hierarchical, rather as evidence that caste is not 'essentially' anything at all.

Caste groups, as we have accounted for them, are now coming to sound suspiciously like ethnic groups as described by urban anthropologists and sociologists. Like ethnic groups, castes are groups within the modern polity which are largely (though not always rigidly) endogamous. Membership is acquired by birth and offers a sense of identity which is not just a translation of material class interests. We may agree with Shah (1982:31) that there is not a great deal to be gained by calling castes ethnic groups, on the grounds that to do so would be to deny the specific features of the caste system altogether. Members of castes will often describe their sense of distance from other castes in terms of culture (other castes have different 'values', different ways of doing things) but to privilege 'cultural difference' over 'differential ritual status' would perhaps be to throw the baby of

19

hierarchy out with the bath water of India's supposed uniqueness. However we can certainly say that caste in the modern urban setting (and in some rural settings also) functions *like* ethnicity in other modern polities, in the sense that it provides a level of identification intermediate between the family and the state which may on occasion provide a basis for general political mobilisation or the establishment of formal associations with more specific goals.

Conclusion

Our concern in this book has not been to propose an alternative theory of caste to replace conventional anthropological approaches, but simply to hint at what a post-Dumontian theorisation of caste might look like. The papers in this volume suggest two points of departure.

On the one hand caste can be seen as one among several principles of classification which can be drawn upon for particular purposes. If caste is no longer to be privileged then the interesting questions turn out to be 'middle range' questions like 'when is purity emphasised rather than other notions about status, such as honour?' and 'who uses the language of caste to whom and when?' Perhaps we need to write multiple descriptions of events in one location using models derived from a range of South Asian discourses.

This is not to diminish the empirical importance of caste or its impact upon the lives of individuals – the contribution of Shukra should convince us that to suggest this would be to deny the lived reality of Indian society. Nor do we wish to replace a holistic vision of Indian society with a post-modernist vision of decentred fragmentation. To say that people in South Asia draw upon and mobilise a range of cross-cutting ties and identifies is to say no more than that in this respect they are like people in other large modern polities.

Another line of theorising suggested by contributions to this volume would retain questions of social structure in central place. What are the ecological and social parameters for particular types of kinship of caste systems? Quigley refers to altitudes above which 'castes' are not found because the local economy is too impoverished to sustain them, and other writers have seen caste as depending upon the existence of a disposable surplus within a certain type of society. Alavi (1994, forthcoming) has pointed out that South Asian areas such as the Indus plain, with low rainfall and other specific ecological features, have remained impervious to both caste ideologies and Brahmanism, first adopting Buddhism and later Islam. They were not sufficiently fertile or productive to produce complex divisions of labour or highly stratified systems. Or we may ask the kinds of questions which have been raised in this Introduction, questions about the role of identity and ascription in the modern polity.

But to provide answers which are capable of contributing to the development of general social theory anthropologists will need to surmount the notion of the incommensurability of Hindu society without losing sight of the cultural specifics of local forms of caste. That is, they must recover the comparative genius which they seem to have lost on their way to the subcontinent.[6]

Notes

1 In the preceding paragraphs we have been referring to anthropological and sociological work on South Asia carried out by social scientists from Europe and America. In the subcontinent the academic lines of fissure are quite differently drawn. Saberwal's discussion of the development of sociology in India touches on the way in which the boundaries between sociology and anthropology are drawn in that country (Saberwal, 1983).

2 We have deliberately used the term 'South Asian' society wherever possible in this essay. Dumont refers primarily to 'Hindu society' and to 'India' as the subject of his study. Whether there is such a thing as 'Hindu society' considered as a unity separate from Muslim society or other religious communities in the subcontinent we regard as open to question (see Searle-Chatterjee's chapter in this volume). And as Quigley's chapter shows, all these issues are relevant in Nepal as much as in India. We have therefore tried to avoid using 'India' as a metonym for a much wider cultural and political region, while leaving open the question of how far what is said in this book might be applicable to, for example, Sri Lanka or Pakistan (issues which we do not have space to address here). Where we have lapsed from these rigorous intentions may the indulgent reader forgive us.

3 We have tried to keep the number of indigenous terms to the minimum, using them only where there is no equivalent term in English or where a word has become common currency in English language social science writing. There are various styles of transliteration for South Asian languages available. We have not imposed any one system on the contributors to this volume, so there may be some minor differences in the way in which indigenous terms are spelt.

4 Debates have raged among both European and Indian logicians about the nature of classification. Is it inevitably affected by the standpoint of the classifier? (See references to Berkeley and Kant in Russell, 1961:625,689 and to Dharmakirti in Matilal, 1986:327,329). Does classification proceed by characterising the nature or essence (*jati* in Sanskrit – the very term popularly

used for 'caste' in much of India!) of an entity, as Kumarila and Jayanta argued? Or does it proceed simply by differentiating it from other entities, as Dinnaga and Santaraksita argued? (See references in Bijalwan, 1977:238–41 and Matilal 1986:401). It is interesting that in the debate among Indian philosophers, those who argued in favour of 'essences' generally accepted the caste system; those who argued that classification is primarily differentiation were generally Buddhists and rejected the caste system!

5 Note that we are not saying that class *is* a culturally empty category in South Asia, only that it is often treated by social scientists as though this were the case. Mitra, in this volume, remarks on the folly of drawing the contrast between class and caste as though caste had no anchorage in an economic system and class no culture. One could argue that the values which Srinivas has termed 'westernization' and the aristocratic values of Rajputs and comparable zamindar groups are manifestations of the cultural dimensions of class.

6 The editors' thanks are due to various colleagues for their part in clarifying our ideas. Special gratitude to Mike Savage of Keele University for constructive comments on our project in this volume and for much encouragement!

References

Alavi, H., (1994, forthcoming), 'The two biraderis: kinship in rural West Punjab', in T.N. Madan (ed), *Muslim Societies in South Asia*, New Delhi: Vikas.

Appadurai, A., (1992), 'Putting hierarchy in its place', pp.34–47 in George E. Marcus (ed) *Rereading Cultural Anthropology*, Durham and London: Duke University Press.

Bailey, F., (1971), 'Gifts and Poison', pp.1–25 in F. Bailey (ed), *Gifts and Poison, The Politics of Reputation*, Oxford: Basil Blackwell.

Banfield, Edward C., (1958), *The Moral Basis of a Backward Society*, New York: Free Press.

Baykan, A., (1990), 'Women between Fundamentalism and Modernity', pp. 134–146 in Bryan S. Turner (ed) *Theories of Modernity and Postmodernity*, London, Newbury Park and New Delhi: Sage Publications.

Berreman, G., (1979a), 'Identity, interaction and social change in India', pp. 58–70 in G. Berreman, *Caste and Other Inequities. Essays in Inequality*, Meerut: Folklore Institute.

Berreman, G., (1979b), 'Self, situation and escape from stigmatised ethic identity', pp. 164–177 in G. Berreman, *Caste and Other Inequalities*.

Béteille, A., (1991), *Society and Politics in India. Essays in a Comparative Perspective*, London and Atlantic Highlands NJ: Athlone Press.

Béteille, A., (1992), 'Caste and family in representations of Indian society', *Anthropology Today*, 8(1): 13–18.

Bijalvan, C.D., (1977), *Indian Theory of Knowledge Based on Jayanta's Nyayamanjari*, Delhi: Heritage.

Boddy, J., (1989), *Wombs and Alien Spirits. Women, Men and the Zar Cult in Northern Sudan*, Madison, Wisconsin: University of Wisconsin Press.

Burghart, R., (1990), 'Ethnographers and their local counterparts in India' in R. Fardon (ed) *Localizing Strategies. Regional Traditions of Ethnographic Writing*, Edinburgh; Scottish Academic Press, and Washington: Smithsonian Institution Press.

Deliège, R., (1992), 'Replication and Consensus: untouchability, caste and ideology in India', *Man* 27(1): 155–174.

Deschamps, J.C., (1982), 'Social identity and relations of power', pp. 85–98 in H. Tajfel (ed) *Social Identity and Inter-group relations*, Cambridge: Cambridge University Press.

Dumont, L., (1972), *Homo Hierarchicus*, London: Paladin.

Dumont, L., (1986), *Essays on Individualism. Modern Ideology in Anthropological Perspective*, Chicago: Chicago University Press.

Eisenstadt, S.N., (1966), *Modernization. Protest and Change*. Englewood Cliffs: Prentice-Hall.

Fabian, J., (1983), *Time and the Other. How Anthropology Makes its Object*, New York: Columbia Press.

Foster, G., (1965), 'Peasant Society and the image of the limited good', *American Anthropologist*, 67:

Freeman, J., (1986), 'The consciousness of freedom among India's untouchables', pp. 153–172 in D.K. Basu and R. Sissons (eds) *Social and Economic Development in India*, New Delhi: Sage.

Giddens, A., (1990), *The Consequences of Modernity*, Cambridge: Polity Press.

Inden, R., (1986), 'Orientalist constructions of India', *Modern Asian Studies*, 20:401–46.

Inden, R., (1990), *Imagining India*, Cambridge MA and Oxford: Blackwell.

Kolenda, P., (1986), 'Caste in India since Independence', pp.106–128 in D.K. Basu and R. Sissons (eds) *Social and Economic Development in India*, New Delhi: Sage.

Mandelbaum, D., (1988), *Women's Seclusion, Men's Honour. Sex Roles in North India, Bangladesh and Pakistan*, Tucson: University of Arizona.

Mencher, J., (1991), 'The Caste System Upside Down', pp. 84–92 in D. Gupta (ed) *Social Stratification*, Delhi: Oxford University Press.

Moffat, M., (1979), *An Untouchable Community in South India*, Princeton: Princeton University Press.

Motilal, B.K., (1976), *Perception: An Essay on Classical Indian Theories of Knowledge*, Clarendon Press: Oxford.

Nagashima, N., (1973), 'A reversed world – or is it?' pp.92–111 in R. Horton and R. Finnegan (eds) *Modes of Thought*, Faber: London.

Parry, J., (1974), 'Egalitarian Values in a Hierarchical Society', *South Asian Review*. 7:95–124.

Pettigrew, J., (1975), *Robber Nobleman. A Study of the Political System of the Sikh Jats*, London: Routledge and Kegan Paul.

Pocock, D., (1973), *Mind, Body and Wealth. A Study of Belief and Practice in an Indian Village*, Basil Blackwell: Oxford.

Raheja, G., (1988), *The Poison in the Gift. Ritual, Prestation, and the Dominant Caste in a North Indian Village*, University of Chicago Press: Chicago.

Russell, B., (1961), *A History of Western Philosophy*, George Allen and Unwin: London.

Saberwal, S., (1983), 'For a sociology of India: uncertain transplants: anthropology and sociology in India', *Indian Contributions to Sociology* (n.s.) 17(2): 301–315.

Said, E., (1978), *Orientalism*, Routledge: London.

Scott, J., (1985), *Weapons of the Weak; Everyday Forms of Peasant Resistance*, New Haven: Yale University Press.

Searle-Chatterjee, M., (1994, forthcoming), 'Urban Untouchables and Hindu Nationalism', *Immigrants and Minorities* Vol. 13.

Shah, A.M., (1982), 'Division and hierarchy: an overview of caste in Gujerat', *Contributions to Indian Sociology*, 16(1): 1–33.

Sheth, D.L., (1991), 'The future of caste in India; A dialogue', *Contributions to Indian Sociology* (n.s.), 25(2): 9–19.

Srinivas, M.N., (1966), *Social Change in Modern India*, Berkeley, LA: University of California Press.

Weiner, M. (1962), *The Politics of Scarcity*, University of Chicago Press: Chicago.

Is a theory of caste still possible?

Declan Quigley

Abstract

A theory of caste must offer a way of ordering the facts in such a way
that it does not diminish the significance of some or ignore others. It
must also be comparative. Caste organisation is found in some parts
of South Asia but not all. Equally, structural parallels may be found
in many other parts of the world and one should not therefore assume
that the defining characteristics of caste are unique to Hindu communities or to the ideology of Brahmanism. What is needed is a theory
which explains why all of the traits associated with caste are found
together where and when they are, whether in South Asia or elsewhere.

Various theories of caste are reviewed in this chapter before coming
to the conclusion that one of these makes much more sense of the historical and ethnographic evidence than the others. Most theories
depict castes as arranged in a ladder-like vertical order. Sociologists
have tended to emphasise this 'stratification', regarding the ideological
and ritual manifestations of caste, such as the pervasive concern with
purity and impurity, as epiphenomenal. Anthropologists have generally avoided this error but have faced other intractable problems.
Some see caste as a recent colonial artefact, others as an ancient
indigenous category. Many are heavily influenced by the ideological
reductionism of Dumont's theory of Hindu society. On the other
hand, Dumont's analysis raises so many problems that some have
attempted to retreat from theory and restrict their studies to ethnographic description.

The argument here is that caste results from an uneasy stalemate
between the pull of localised lineage organisation and the forces of
political, ritual and economic centralisation encapsulated in monarchical institutions. Caste systems are the product of a certain degree of
centralisation which involve the organisation of ritual and other services around the king and dominant lineages. The central institution is

(as Hocart suggested) the monarchy, and not (as Dumont suggested) the *Brāhman* priesthood. The removal of Hindu kings in India with the advent of colonialism does not negate this thesis, for it is a specifically western view of kingship which allows for only one monarch within a territory. Kingship (and the configurations of castes associated with it) was always reproduced at the court of lesser chiefs, and is still replicated today in the households of members of dominant castes.

Introduction

There is a considerable gulf between the ways in which sociologists and anthropologists typically look at caste.[1] Sociologists tend to regard caste, in a regrettably truncated fashion, as an extreme form of social stratification which is a kind of sociological opposite of class: 'Open and closed stratification systems are sometimes described by the terms *class* and *caste*' (Chinoy, 1967:178).[2] Caste is frequently equated with Hindu social organisation through the misleading epithet 'the Indian caste system' and sociologists usually home in on the fact that where there is caste, 'an individual's social position is fixed at birth and cannot be changed' (Giddens, 1989:735). When sociologists use the concept to refer to situations outside of India, this is normally in cases where racial segregation occurs, as in the southern states of the USA following the abolition of slavery or the more contemporary situation in South Africa.[3] What is common to both situations, it is argued, is the cultural insistence on maintaining the 'purity' of certain groups by establishing inviolable boundaries, particularly with reference to intermarriage.

Such a perspective is of limited value. In the first place, the kind of ethnic separation referred to above normally concerns a very small number of groups, usually two or three, whose opposition to each other is crude and straightforward. In a typical caste system, however, it is not unusual for a score or more castes to be bound together in very complex relationships.[4] Moreover, the kind of ethnic cleansing which we associate with former Yugoslavia is undoubtedly also motivated by a concern for 'purity', as is the Mediterranean 'honour and shame' complex, but we would never think of describing either as a caste system.

To characterise caste systems baldly as forms of stratification is also to leave out most of what is really intriguing about them. In particular it tells us nothing about the seemingly endless flow of ritual and ritual prohibitions which preoccupy all members of caste-organised communities in their everyday activities, for example those revolving around the preparation and consumption of food. Nor does it account for the existence of untouchability, an institution which causes many egalitarian Westerners, and increasingly Indians themselves, to condemn caste out of hand as a barbarous institution which has no place in the modern world.

A further difficulty with the stratification approach is the implication that all castes are arranged, one above the other, in a relatively unambiguous way like a football league table. This is often coupled with a somewhat distorted view of the two Indian concepts most closely associated with the word 'caste', namely *varṇa* and *jāti*:

> The *varṇa* consist of four categories, each ranked differently in terms of social honour. Below these four groupings are the 'untouchables', those in the lowest position of all. The *jāti* are locally defined groups within which the caste ranks are organized . . . Those in the highest *varṇa*, the Brahmins, represent the most elevated condition of purity, the untouchables the lowest. (Giddens, 1989:213).

This simple description, while accurately reflecting the most common conceptions of caste both among Hindus and among those who comment on them, contains a number of misrepresentations. In the first place, the concept of *varṇa* refers to four basic social *functions* (usually defined as priesthood, kingship, generating wealth, and providing service) and not to kinds of social groupings. *Jātis*, which are groups based on kinship and marriage, are not subsets of *varṇas*, any more than English people with the surname 'Smith' are a subset of people who work as smiths.

Secondly, it is problematic to say that Brāhmaṇs are the highest *varṇa* for a number of reasons. There are thousands of Brāhmaṇ castes (*jātis*) whose members continually dispute each others' status. If some of them enjoy greater prestige than others, as they themselves always state, the criterion for this must be something other than assimilation to the Brāhmaṇ *varṇa*. Another difficulty is that those Brāhmaṇs who are priests are often seen as subordinate to those whose rituals they perform and whose status they thereby legitimate: paradigmatically, the kings and landowning nobility who are identified with the *ksatriya varna*. Priests are often portrayed as vessels or scapegoats who, through ritual, take away the sin, evil and death of their patrons. Parry's work on the Mahābrāhmaṇs of Benares (especially 1980, 1986) provides one of the best examples of this and is supported by the work of Raheja (1988a) and Levy (1990) among others.[5] In any case, only a minority of Brāhmaṇs actually work as priests so it is not self-evident that the status of all Brāhmaṇs is determined by this particular function, as is often claimed.

The implication that there is an automatic correspondence between *varna* and *jāti* is also unwarranted because there is often a certain amount of dispute about which *varna* a particular *jāti* should be identified with. Parry's representation of the caste hierarchy in Kangra in north-west India is a particularly good illustration of this. Here, he says, a number of castes whose *varna* is perceived by others as *śūdra* see themselves as either *kṣatriya* or *brāhman* (Parry, 1979:110, Table 14). Such discrepancies between self-representation and representation by others are, I believe, a common feature of caste-organised communities.

In short, then, the conventional portrayal of caste, as one might find it in a standard textbook of sociology, or, one should add, as one might find it in the accounts of many Hindus themselves, is riddled with problems. Anthropological theories of caste have also run into a number of difficulties. There is widespread agreement that the most important theoretical statement on the subject in recent times has been Louis Dumont's *Homo Hierarchicus* (1980) and a glance at any bibliography on caste will immediately reveal that the influence of this book has been unparalleled. Yet Dumont's theory has been the focus of sustained criticism for more than a quarter century, to the point where it is no longer clear how much, if any, of it remains tenable.

Some anthropologists have tried to sideline the theoretical problems by sticking to what they can actually observe on the ground during prolonged periods of fieldwork, as if ethnographic description and theoretical abstraction belong to mutually exclusive zones. At a recent international workshop on 'Caste Today', for example, the implications of recent ethnographic and historical research for the theory of caste were markedly absent from virtually all of the workshop's deliberations.[6] Where theory did appear, as in the question of the relation between caste and colonialism, the central issue was not confronted. Some claimed, following the deconstructionist fashion, that caste was a relatively recent colonial artefact deriving from the classificatory obsessions of census-makers. Others argued, or implied, that caste is an ancient Hindu principle enshrined in classical Hindu texts.[7] It cannot, of course, be both.

It should be obvious that it is impossible to divorce sociological theory from ethnography and history: even to introduce the word 'caste' is to imply a particular way of cutting up the world which relies on certain theoretical presuppositions. More obviously still, if anthropologists working in different regions are to compare their findings, there is no option but to turn to theory. As in the study of any social institution, to be comparative is to be theoretical and to be theoretical is to be comparative.

Why should there be such difficulty in providing a theoretical explanation of caste when an enormous amount of ethnographic and historical evidence on the subject has been produced over the last forty years or so? There are, I believe, a number of interrelated reasons for this which can be summarised as follows:

1 Most theories of caste appear to involve an unjustifiably arbitrary selection of evidence.[8] Since it appears to many that it is the facts themselves which are inconsistent, a common approach has been to ignore those elements which are awkward and to present the allegedly overwhelming picture suggested by those facts which are retained. The objection to this is that the awkward facts still remain, even if they are hidden.

2 While Dumont's *Homo Hierarchicus* has been criticised endlessly, many continue to argue, or imply, that his basic premises are undeniable (see, eg, Deliège, 1993). Given the difficulty of constructing an alternative theory using the same premises, or of finding alternative premises from which to begin, the majority of recent commentators on caste have preferred to concentrate on particularistic historical or ethnographic studies. However, this retreat from theory has not been any less problematic since, whatever is presented, some selection or prioritising of material is inevitable: it is impossible to write about caste without betraying an endorsement of one theoretical position or other.

3 The claim is often made that caste is unique to either India or Hinduism, thus making comparison with other social forms elsewhere difficult, if not altogether undesirable.

4 Caste is seen by some as being quintessentially a traditionally village phenomenon while others see it as a colonial invention

29

which exists more in the minds and classificatory needs of imperialist foreigners than it does as an ethnographic or historical reality. Apart from being mutually contradictory, both of these perspectives are too limited in their purview to provide an adequate explanation of the range of phenomena which are associated with caste.

The remainder of this article will explore these problems. I will argue that a consistent theory of caste is not as elusive as it has often been made to appear, and that the difficulty is not with the facts, but in finding a way of ordering them which does not diminish the significance of some or ignore others.

Discarded theories of caste

Before coming to Dumont's theory of caste, which deserves special consideration, let me briefly mention four other approaches to the subject which should be rejected. In fact all of them have been dismissed many times before but they have an insidious way of resurfacing and two of them are still in popular circulation. (By 'popular' I mean both in the minds of many who practise caste and in the minds of many of those who study them.)

The first theory which we can dispense with is that caste is a product of race, although an important qualification must be added before we throw out the idea altogether. The connection between caste and race was made by some of the earliest outside commentators on India who related it to the Aryan invasion of India and to the fact that members of Brāhman castes were often light-skinned while members of peasant and low castes were often dark-skinned or displayed other 'aboriginal' traits.[9] There is some basis in reality for this observation, but it is of limited value for an explanation of caste. Over the centuries certain populations were undoubtedly subjugated by others and the historical remnants of this can still be seen clearly in many places. But for the most part there is no obvious connection between caste and racial characteristics and in any case, the complexity of caste systems cannot be explained by a marker as crude as race. The often-made comparison with racial segregation does not explain why one should need such a plethora of castes in any locality.

The second theory, though false, is still widely believed. This is the idea that there is an inherent connection between caste and occupation which explains how caste systems work in general.[10]

There are two reasons why this connection is not a sufficiently good guide. The first is that it is never the case that *all* members of a given caste perform a particular occupation. A very common situation is that a particular caste is associated with a particular occupation, for example, being a priest or barber or potter, but that many (perhaps even all) members of the caste are agricultural labourers, or work in nearby towns as clerks or rickshaw drivers or whatever, or are employed by the military in some more or less distant garrison.

So while a couple may be referred to as Mr and Mrs Potter (ie, they are designated as members of the local Potter caste), they may in fact have never made a pot in their lives. This will no deter others from saying about them: 'Our sons cannot marry their daughters because they are Potters and we are Tailors [for example]' even though the Tailors in question have never sewn cloth but are in fact minor civil servants in a local government office, or members of a musical band performing Hindi film music at weddings and other social occasions. And, by extension, the same statement will be made by members of other castes. The general principle, then, is that a Mr Potter need not be a potter, a Mr Brāhman need not be a priest, and so on.

The second reason why the correspondence between caste and occupation is a poor guide to the working of caste is that many people who perform the same occupation belong to quite distinct castes. This is particularly obvious with relation to two classes of work: agricultural labour and the priesthood. Given that the vast majority of the population of the Indian subcontinent work on the land but are divided into thousands of castes, it is obvious that this occupation does not, by itself, provide a very clear indicator of caste membership. It is also evident that many groups perform priestly activities but see themselves as completely separate from each other and different in caste status. (For examples at either end of the Indian sub-continent, see Levy, 1990 and Fuller, 1984.) In fact it is quite common for some priestly groups to regard others performing ritual activities as kinds of Untouchables.

A third theory which runs into difficulties is favoured by some comparative sociologists. This revolves around the idea that caste is fundamentally about dominance and exploitation and any talk of pollution concepts as the criterion for distinguishing between castes is mere ideological obfuscation. On this argument, Brāhmans are at the top and Untouchables are at the bottom not because of their respective degrees of purity, but because of their respective degrees of material or economic power. The work of Gerald Berreman is one of the best examples of this kind of argument though there is a similar, if more subtle, version in the writings of the Indian sociologist André Béteille.[11] The reason that this explanation does not hold is simply that economic power and ritual status do not always coincide. There are Brāhmaṇ castes whose members are very poor and there are castes which are seen as low or even Untouchable whose members are in fact quite wealthy in comparison with the rest of the population.[12] There also frequently appears to be some kind of in-built mechanism which inhibits any easy conversion of acquired wealth into higher caste status. Against this it must be said that conquering groups always enter a local caste system with *kṣatriya*, or kingly, status even if they were previously regarded as 'barbarians' or outside the pale of the local caste system altogether.

Perhaps the strongest argument against the idea that there is a straightforward correspondence between caste status and economic position is that if this were so, it is doubtful if we would notice anything distinctive about caste systems or have any reason for using the word 'caste' in the first place.

A fourth theory which has little to recommend it is the kind of argument advanced by E.R. Leach (1960) in an essay entitled: 'What do we mean by caste?' Leach argued that in caste systems every group has its place, and the element of competition among them had been largely removed, resulting in harmonious, integrated systems. While caste systems *are* often well integrated, this does not mean that competition for status is lacking.[13] On the contrary, the institution of hypergamy in north India, which is widespread among landowning castes, is nothing other than a competitive marriage strategy where the goal is to improve one's status at the expense of others. Other examples of refusing to accept one's place include the construction of false genealogies (Shah & Shroff, 1958), name-changing in order to make it appear that one 'really' belongs to a higher caste (Rosser, 1966), moving to another locality in order to assume a new identity (Caplan, 1975), and conversion from Hinduism to Christianity and Buddhism (Isaacs, 1964; Juergensmeyer, 1982). In short, the idea that castes always meekly accept their status position is unfounded.

What remains of Dumont's theory of caste?

Another argument against seeing caste as a form of social stratification is that this perspective smuggles in a modern, individualistic, 'Western' set of values which is inappropriate where traditional, 'holistic' values prevail.[14] This is one element of Dumont's position which seeks to restore the indigenous values of caste to their rightful place. Dumont claims that two oppositions form the ideological basis of caste. The first of these is between purity and impurity which, he argues, is manifested most clearly in the location of Brāhmaṇs and Untouchables respectively at opposite poles of the caste system. The second opposition is between (ritual) status and (secular) power and this shows itself, he states, most clearly in the respective positions of the *brāhman* and *kṣatriya varnas* in the ancient Vedic texts, or in the respective positions of priest and king (or priestly caste and dominant caste) on the ground. There is, says Dumont, an ideological disjunction such that power is subordinated to status, the king to the priest, because it is through religious values that the whole system gains its meaning, and the Brāhman priest is the repository of these values.

At first sight this way of looking at things seems appealing because it appears to account for the 'fact' that Brāhmaṇs are the highest caste. However, on closer inspection the concept of Brāhmaṇs being supreme because of their superior purity (Dumont, 1980:56) is difficult to sustain. As I have already mentioned, there is a widely held belief that priesthood is a defiling activity, the idea being that through rituals which are performed for a patron the officiant takes away the patron's impurities leaving the patron pure, at least momentarily.[15] The fact of there being many different kinds of priest, not all of whom are Brāhman by caste, presents another problem. Men of Barber caste, for example, often perform ritual activities for lower castes which are strictly analogous to those performed by Brāhmaṇs for higher castes (Parry, 1979:59). And, as Raheja (1988a:20) has pointed out, affines are sometimes called to perform priestly duties when a Brāhman cannot be found.

Most intriguingly, there is a category of Brāhmaṇs, in north India referred to as Mahābrāhmaṇs (literally 'great' Brāhmaṇs) whose function is to perform funerary rituals. This is a particularly despised group because they are seen as being permanently defiled by the death pollution they take on themselves (Parry,

1980:94). The problem for a theory of caste which would have Brāhmaṇs at one pole and Untouchables at the other is that the Mahābrāhmaṇs are seen as both at the same time! Their ethnographers tend to dispel the ambiguity by arbitrarily assigning them either very high or very low status but this really amounts to a sleight of hand (see Quigley, 1993:81). Moreover, the same apparent paradox applies in a much more understated way, I would argue, to the members of *all* those castes, whether Brāhmaṇ or other, who work as priests. It is no coincidence that Brāhmaṇs who follow some profession other than priesthood widely regard themselves as superior in caste status to Brāhmaṇs who function as priests (see, eg, Fuller, 1984:59). Dumont's opposition between pure and impure, which he equates with the opposition between Brāhmaṇ and Untouchable, is, then, suspect though there is no denying that Hindus are constantly preoccupied by pollution concerns and this must be explained.

What of Dumont's other opposition, between status and power, or between priest and king? The main difficulty with this concept is that it only works at the level of ideology, and then only if one is extremely selective and listens to certain voices and not others (see also Burghart, 1978). Dumont's thesis depends primarily on the idea that 'power in India became secular at a very early date' (Dumont, 1980:76) but this is simply not sustained by the evidence, whether from texts or from ethnography. Kings always retained a central position in the rituals they patronized and their functions were replicated on a lesser scale by the well-to-do members of dominant castes, a situation which has not changed with the collapse of Hindu kingship in the face of colonialism. The argument has been put succinctly by Raheja:[16]

> Kingship no longer exists, but it has been, perhaps, replaced by the ritual centrality of the dominant caste as it has been described in the Pahansu [village of her fieldwork] ethnography. There, as in many of the textual traditions on kingship, the Brāhmaṇ is hierarchically superior, yet the dominant landholding caste stands at the center of a complex ritual organisation that permeates nearly every aspect of the everyday life of the village. (Raheja, 1988b:517).

Dumont is well aware that his theory does not apply to the observable facts on the ground: 'In theory, power is ultimately subordinate to priesthood, whereas in fact priesthood submits to power' (Dumont, 1980:71–2). But the solution to this apparent contradiction, he insists, is to understand caste as a structure of ideas, not as something which can be grasped by looking at particular territories (Dumont, 1980:154). The difficulty with this argument is that Dumont is simultaneously asking us to consider an actual place (India) which exists in space and time: we are asked to be empirical when it suits his theory and something less than empirical when the facts appear to contradict it.

In spite of these difficulties, there is a legacy from Dumont's theory which students of caste ignore at their peril, and some recent alternative interpretations of caste such as those of Klass (1980), Hall (1985) and Baechler (1988) are seriously flawed in this regard. Among the most important of Dumont's ideas are the following:

• The 'holism' of caste systems is in direct contrast to the individualism which is the dominant ideology of the modern West.
• One cannot talk about castes in isolation, only in relation to other castes. This means that one must have some kind of theory of a system of relations. Also, since this system is repeatedly found in a very large number of localities, there must be an underlying structure which gives rise to this.
• The relation between priest and king (or priests and dominant castes) is central.
• The connections between priesthood, purity and impurity are also central.
• Given the endogamous character of castes, the role of kinship and marriage obviously requires careful attention.

The basic elements of caste organisation

Perhaps the most widespread idea of all about caste is that it is exclusive to Hinduism and this is why it is found only in India or in places where Hindus have migrated. This idea is impossible to counter if, following Weber (1958:29–30), caste is defined in terms of one's position relative to Brāhmaṇs. But virtually all of the institutions which one associates with caste are found in different degrees in other societies at different periods of history. The most obvious of these are:

• recruitment to one's social position at birth;
• kinship organisation in terms of lineages;

- differentiation between noble (or kingly) lineages and others;
- endogamy such that marriage tends to be within a restricted group of lineages;
- pervasiveness of ritual as a mechanism for structuring social relations;
- pollution concepts which place an ideological stress on the purity of women, or of lineages, or of kings, or of priests;
- monarchical institutions, whether material (palace complexes, monuments to kings and royal deities), social (courtly lineages and royal retainers), or ideological (royal rituals, chronicles);
- untouchability and scapegoatism.

To explain caste is to explain why and when all of these traits are found together when only some of them are found elsewhere. To begin with the premise that all of the defining characteristics of caste are unique to India or to Hinduism, as has been far too uncritically accepted from at least Weber on, is to be much too selective in deciding what it is that defines caste and to deny the possibility of any kind of fruitful *positive* comparison with other places and other eras.

Even if one were to avoid groups which have converted from Hinduism for political reason, one could still find South Asians who practise caste but profess a different religious identity – Muslims in Pakistan (Barth, 1960) or Buddhists in Nepal (Gellner, 1992) for example. One must also recognise that there are Hindus who argue that caste is not part of their religion. And there are Hindus who *claim* to have nothing to do with caste but who clearly maintain its existence – for instance, by refusing to eat or intermarry with people they deem beneath them.

Recently André Béteille (1991, 1992) has argued that the Indian urban middle classes are moving away from caste and that 'family' is becoming the more important institution. Apart from the fact that he presents virtually no evidence for this claim, it is clear that there are still limits to who is regarded as an acceptable marriage partner. By and large Béteille seems to be referring to the intermarriage of members of Brāhman and dominant castes which formerly would have been separated territorially and politically but now find themselves thrown together in all of the institutions of a modern state. While the barriers to intermarriage may be coming down among these groups, this does not mean that they will marry into other castes which they continue to regard as inferior. In any case, to say that 'family' is now becoming more important is not of itself to indicate any sea-change since family pedigree is precisely what caste has always been about. As Hocart put it: 'Castes are merely families to whom various offices in the ritual are assigned by heredity' (Hocart, 1950:20). I will return to this idea below.

It is obvious that caste continues to play a significant role in the contemporary political arena, but among educated people this is widely seen as shameful and completely inappropriate in a modern, democratic state. Béteille argues that '[it] may safely be assumed that in India today, everyone is prepared to speak publicly in support of equality, but none in support of hierarchy or inequality' (Béteille, 1991:3). This conclusion flies in the face of a huge body of recent ethnographic material. While it is undoubtedly correct to point out that there is an increasing *distaste* for the values of caste among the educated middle class, the institution itself does not appear to be in decline. In the last two decades alone, scores of ethnographies from all over South Asia have made clear that caste continues to be the bedrock of social organisation for hundreds of millions of people. While there is perhaps increasing ambiguity surrounding the ideology of caste, it would appear that inequality, far from being regarded as invidious, continues to be seen pervasively as normal, inevitable, even 'natural'.

This is not to deny that there have been significant changes in the ways in which caste manifests itself during the last century. For example, where caste blocs appear today, uniting previously disparate groups, this is a modern development which would have been inconceivable in the not very distant past. A good illustration of this is found in the mass conversions to Buddhism stimulated by Gandhi's contemporary and rival Ambedkar.[17] Himself an Untouchable, Ambedkar sought to raise the status of other outcastes by breaking their attachment to Hinduism. But this could never have been achieved without the apparatus of modern communication, transport networks, and education, the bases of which were laid down during the period of colonial rule. And it could not have happened if the British had not decapitated the myriad local systems of political allegiances which underpinned pre-colonial caste systems by establishing new foci of political legitimacy and identity. Given the opportunities to organise collectively, Untouchables and others did so with a vengeance. It is not that they lacked the will to improve their position under the old régime; more often than not, political and economic structures deprived them of the means, primarily literacy and mobility.[18]

This does not, however, mean that caste is paradigmatically a product of the traditional Indian village. One of the most entrenched fallacies in the literature on caste, this notion stems from a distorted colonial view of India as a land of village republics and from the fact that most detailed ethnographic work on caste has been done on village communities which are of manageable size for a field researcher working alone.[19]

The mistake has been fuelled by a frequent failure to consider the historical and ideological relationship between village and town, the former being, literally, a reflection of the latter. In an article which draws attention to this mirroring quality, Pocock argues that both in theory and in fact the traditional Indian city stands for completeness. It is a microcosm of the cosmos and provides the most complete expression of moral values and social order because it is the locus of maximum caste activity. It is also the place where the king is to be found, the main function of the king being 'the maintenance of caste order' (Pocock, 1960:66). Rowe echoes this when he writes that:

> The distinguishing mark of a town or city in the ancient texts
> . . . was that *only* there did one find all the castes resident . . .
> The founder of a village or petty kingdom of several villages
> . . . fulfilled the same role but on a minor scale. And the
> village socioeconomic system . . . reflected the arrangements of
> the city on a lesser scale. (Rowe, 1973:213).

Perhaps the best extant examples of this connection between caste and preindustrial urbanism are to be found in the social organisation of the Newars of the Kathmandu Valley in Nepal, the seat of a complex, urban civilization for more than a millennium. One reason for this is that the 'Valley', in reality a circular bowl surrounded by Himalayan foothills, is extremely fertile and while the majority of the population have traditionally been agriculturalists, the area has always been capable of supporting a large population many of whom could be engaged in occupations other than producing food. As a gateway between India and Tibet, the strategic location of the Kathmandu Valley also made it an important trading centre. Over the centuries, the combined wealth of commerce and agriculture was converted into impressive temple, palace, and domestic architecture as well as being channelled into the competitive patronage of ritual which required a plethora of religious specialists.

Moreover, unlike India, Nepal was never colonized by either the Muslims or the British. In the small city-kingdoms of the Kathmandu Valley, caste has flourished for centuries among both Hindus and (Mahayana) Buddhists, with Hinduism, as Gellner (1992:55) observes, being the religion of the rulers.

While there is not space in this short article to give even a potted description of the complex history and sociology of the Kathmandu valley, one can point to some of the main features which underpin its caste organisation.[20] These same features are, I believe, at the basis of caste everywhere, even if not always in such a clear, or complete, form.

Any description of caste organisation must rest on two preliminary observations. The first is that to be a member of a caste, one must first be a member of a lineage for it is groups of lineages which we recognise as castes by their agreement or refusal to intermarry, interdine, or perform certain rituals together.[21] The second observation is that caste systems are only possible given a certain measure of territorial centralisation in regions which are capable of sustaining a complex form of social organisation – river basins and other fertile areas are typical. One does not normally find caste systems in deserts or high mountains and it is no accident that in Nepal, for example, caste organisation typically evaporates at approximately 4,000–6,000 feet above sea level where the land becomes progressively infertile and populations begin to depend on pastoralism to augment their meagre agricultural resources.

Caste, I would argue, results from a kind of uneasy stalemate. On the one hand, there is the pull of the lineage, institutionalised in the various ways in which lineage members exert control over one another – by restricting marriage choices, in the observance of periods of mourning when fellow lineage members die, by taking part in each other's life-cycle rituals (marriage, caste initiation, and so on), and through periodic collective worship of lineage deities. On the other hand, there are the forces of economic, political, and ritual centralisation, encapsulated in monarchical institutions. Among these, the most striking are the often spectacular palace-temple complexes and rituals such as Dasai which are traditionally linked to royal power and which provide a means by which lineage and caste divisions can be transcended as communities come together in common devotion and celebration.[22]

If lineage principles were so strong as to inhibit any kind of developed centralization (as in the paradigmatic forms of segmentary organisation), then clearly caste could not take root since it depends on a complex division of labour which must be based on something other than kinship. If, on the contrary, centralisation were to be so effective that recruitment for the performance of various social functions was always based on principles other than kinship, then obviously caste could not flourish either. The weakening of caste among urban professionals in modern India reported by Béteille, though exaggerated, certainly indicates this.

I have already pointed out some of the dangers in representing the order of castes in any local caste system as an unambiguous perpendicular ladder with Brāhmaṇs at the top and Untouchables at the bottom. Many of the difficulties in constructing an adequate theory of caste seem to me to be the result of being imprisoned by this ladder-like representation which one is led to almost inescapably if one starts with the notion that every caste can be said to be 'higher' or 'lower' than every other caste. An alternative representation which does not give rise to this problem focuses rather on the fact that caste systems are relatively centralised forms of political organisation: Figure 1 gives a simplified model of this.[23]

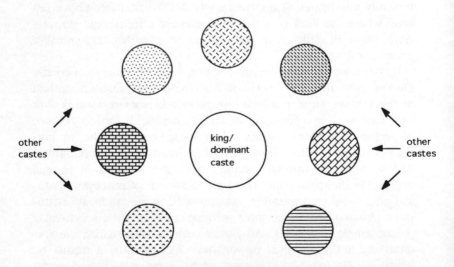

Figure 1 *The general structure of caste systems*

This model is of course grossly simplified, and particularly in two respects. Firstly, it is not only dominant caste households which are able to attach other castes to themselves. To a greater or lesser extent, households in every caste will attempt to replicate this pattern by using their resources to employ members of other castes (or sometimes other, usually affinally related, lineages within the same caste) to perform various services for them. Obviously, the greater one's resources, the greater will be one's capacity to do this. But virtually no household is so poor that it cannot at least occasionally afford to retain others to perform specialised ritual functions – at funerals, weddings, or caste initiation ceremonies for example.

Secondly, the model might give the impression that each caste is an undifferentiated bloc when the reality is more complex. Different lineages and different households within each lineage may vary substantially in their wealth and this may have important ramifications in terms of internal status differentiations within the caste. For example, the formation of *de facto* sub-castes is not uncommon when certain lineages attempt to set up more or less exclusive marriage circles within the caste and begin to call themselves by a particular name which sets them apart from their erstwhile caste fellows.[24] Over time these groups may become recognised by some as separate castes even though their *de jure* claims to such status may be seen as rather shadowy by others.

A number of other qualifications should be borne in mind when looking at the simplified model depicted in Figure 1. For example, castes vary enormously in size. Typically, the largest castes are the dominant landholding groups and those who provide the bulk of the agricultural labour while other castes providing specialist services are frequently very small. While the members of most castes, because of their attachment to the land, will see themselves as belonging to one caste system only, others, particularly merchants, may well function in more than one community and may thereby attain a certain degree of autonomy from dominant landowning castes.

It would be impossible to present a model which showed either the ideological or physical distances of different castes from the centre. Some castes, or some lineages within certain castes, will legitimately claim to be nearer to the (royal) centre either in terms of their kinship pedigree (perhaps some among them have married into noble lineages), or in terms of the privileges they enjoy. The castes which supply the king's priests will undoubtedly claim higher status than the castes which supply the farmers' priests. Untouchables are frequently represented as being outside the community altogether and in fact must often live physically apart from other castes. This is because their primary function is to act as scapegoats and to take out pollution (ie whatever threatens social order) to beyond the community's limits. Finally, it is also possible that there will be others somewhere in the vicinity (renouncers, independent sects, members of other ethnic groups) who cannot be accommodated easily within the local caste system.

In spite of these qualifications, the underlying structure of caste organisation is as Hocart (1950) portrayed it. The central institution for comparative purposes, he claimed, is kingship (and its associated ritual). For Hocart, castes are essentially 'families' which perform hereditary functions in order to ensure that the king and nobles remain free from pollution (1950:17,20). Whereas Dumont claims that the ideological pivot of caste is the priest's purity, Hocart argues that it is the purity of the king and nobles. There is another, more subtle, but very significant, difference between the two views which explains Hocart's reasoning.

For Dumont, the priest is highest because he *is* pure. Yet even if we were to restrict this claim to the realm of ideology, Hindu views concerning the purity of priests are extremely ambivalent. as one eminent Sanskritist has concluded, if a Brāhmaṇ does not wish to compromise his purity, the one thing he must *not* do is function as a priest (Heesterman, 1985:38). For Hocart, however, it is not that the king and nobles *are* pure but that they *should be* pure because they provide a model for others. From this perspective, the priest is an instrument or vessel who facilitates the king's kingship or the noble's nobility: caste organisation, which requires some members of all non-noble lineages to provide ritual services, is a continual striving to make this possible.

Where Dumont argues that the underlying structure of caste is in the ideology, I would argue that the ideological representations made by Hindus are irretrievably contradictory. The common structure underlying caste systems is rather to be found in constraints given by kinship on the one hand and kingship on the other, both of which are set against a particular material backdrop which allows a territorially limited kind of centralisation to develop,

It is not only the historical experience of Nepal which belies the claim of a growing number of scholars that caste emerged out of the colonial experience in India.[25] The removal of Hindu kings in India heralded the superimposition of new forms of political authority and new forms of political association. But the traditional institutions of kingship, on which caste organisation depends, have proved much more resilient and remain, as they have been for centuries, encapsulated in the political and ritual centrality of dominant landowning castes. Here it is partly the Western conception of kingship which is at fault for it tends to characterise kingdoms as having a single monarch. The traditional Hindu view has always been much more elastic, allowing for 'little kings' and 'great kings' as reflected in such epithets as *mahārājadhirāj*, 'great king of kings', which is still today the title of the king of Nepal.

No-one has done more to elucidate the concept of 'little kings' than Nicholas Dirks in his historical study of the former princely state of Pudukkottai in the Tamil-speaking region of southern India. He argues convincingly that 'until the emergence of British colonial rule in southern India the crown was not so hollow as it has generally been made out to be. Kings were not inferior to Brāhmaṇs; the political domain was not encompassed by a religious domain' (Dirks, 1987:4). Unfortunately Dirks confuses representations of caste in the colonial and postcolonial periods, particularly those of Weber and Dumont, with caste as it actually was under British rule and has been since Independence. Paraphrasing Dirks, one might say that even at the end of the twentieth century, kingship in India is not as hollow as it is generally made out to be.

Notes

1 Many sociology textbooks treat caste in a surprisingly cursory way given that it is an institution which continues to affect the lives of a huge swathe of the world's population. Hamilton and Hirszowicz(1987:90–9) provide a very readable introduction to some of the central debates. Possibly the best short introduction to the subject is the *Encyclopaedia Britannica* entry by Marriott and Inden (1985). Deliège (1993), which is very heavily influenced by the work of Dumont, also offers a good review of the issues.

2 See also Berger and Berger (1972:144) and Davis (1948:377–8).

3 See Dumont (1980:214–5, 247-66) for references on this and his argument that caste and racism should be carefully distinguished.

4 Among the Newars of Nepal, where I did my own fieldwork, there were traditionally said to be sixty-four castes.

5 The implications of priests being scapegoats are discussed in Quigley (1993:ch.4).

6 The workshop was held at The School of Oriental and African Studies, London on 12–13 July 1993.

7 Compare the following statements which have been made by three of the workshop's participants:

'Caste has existed for thousands of years: Sanskrit literature provides us with irrefutable proof of this' (Deliège, 1993:9; my translation from the French).

'It is increasingly clear that colonialism in India produced new forms of society that have been taken to be traditional, and that caste itself as we now know it is not a residual survival of India but a specifically colonial form of civil society' (Dirks, 1992:59).

'Despite the many changes which historians are now beginning to bring to light, a certain correspondence prevailed for nearly two thousand years between the actual division of society into castes and subcastes and what people considered to be right, proper and desirable from the social point of view . . . In the traditional order, caste was an integral part not only of Hindu law but also of Hindu religion' (Béteille, 1992:16).

8 Klass (1980) provides a review of some of the main theories.

9 See especially Risley (1891, 1908) and the critiques of Ghurye (1932), Dumont (1980:349–50, fn.15c), Pinney (1989), Inden (1990:77), and Dirks (1992).

10 An interesting report on the politicisation of 'backward castes' which appeared in the English newspaper *The Guardian* just as I was finishing this paper is fairly typical of the misleading connection made between caste and occupation (see Rettie, 1994).

11 Berreman (1979), Béteille (1965). See also Meillasoux (1973), Mencher (1974), and the article by Rosser (1966) which I have looked at elsewhere: Quigley (1986), (in press)1, and (in press)3.

12 An example of the latter from my own fieldwork would be the Nay caste of Kathmandu, many of whom are butchers who have become very wealthy in recent years due to the rising demand for meat among the growing, and increasingly affluent, population.

13 Levy's *Mesocosm* (1990) is a good example of a highly integrated, though extremely complex, caste system in an urban environment.

14 Alan Macfarlane (1992/93) presents a useful summary of Dumont's ideas on individualism and points to a basic contradiction. While Dumont asserts that individualism is a concomitant of the modern rise to primacy of the economic sphere, he also wants to claim an ancient pedigree for the roots of individualism which he finds in early Christianity.

15 Some have argued that it is really *inauspiciousness* which is being absorbed by the priest rather than *impurity* and that one ought to draw a distinction between these two concepts (Raheja, 1988a). My own view is that while this distinction is important in certain contexts (in the same way that 'dirt' and 'evil' are not the same thing), this has no bearing on the structure of caste relations.

16 Raheja (1988b) provides a breathless review of the literature on this subject, most of which I agree with. Where I would disagree is in her assertion (which seems to derive from Marriott's, eg 1968, transactionalism) that social life in India, as elsewhere, 'is semiotically constructed' (Raheja, 1988b:519). This leads her to adopt an approach which depends much too heavily on the differences in what people say in different contexts at the expense of emphasising the underlying structure of inter-caste relations.

44

17 Juergensmeyer (1982) provides a very readable account of the movement against untouchability in the Punjab which includes a chapter on Ambedkar's influence.

18 In India, movements which took off from about 1910 included the All India Depressed Classes Association, the All India Depressed Classes Federation, the Adi Dravida movement in the south which proclaimed that the Untouchables were the original inhabitants of India, and movements like Ad Dharm and Adi Hindu in the north which worked on variations of this theme. The Untouchables were not, of course, the only ones to realise their political clout and the Congress Party, as the main nationalist grouping, was very keen to make sure that Untouchables did not hive off and form a separate, powerful constituency.

19 See Dumont (1966) on the genesis of the idea of the Indian 'village community' and Fuller (1977:111) for an argument that 'the archetypal "traditional" village, with its *jajmani* system and local political structure centred on the dominant caste, is not traditional at all, but was, as Cohn (1970:45) suggests, mainly a creation of the British Raj'.

20 Since the mid-1950s, a huge amount of research has been carried out by anthropologists, historians, geographers, and others in the Kathmandu Valley. Among the works which are particularly relevant to the present discussion are: Fürer-Haimendorf (1956), Toffin (1984), Gutschow & Michaels (eds) (1987), Levy (1990), and Gellner & Quigley (eds) (in press).

21 Kolenda (1978) is particularly clear on the lineage basis of caste. I will not confuse the issue here by bringing in the relation between castes and 'subcastes' – see Dumont (1980:60–4).

22 Recent discussions of the centrality of Hindu kingship and royal rituals include Dirks (1987), Raheja (1988b), Galey (1989), Yalman (1989), Fuller (1992, ch.5), Quigley (1993, ch.6), and Toffin (1993). I am particularly sorry that I did not come across Yalman's short but powerful article before writing *The Interpretation of Caste*. In a rather critical review of my book which makes a bewildering number of misrepresentations, Good claims, among other things, that much of my argument about caste is inapplicable to South India and Sri Lanka (Good, 1993). Yet my position is very similar to that of Yalman who writes: 'If we can demonstrate that there is a caste system in Sri Lanka, that the king who controls the caste system is merged into the gods, that the palace is a temple and that this connection between royalty and divinity is not primarily Buddhist, but also obtains for kings and temples of South India, then it is clear that Dumont's theory will have to be seriously re-examined' (Yalman, 1989:143).

23 I have given a number of alternative representations of this model, illustrating how a caste system appears to different castes, in Quigley (1993:153–6).

24 For examples of internal differentiation within the Rajputs of northern India and the Sresthas of Nepal, see Parry (1979) and Quigley (in press 1, in press 3) respectively.

25 Dirks, for example, writes that 'colonialism in India produced new forms of civil society which have been represented as traditional forms; chief among these is caste itself' (Dirks, 1989:43). See also Cohn (1970:45), Fuller (1977:107–112), Dirks (1992:61), and Inden (1986, 1990:49–84). Both Dirks and Inden are heavily influenced by Said (1978). Dirks's description of caste as a 'trope' inspired by the classificatory needs of colonialists (Dirks, 1992:56,76) greatly trivialises its sociological significance.

Declan Quigley

Bibliography

Baechler, J., (1988), *La Solution Indienne: Essai sur les Origines du Régime des Castes*, Paris: Presses Universitaires de France.

Barth, F., (1959), 'The System of Social Stratification in Swat, North Pakistan', in E.R. Leach (ed.), *Aspects of Caste in South India, Ceylon and north-West Pakistan*, Cambridge: Cambridge University Press.

Berger, P.L. and Berger, B., (1972), *Sociology: A Biographical Approach*, New York: Basic Books.

Berreman, G., (1979), *Caste and Other Inequities. Essays in Inequality*, Meerut: Folklore Institute.

Béteille, A., (1965), *Caste, Class and Power*, Berkeley: University of California Press.

Béteille, A., (1991), 'The reproduction of inequality: occupation, caste and family', *Contributions to Indian Sociology*, NS 25(1):3–28.

Béteille, A., (1992), 'Caste and family in representations of Indian society', *Anthropology Today*, 8(1): 13–18.

Burghart, R., (1978), 'Hierarchical Models of the Hindu Social System', *Man*, NS 13:519–36.

Caplan, L., (1975), *Administration and Politics in a Nepalese Town*, London: Oxford University Press.

Chinoy, E., (1967), *Society: An Introduction to Sociology*, New York: Random House.

Cohn, B.S. (1970), 'Society and social change under the Raj', *South Asian Review*, 4:27–49.

Davis, K., (1948), *Human Society*, New York: Macmillan.

Deliège, R., (1992), 'Replication and Consensus: untouchability, caste and ideology in India', *Man* 27(1): 155–173.

Deliège, R., (1993), *Le Système des Castes*, 'Que sais-je?' series no. 2788, Paris: Presses Universitaires de France.

Dirks, N.B. (1989), 'The invention of caste: civil society in colonial India', *Social Analysis*, 25:42–52.

Dirks, N.B. (1992), 'Castes of mind', *Representations*, 37:56–78.

Dumont, L., (1966), 'The Village Community from Munro to Maine', *Contributions to Indian Sociology*, IX:67–89.

Dumont, L., (1980), [1966] *Homo Hierarchicus: The Caste System and its Implications*, Chicago: University of Chicago Press.

Fuller, C.J., (1977), 'British India or Traditional India? An Anthropological Problem', *Ethnos*, 42(3–4):95–121.

Fuller, C.J., (1984), *Servants of the Goddess: The Priests of a South Indian Temple*, Cambridge: Cambridge University Press.

Fuller, C.J., (1992), *The Camphor Flame: Popular Hinduism and Society in India*, Princeton: Princeton University Press.

Fürer-Haimendorf, C., von, (1956), 'Elements of Newar social structure', *Journal of the Royal Anthropological Institute*, 86(2):15–38.

Galey, J.-Cl., (1989), 'Reconsidering Kingship in India: An Ethnological Perspective', *History and Anthropology*, 4:123–87, volume reprinted in 1990 as J.-Cl. Galey (ed.) *Kingship and the Kings*, Chur: Harwood Academic Publishers.

Gellner, D.N., (1982), 'Max Weber, Capitalism and the Religion of India', *Sociology*, 16(4):506–43

Gellner, D.N., (1992), *Monk, Householder, and Tantric Priest: Newar Buddhism and its Hierarchy of Ritual*, Cambridge: Cambridge University Press.

Gellner, D.N. & Quigley, D., (eds) (in press), *Newar Society: A Collaborative Ethnography of a Complex Caste System*, Oxford: Clarendon Press.

Ghurye, G.S., (1932), *Caste and Race in India*, London: Kegan Paul.

Giddens, A., (1989), *Sociology*, Cambridge: Polity Press.

Good, A., (1993), 'Polemic against Dumontian Orthodoxy', Review of Quigley (1993) in *Current Anthropology* 34(5):797–8.

Gutschow, N. and Michaels, A., (eds), (1987), *Heritage of the Kathmandu Valley*, Sankt Augustin: VGH Wissenschaftsverlag.

Hall, J.A., (1985), *Powers and Liberties: The Causes and Consequences of the Rise of the West*, Oxford: Basil Blackwell (published by Penguin, Harmondsworth in 1986).

Hamilton, M. and Hirszowicz, M., (1987), *Class and Inequality in Pre-Industrial, Capitalist and Communist Societies*, Sussex: Wheatsheaf & New York: St Martin's Press.

Heesterman, (1985 [1964]), 'Brahmin, Ritual and Renouncer', in *The Inner Conflict of Tradition: Essays in Indian Ritual, Kingship, and Society*, Chicago: University of Chicago Press.

Hocart, A.M., *Caste: A Comparative Study*, London: Methuen.

Inden, R., (1986), 'Orientalist constructions of India', *Modern Asian Studies*, 20:401–46.

Inden, R., (1990), *Imagining India*, Oxford: Blackwell.

Isaacs, H.R., (1964), *India's Ex-Untouchables*, New York: Harper & Row.

Juergensmeyer, M., (1982), *Religion as Social Vision: The Movement against Untouchability in 20th century Punjab*, Berkeley: University of California Press.

Klass, M., (1980), *Caste: The emergency of the South Asian Social System*, Philadelphia: Institute for the Study of Human Issues.

Kolenda, P., (1978), *Caste in Contemporary India: Beyond Organic Solidarity*, London: Benjamin/Cummings.

Leach, E.R., (1960), 'What should we mean by caste?', in E.R. Leach (ed.), *Aspects of Caste in South India, Ceylon and North-West Pakistan*, Cambridge: Cambridge University Press.

Levy, R. with the collaboration of K.R. Rajopadhyaya, (1990), *Mesocosm: Hinduism and the Organisation of a Traditional Newar City in Nepal*, Berkeley: University of California Press.

Macfarlane, A.D.J., (1992/93), 'Louis Dumont and the origins of individualism', *Cambridge Anthropology*, 16(1):1–28.

Marriott, M., (1968), 'Caste ranking and food transactions: a matrix analysis', in M. Singer and B.S. Cohn (eds), *Structure and Change in Indian Society*, Chicago: Aldine.

Marriott, M. and Inden, R.B., (1985) [1974], 'Social Stratification: Caste', entry in *Encyclopaedia Britannica*, 15th edn., vol. 27:348–56.

Meillasoux, C., (1973), 'Y a-t-il des castes aux Indes?', *Cahiers Internationaux de Sociologie*, 14:5–23.

Mencher, J., (1974), 'The Caste System Upside Down, or the Not So Mysterious East', *Current Anthropology*, 15(4):469–93.

Moffat, M., (1979), *An Untouchable Community in South India*, Princeton NJ: Princeton University Press.

Parry, J.P., (1979), *Caste and Kinship in Kangra*, London: Routledge & Kegan Paul.

Parry, J.P., (1980), 'Ghosts, greed and sin: the occupational identity of the Benares funeral priests', *Man*, NS 15:88–111.

Parry, J.P., (1986), '*The Gift*, the Indian Gift and the "Indian Gift"', *Man*, (N.S.) 21:453–73.

Pinney, C., (1989), 'Representations of India: normalisation and the "other"', *Pacific Viewpoint*, 29(2):144–162.

Pocock, D.F., (1960), 'Sociologies: urban and rural', *Contributions to Indian Sociology*, iv:63–81.

Quigley, D., (1986), 'Introversion and isogamy: marriage patterns of the Newars of Nepal', *Contributions to Indian Sociology* (n.s.) 20(1):75–95.

Quigley, D., (1993), *The Interpretation of Caste*, Oxford: Clarendon Press.

Quigley, D., (in press 1), 'Social mobility and social fragmentation in the Newar caste system', in S. Lienhard (ed.), *Change and Continuity in the Nepalese Culture of the Kathmandu Valley*, Turin: CESMEO.

Quigley, D., (in press 2), 'Caste organisation and the ancient city', in D.N. Gellner & D. Quigley (eds), *Newar Society: A Collaborative Ethnography of a Complex Caste System*, Oxford: Clarendon Press.

Quigley, D., (in press 3), 'Sresthas: Heterogeneity among Hindu Patron Lineages' in D.N. Gellner & D. Quigley (eds), *Newar Society: A Collaborative Ethnography of a Complex Caste System*, Oxford: Clarendon Press.

Raheja, G.G., (1988a), *The Poison in the Gift. Ritual, Prestation, and the Dominant Caste in a North Indian Village*, Chicago: University of Chicago Press.

Raheja, G.G., (1988b), 'India: Caste, Kingship and Dominance Reconsidered', *Annual Review of Anthropology*, 17:497–522.

Rettie, J., (1994), 'India's oppressed millions awaken', *The Guardian*, March 5th, p.12.

Risley, H.H., (1891), *The Tribes and Castes of Bengal. Ethnographic Glossary*, 2 vols., Calcutta: Bengal Secretariat Press.

Risley, H.H., (1908), *The Peoples of India*, London: W. Thacker.

Rosser, C., 'Social Mobility in the Newar Caste System', in C. von Fürer-Haimendorft (ed.), *Caste and Kin in Nepal, India and Ceylon*, Bombay: Asia Publishing House.

Said, E., (1978), *Orientalism*, Routledge: London.

Shah, A.M. & Shroff, R.G. (1958), ';The Vahivancha Barots of Gujerat: a caste of genealogists and mythographers', *Journal of American Folklore*, 71:248–78, reprinted in M. Singer (ed.) (1959), *Traditional India: Structure and Change*, Philadelphia: American Folklore Society.

Toffin, G., (1984), *Société et Religion chez les Newar du Népal*, Paris: CNRS.

Toffin, G., (1993), *Le Palais et le Temple: La Fonction Royale dans la Vallée du Népal*, Paris: CNRS.

Weber, M., (1958), *The Religion of India: The Sociology of Hinduism and Buddhism*, edited and translated by H. Gerth and D. Martindale, New York: Free Press.

Yalman, N., (1989), 'On royalty, caste and temples in Sri Lanka and South India', *Social Analysis*, 25:142–49.

Caste, democracy and the politics of community formation in India

Subrata K. Mitra

Abstract

This chapter examines debates about the survival of caste in India today. It argues that caste is an institution which has both 'traditional' and 'modern' aspects, both 'primordial' and instrumental dimensions as, indeed, it probably always had. Mitra rejects the view of modernisation theorists, and of secular Indian intellectuals, who consider that caste is just a hangover from a discredited past. Arguing in favour of an instrumentalist, rather than essentialist, view of caste, he suggests that castes may have a useful role in the formation of identity and, as such, may help in the formation of the nation and state. Castes are resources that actors use to promote their own interests. Caste consciousness destroys those very aspects of the caste system which the essentialist view presented as immutable. The continuation of an essentialist perception of caste serves only to drive a wedge between the state and society. It gives rise to the stigma which prevents the law, bureaucracy and media from doing those things that would help transform castes into social organisations available for the creation of a plural and multi-cultural nation. Mitra develops his argument by focusing on three empirical areas: competitive politics, positive discrimination and the market economy.

The puzzle

The ability of castes to survive large-scale social and economic change and to mutate into modern forms like caste associations continues to be a puzzle. That caste 'survives' is clear from several diachronic studies based on fieldwork (Gould, 1990; Mitra, 1982). What remains unclear is exactly which attributes of caste survive and why. Those who argue for its survival constantly slide from one form to another – the traditional endogamous status groups organised around specific occupations – and caste associations, where people come together in order to promote shared interests. Thanks to its liminality, caste appears as the quintessential Janus of Indian politics. It has a *jati* face (*jati* being the Indian appellation of caste), turned towards the *varna* scheme (the traditional four-fold clustering of *jatis*) and through it, to Indian tradition and identity, capable of moving people in ways and areas past the reach of modern institutions. It also has an associational face which links it with the institutional fabric of the modern state. The political actor deftly manipulates both faces in order to generate power through this complex repertoire.

Interpreting caste therefore leads to the larger issue of how to relate the ontology of *jati* and *varna* (of which the English concepts caste and the caste-system are but inadequate representations) to the moral basis of society and state in India. Here, the battle lines are clearly drawn. The essentialist view holds that castes, ensconced in the *varna* scheme, are the bedrock of Indian tradition. The secular modernists of India, on the other hand, view caste as synonymous with underdevelopment, hierarchy and prejudice. They wish to jettison it altogether. Essentialists, whose instinctive and political sympathies are for preserving the pure spirit of Indian civilisation in amber, ridicule such attempts as derivative and, ultimately, self-defeating. That caste survives as a key factor of everyday political life *and* mutates, serves only to raise further questions about both the rival schools.

The interpretation of caste undertaken in this article is underpinned by the larger objective of a general revaluation of endogenous institutions in post-colonial societies. These institutions and practices, condemned to the dust heap of history by many modernisation theorists, are central to the formation of identity, nation and the state. This chapter has two main parts: Part I which juxtaposes an instrumental view of caste against the essentialist view that depicts it as the immutable essence of an ageless Indian society, and Part II which provides some empirical evidence from contemporary Indian life in support of the instrumental view of caste. This alternative view of caste suggests that, rather than being the essence of Hinduism, caste is a resource that political actors use in order to negotiate their status, wealth and power. This is examined with reference to three specific empirical issues: caste and competitive politics; caste and positive discrimination; and caste and the market economy. Through these examples it will be shown that the interpenetration of the traditional society and the modern state is brought about through the agency of caste and is the basis of its resilience.

PART I

The essentialist view of caste

Popular and scholarly perceptions of caste present it as an essentially Hindu institution. 'In its most literal interpretation', caste is perceived as 'an exclusively Indian phenomenon', not paralleled by any other institution elsewhere in its 'complexity, elaboration and inflexibility'. It 'moulds the psychology of the people', 'predetermines an individual's or family's pattern of behaviour in society' and 'plays a major role in the choice of leadership particularly in rural areas'. Further, 'from the individual's point of view, caste provides him with a fixed social status, limits his choice in marriage, determines his occupation and dictates to him the customs to be observed in the matter of diet, ceremonies and rituals at birth, initiation and death' (Chambers, 1951:150). This view of caste as a unique and enduring institution is reinforced by a long tradition in anthropology. 'Caste' as Hutton writes, 'no doubt keeps changing, and customs come and go; the pattern alters, but the principles that govern it, the frames that hold the pattern so to speak, are exceptionally constant for a human institution' (Hutton, 1950:151).

The popular perception of caste is informed by its depiction as a fixed presence, not contingent on the material basis of society, but, instead, exerting a decisive influence on it. It is supposed to derive its power from deeply ingrained beliefs in the Hindu psyche. These views were put together by Kroeber who described the caste systems as 'systems of social stratification, examples of ranked aggregates of people, that are unusually rigid, birth-ascribed, and permit no individual mobility' (Kroeber, 1930:254). Further, 'the hierarchy entails differential evaluations, differential rewards, and differential association'. Castes are discrete, bounded and ranked entities. In a caste system, 'everyone belongs to a caste and no one belongs to more than one caste' (Berreman, 1968:334).

Many students of Indian society find a transcendental explanation for the existence of the social order in the ideology of caste.

In terms of its composition, Hindu society is seen by them as uniquely based on caste, and, thus, necessarily different from their non-Hindu and European counterparts. Some of these views, attributed primarily to Dumont (1980) have been summed up by Quigley in terms of a set of falsifiable propositions: (1) The Hindu world is made up of a number of castes; (2) Castes are closed social groups: one may only marry within one's caste and the children of the marriage belong to the caste of their parents. In this way the system is perpetuated *ad infinitum*; and (3) Castes are hierarchically ranked on a purity-pollution scale [invariant in space and time] according to their traditional occupations (Quigley, 1993:1).

Seen thus, the political role of caste is theoretically unproblematic. Its existence is meant only to provide political reinforcement to an essentially hierarchic view of Hindu society, based on the predominant concern of ridding oneself of pollution, guided by a desire for liberation from the nexus of rebirth (*moksha*). It is easy to see why this essentialist view of caste as a social institution arouses such passionate debate. As an ideology of state-society relations, it is in many ways the opposite of the concept of equality that India's secular intellectuals consider to be the core value of the Indian state. For political reformers and intellectual advocates of modernity, caste comes across as a vestige of tradition irrevocably opposed to the modern world of democracy, social justice and economic growth.[1] This view of caste, ardently espoused by many educated Indians, continues to underpin the debate on such contentious issues as religion, identity and, of course, the caste system itself.

This radical polarisation of the two views of caste continues to plague research on social change. The literature is split into hyper-empirical village studies on the one hand and unpromisingly abstract theoretical constructs on the other. Another manifestation of this sterile debate is the ongoing feud between the advocates of caste against class as if caste had no economy and class no culture. Conflicting theories of the origin of caste are indicative of this theoretical impasse. Hindu mythology ascribes the origin of the four *varnas* to a mythical deity: the Brahmins sprang from his mouth, the Kshatriya from his arms, the Vaishya from his thighs, and the Sudra from his feet. The mythological view is contested by the racial approach, according to which caste arose out of race contacts between light skinned Aryans and dark skinned Dravidian and the subsequent divisions were based on the purity of colour (*varna*). Yet another view attributes the development of the caste system to tribalism and holds that 'caste is little more than an ordinary class society made rigid.' 'Caste is immobile class, class is mobile caste' (Prasad, 1986:776).

In spite of the variations in their empirical reasoning, each of these accounts points in the direction of the essentialist paradigm where society is divided into a set of rigid, hierarchical groups bound together in an immutable bond, justified in terms of the moral superiority of the clean castes to those considered unclean. The essentialist view of Indian society became a point of reference for competing political lines within India's freedom movement. Reacting against it, 'modernists' like Jawaharlal Nehru saw the caste system as 'the main source of India's social, political and even moral degeneration' (Parekh, 1991). The Hindu nationalist reaction was more complex. One section was keen on the revival of Hinduism in its pure form and drew its support from the upper social strata. The other section whom Parekh calls the 'critical traditionalists' included leaders like Vivekananda, Tilak and Gandhi. 'While acknowledging that castes had divided the Hindus and degraded large sections of them, they insisted that they had also held the Hindu society together, preserved some of its central values, and been a source of moral, social and emotional support.' Parekh adds, 'The critical traditionalists thought that if castes could be transformed into open, non–hierarchical and voluntary organisations and thus purged of their ugly features, they would fit into and indeed become the healthy basis of a modern and secular India' (Parekh, 1991).

A critique of the essentialist view of caste

Critical traditionalism, particularly the ideas of Gandhi, has had a significant though limited impact on the scholarly writings on Indian politics and the role of caste in it. An early example of this genre, critical of the essentialist paradigm, is the *Modernity of Tradition* by Lloyd and Susanne Rudolph. In this seminal book, the Rudolphs suggested that 'tradition' and 'modernity' need not necessarily be in contradiction, that a synthesis is possible, even desirable. Referring to the almost infinite ability of tradition to adapt and therefore survive, the Rudolphs commented:

If tradition and modernity are seen as continuous rather than separated by an abyss, if they are dialectically rather than dichotomously related, and if internal variations are attended to and taken seriously, then those sectors of traditional society that contain or express potentialities for change from dominant norms and structures become critical for understanding the nature and processes of modernisation (Rudolph and Rudolph, 1967:8).

In their *Modernity of Tradition* and their research on caste associations, the Rudolphs pointed to the ability of traditional institutions to act as a vehicle for modern functions. However, the inability to specify caste-actors as a hinge group, who draw strength from both tradition and modernity and create new norms in the process, gave their findings an appearance of eclecticism, born out of an indulgence towards India's tradition rather than rigorous theoretical analysis. Their assertion of the potential for modernity hidden within tradition was seen as an acknowledgement of India's fundamental difference from western societies and, thus, an affirmation of her uniqueness. Given a choice between ascriptive, hierarchy-bound tradition and egalitarian and individualistic modernity, the Rudolphs gave the impression of arguing on both sides of the issue. Their position was severely criticised by Fox who referred pointedly to the tautological implications of their formulation. 'If aspects of the traditional survive', said Fox, 'it is because they had this potentiality; if they do not, it is because they lacked this potential ability' (Fox, 1970).

Fox's criticism of the Rudolphs' position gave a clear indication of the methodological difficulty of describing phenomena like caste in terms of cultural categories extrinsic to the culture in which it is endogenous. When tradition and modernity are seen as dichotomous categories and caste is seen as the essence of Indian tradition, the terms of social science discourse, based on cultural assumptions of individualism, limited government and secular power, are scarcely in a position to analyse them. Inden refers to their problem of cognition as typical of post-colonial societies where a traditional society and modern state face one another in mutual incomprehension. From this perspective, the roots of caste wars and communal conflicts go back to the manner in which the secular principle was enshrined within the constitution and the spirit in which it was implemented. From the beginning, despite the end of foreign colonial rule, no consistent attempts were made to derive the principle of government from local and regional cultural and political traditions in India. The result, as Inden reminds us, was a 'nation-state that remains ontologically and politically inaccessible to its own citizens. Its government continues to be just like its immediate British Indian ancestor, merely a neutral enforcer of unity on a morselized society, continually in danger of being pulled apart by centrifugal forces' (Inden, 1990:197).

Caste associations, neo-castes and religious communities with a multiplex role are empirical phenomena whose anomalous presence at the heart of Indian politics raise basic issues for a theoretical understanding of Indian society. An anti-essentialist view which takes actors seriously and seeks to understand the political reality through categories intrinsic to the society will be of greater use in understanding the political evolution of Indian society. The limitations of space force a selection of evidence. However, a more comprehensive approach on these lines, which makes for cross-cultural comparability without sacrificing cultural content, can be derived from three bodies of evidence, corresponding to (a) the cultural pluralism of Indian society seen in the omnipresence of caste which is not unique to Hindus (b) a study of social stratification and the role of secular power in its maintenance and (c) social interaction and the management of conflict.

Caste among non-Hindus

To untutored western eyes, (in this case the Portuguese and subsequently, the British conquerors of India) the key concepts of Brahminical Hinduism such as *dharma, karma, moksha,* and *maya* provided a sense of ideological cohesion to understand the apparently fragmented and occasionally contradictory processes of India. The misperception of caste hierarchy as the basic foundation of the social process led to the understanding of Indian society as ageless and static. It gave rise to two traditions of caste research. The earlier, indological tradition was based mostly on sacred texts, written by Brahmins, providing an ideological justification for the hierarchical nature of the caste system, based on close correspondence between status and varna. This knowledge is part of the orientalist tradition. Subsequently, the secular modernist reaction to essentialist thinking led to fieldwork based studies which specified caste as social stratification and advocated its reform. Both traditions were essentialising Indian experience in terms of a European paradigm. Thanks to the new genre of writers like Inden (1990) and Scott (1985) who emphasise the role of the actor as an agent of his own destiny, what we need is to understand caste in terms of categories drawn from the lifeworld of the individual, placed in the context of the local arena. Thus perceived, castes reappear as communities, the main vehicle of upward mobility, of social groups who entered the political process after independence.

Historical research, as well as fieldwork, since independence show that the caste system in India was not confined only to the Hindus nor was it invariant in time and space, even for those nominally belonging to the same religion. All important communities, including Muslims, Christians and Sikhs have some sort of caste scheme. These schemes are patterned after the Hindu system, since most of them originally came from Hindu stock. The large-scale conversions that have been going on for centuries have not greatly modified Indian caste society. Thus traditional Hindu commensal and connubial rituals, though generally rejected in the Islamic or Christian religious texts, nevertheless exist in these communities in India. Among the Muslims, groups such as the Sayid, Sheikh, Pathan and Momin function as exclusive endogamous caste groups. A similar stratification can be observed among the Christians who are divided into a number of endogamous groups, including Chaldean Syrians, Jacobite Syrians, Latin Catholics, Marthomite Syrians, Syrian Catholics and Protestants. Even among the Catholics, the Syrian Romans and the Latin Romans generally do not intermarry. The Christians have not wholly discarded the ideal of food restrictions and pollution by lower caste members. When lower caste Hindus were converted to Christianity, a generation or two ago, they were not allowed to sit with high caste Christians in Church, and separate churches were erected for them. The Buddhists also have their own mutually exclusive social groups. Caste is, thus, indicative of India's local and regional variations and her cultural plurality and not a finely graded *dharmic* nexus through which Hindus realise their *karma*.

Force and the maintenance of caste systems

The essentialist view paints the picture of a homeostatic society where different groups are organically linked. The anti-essentialist view does not deny the existence of society nor the complementarity of needs for which social transaction provides a mechanism of exchange. It only suggests that status inconsistency is an inevitable byproduct of this process, so that, at least in the short run, the role of force is indispensable for the maintenance of the caste system. Caste societies are not homeostatic; they generate enormous conflict and have to be maintained by force. Hence, politics becomes the cutting edge, society's method of 'self-correction' (Nandy, 1918:50). The role of force in the maintenance of local caste systems and its collapse through the organisation of countervailing force can be seen in Robinson (1991), Béteille (1983), and Frankel and Rao (1991, 1992).

Sociocultural change brought about through the instrumentality of caste provides further evidence for an anti-essentialist position. Within caste systems there is constant mobility striving. It is generally sought through 'status emulation' as groups attempt to imitate their social superiors (for example, 'Sanskritisation' in India). Mobility striving, while intrinsic in caste systems, is a constant threat to the status quo. It is suppressed whenever possible, but the process of suppression is difficult and never completely effective. Commenting on this process of constant contestation, Berreman suggests: 'They [the caste hierarchy] are maintained not by agreement but by sanctions. It takes much physical and psychic energy to maintain an inherently unstable, conflictive situation in a semblance of working order. The high-status groups must suppress mobility striving among others; rules restricting social interaction must be enforced; the purity and integrity of the group must be maintained; a myth of stability must be supported in the face of overt disconfirming evidence. On the part of low-status people, self-respect must be maintained despite constant denigration; resentment must be suppressed or carefully channelled' (Berreman, 1968:338).

The regeneration of caste-systems

If, as the essentialist approach suggests, the caste system is rigid, static and ageless, how do new castes ever arise? The explanation given for its theoretically static structure and the social reality of change can be found in the concept of status summation. The multiple roles played by individual members of a caste are equivalent in the status they confer. Thus a person of high ritual status tends also to be of high economic, political and social status. These statuses tend to coalesce, and people are thus enabled as well as enjoined to interact with members of other castes in an unambiguous, consistent and hierarchical manner. Part of the dynamics of caste organisation is the tendency for status incongruities, when they occur, to be rectified. Castes maintain themselves by generating their specific internal culture, network, method of communication and political order. Caste systems are maintained by defining and maintaining boundaries between castes. They are threatened when boundaries are compromised.

Evidence from historical research of the evolution of the caste system presents a contrasting image which is radically different from the essentialist view of unchanging Indian society. In the first of his three volumes Gould (1990) explores the origin of the caste system in terms of the 'sacralisation' of the occupational order and 'occupationalisation' of the sacred order in pre-industrial India, leading to the creation of an intricate social nexus. Professor Gould shows how urban professionals as well as rural politicians draw on the cohesive functions of caste in the course of their everyday political transactions. The result is a continuous creation of new social groups. These have been unsatisfactorily labelled as caste associations, because they are rarely formal enough to merit being called associations and while they might use the idiom of caste as a vehicle, caste is not the cause of their origin. It is best to understand the creation of new social groups in terms of political communities and *jatis*.

PART II

Sacred beliefs and secular power

The essentialist view of caste suggests a static social structure where the desire to avoid pollution provided a transcendental basis for the material organisation of society. A corollary of this view is the subordinate role of secular power in relation to those in charge of spiritual matters. Thus, the pure should rule the impure; the raja should be the ritual inferior of the Brahmin. A brief review of the literature shows that the situation was much more complex and regionally varied. Belief was never considered absolute or in the abstract but only in reference to practice.

'There never was any question of a subject's being entitled to put his beliefs into practice if society objected, for all *adhikaras* [which in its original usage implies both a right and a duty] came into existence within the sphere of a society and when societies became numerous or complex the king kept the balance within or between them. The king's failing to do this could not be contemplated: it meant the end of the dharmas and the Rule of the Fish [*matsyanyaya*]' (Derrett, 1978:560). The holy texts of Hinduism both ordained and approved of intervention by the temporal power and assemblies in the social and moral life of the community. 'When Manu tells us that different customs prevailed in different ages he suggests that the social code is not a fixed but a flexible one. Social customs and institutions are subject to change.' Derrett adds further that 'the state may determine what the law is within the general framework of *dharma*'. Political authority within the Indian state tradition required the mutual accommodation of the King and the Brahmin, responsible, respectively, for secular power and sacred beliefs. In the Indian tradition, 'the regnus (*kshatra*) could not subsist on its own without the sacerdotium (*brahma*) which provided its principle of legitimacy.'[2] The role that the king as the representative of secular power plays in the interpretation of the codes of good conduct, sometimes in collusion and occasionally in competition with the Brahmin, shows that the position of neither was absolute or fixed within a social hierarchy. Referring to this, Quigley suggests that 'the entrenched ideal that "Brahmins are the highest caste" has done most to hinder an alternative formulation of how the caste system works' (Quigley, 1993:169).

However, though secular power was far from being necessarily subordinate to Brahmins, the position of the king, unlike in traditional China or Japan, was neither fixed nor absolute. Its existence, though distinct, was necessarily insecure. Shulman warns us: 'At the heart of South Indian social symbolism we find the enticing but enigmatic figure of the king. As in the classical North Indian sources studied by Heesterman, the royal role is seen in medieval southern sources as profoundly problematic; hence the profusion of stories that deal with its endlessly varied aspects. In South India, kingship is less a fact than a concern, a congealed longing always in danger of dissolving back into despair.' (Shulman, 1985:15).

Macro Politics, Micro Society

The essentialist view presents Indian society as an internally undifferentiated whole which is politically self-sustaining (Dumont, 1980). The anti-essentialist view advocated here recognises the relative autonomy of politics, considerably reinforced since the growth of representative politics. Local caste hierarchies were greatly affected by the onset of British rule when new institutions and market forces started affecting the balance of power. India's British rulers set up a complex institutional structure to administer sacred beliefs and sacred property. Under the overall authority of the colonial state, Hindu and Muslim rulers – and failing that, other intermediaries and civil servants – were appointed as administrators. At the level of ideological abstraction, the colonial theory of caste attributed to it a dual role. Thus, on the one hand, it was seen as static, symbolic of Indian hierarchy and spirituality, best left to itself or in Indian hands. It was also seen as essentially social, fragmented and incapable of producing a political centre. This became a self-serving argument for colonial rule (Parekh, 1989:26). Nevertheless, in an eloquent testimony to the relationship between the local caste system and secular power at the level of high politics, the spread of British rule set in motion an inexorable process of change. The process was further exacerbated after independence. We shall examine the relationship between changes in the higher reaches of the political system and the market with community formation at the local level with reference to three specific areas: (a) caste and political competition; (b) the politics of positive discrimination; and (c) caste and the economy.

Caste and competitive politics

The introduction of limited franchise under British rule had already created a stir among the Indian electorate. The ensuing competition and the differential mobilisation by untouchables had led to a strong reaction among the Congress leadership which saw the communal electorate as an attempt by the British to divide and rule. One of the legacies of the Poona Pact, which symbolised a historic rapproachment between the leaders of the untouchables and the Congress leadership, was to set aside a quota for the representatives of the untouchables. The second legacy was the knowledge that local hierarchy could be renegotiated at the level of high politics through competitive electoral mobilisation. The lesson was not lost on the electorate, particularly among the less privileged sections after independence when universal adult suffrage was introduced in one fell swoop. There was an initial interlude during which the locally dominant castes transformed the *jajmani* relations into a veritable vote bank through what the Rudolphs have called vertical mobilisation. However, intra-elite conflict and land reforms, which helped further loosen the dependent relations between the locally dominant caste and those who worked for them, quickly led to a situation of factional conflict and short–term political alliances, called differential mobilisation. By the 1960s, electoral mobilisation had led to a new phenomenon called horizontal mobilisation whereby people situated at comparable levels within the local caste hierarchy came together in caste associations. One consequence of horizontal mobilisation was the formation of new parties like the Republican Party, the Bahujan Samaj Party primarily supported by former untouchables or the various *kisan* parties, and movements like the Lok Dal which draw their support mainly from the 'other backward classes', to use an official Government classification. These aggressively promoted sectional interest through the electoral arena.

One of the main consequences of four decades of competitive electoral politics on the local caste hierarchy has been to render all inherited relations of power necessarily contestable. The congruence of status, power and wealth, tenuous even at a period when little recourse for status negotiation was available outside the local arena has been thrown out of sync so that, as Washbrook reminds us, '. . . the merest sight or smell of privilege in any area of society instantly provokes antipathetic response among those who see or smell it. No privilege is inherently legitimate and no authority exists uncontested' (1989:227).

For ease of presentation, we can conceptualise the role of caste as a factor in political behaviour in terms of an analytical scheme (Table 1). Membership of a caste, ensconced within the local caste hierarchy, can be perceived by some of its members as an obligation to support their social superiors. In terms of Indian voting behaviour, this has been conceptualised as vertical mobilisation. However, when members of a caste come together to promote shared economic interests, it is called horizontal mobilisation. As the logic of political participation has made its headway steadily through the Indian electorate and the percentage of people taking part in elections has grown, 'vote banks', which functioned on the basis of vertical obligation, have become progressively rare. As things stand now, it is common to find factions – short–term political alliances – where voters follow their own interests and utilise all political resources at their command, including the membership of a caste.

The scenario of contestation that Washbrook describes from the case of Tamil Nadu is repeated daily in all parts of India (Haynes & Prakash, 1991).Underneath the violence and atrocities perpetrated in its name, caste is alive and well as a factor in electoral mobilisation. Does caste consciousness perpetuate inherited caste related inequalities? What might sound counter–intuitive is one of the enigmas of caste, for caste consciousness in fact destroys precisely those attributes of the caste system, such as traditional social obligations, hierarchy, and dominance, which the essentialist view presented as necessarily fixed in time and space. The point will be discussed at greater length below.

Table 1 *Caste and political competition*

Value	Norm	Modality	Structure	Mobilisation Process
Primordial (essence)	Obligation	Jajmani	Vote banks	Vertical
Rational (agency)	Interest	Political organisation	Multi-caste Caste associations	Differential Horizontal

Caste and positive discrimination

Caste is conceptualised in the Indian constitution as the principal factor behind social hierarchy, inequality and social closure. Rather than banishing it altogether by a constitutional fiat, the constitution combats it in two distinct but related ways. The constitution specifically outlaws caste as a cause of discrimination along with gender, race, place of birth. Article 15, in laying down the norms of the right to equality for all citizens, provides for equal access to all aspects of political as well as civil life:

15(1): The State shall not discriminate against any citizen on grounds only of religion, race, caste, sex, place of birth or any of them.

15(2): No citizen shall, on grounds only of religion, race, caste, sex, place of birth or any of them, be subject to any disability, liability, restriction or condition with regards to –

(a) access to shops, public restaurants, hotels and places of public entertainment; or

(b) the use of wells, tanks, bathing ghats, roads and places of public resort maintained wholly or partly out of State funds or dedicated to the use of the general public.

The practice of untouchability is prohibited by the constitution. 'The enforcement of any disability arising out of "Untouchability" shall be an offence punishable in accordance with law; (Article 17). The provision was given considerable force by the Untouchability Prohibition Act of 1955 which has subsequently been amended to give it even greater force. The new law, called the Civil Rights Act, is much more far-reaching in its scope.

In the second place, the constitution provides for a range of political and legal instruments to combat past inequalities through positive discrimination in representation, public services, allocation of educational, economic and social facilities. A subsection of the fundamental provision for equal rights lays down categorically: 'Nothing in this article . . . shall prevent the State from making any special provision for the advancement of any socially and educationally backward classes of citizens or for the Scheduled Castes and the Scheduled Tribes.' In addition, the constitution has provided for administrative machinery to watch over the interests of the former untouchables, tribes and backward classes.

Not surprisingly, this has led to considerable political agitation by social groups who feel unjustly dispossessed of what they consider their fair share of the national wealth. The backlash against reservation policies has been fierce and widely spread. The rhetoric of the anti-reservation movement, couched in the abstract language of merit and equality, both of which are supposedly violated by affirmative action, should be familiar to those who have followed similar movements in other cultures. The unique element, which on the face of it appears eminently plausible, is that while the idea of positive discrimination is both noble and necessary, by choosing caste as the basis of special privilege, a fresh lease of life is given to an institution which really ought to disappear. This argument, which has been discussed at length in the literature on reservation (Kaul, 1993; Mitra, 1990) is based on an inadequate understanding of the dialectics of caste and caste consciousness.

The main achievement of the double instruments of legal equality and positive discrimination has been to sever the psychological link between *jati* and occupation. That some former untouchables do in fact succeed in securing high positions in public life gives credibility to the symbolic value of the policy. The instrumental role that caste plays both in raising consciousness and electoral mobilisation actually undermines the ideological basis of the *varna* scheme. Thus, 'while legitimizing caste at one level, it [the reservation policy] subtly undermined it at another level. Dissociated from its material roots, the consciousness of caste becomes purely formal, a badge of politically convenient self–classification to be manipulated and waved when necessary. [Now] A Chamar does not automatically and instinctively *think* of himself as a Chamar: rather he now presents himself as one to secure certain advantages. His being is detached from his self-consciousness, and that is a remarkable gain. Caste consciousness is a ladder he uses to climb out of a social cul-de-sac, and having got to the top he kicks it away. The dialectic of reservation is far more subtle than is generally appreciated' (Parekh & Mitra, 1990:106–7).

Caste and market transactions

So far, caste has been conceptualised as a specific feature of a traditional economy based on subsistence. Many advocates of modernisation theory thought that with economic change, urbanisation and industrialisation, the caste system would simply disappear, to be replaced by a class society based on the contradiction between capital and wage labour. That is not what appears to have happened. Under the impact of market transactions, the two faces of caste have interacted to produce economic communities to promote collective interest. Social and economic change have brought about a notion of entitlement, empowerment and enfranchisement. But, rather than necessarily dissociating himself from his social network, the politically conscious individual has found in it a political and economic resource of enormous value, to be made use of in order to enhance his ability to transact in the new, competitive market place of India's modern democracy. The result is a proliferation of modern associations that use traditional ties of *jati* and *varna* to promote collective economic well-being.

A recent report in the media about the formation of a housing association for the exclusive benefit of Brahmins in the State of Karnataka illustrates this point. 'What is your *gotra*? Which sub-caste do you belong to?' These questions sound very silly and are highly deplorable but are asked when you enter the office of this particular housing society. All these questions are to confirm that the person seeking enrolment in the society is a Brahmin. Only when satisfied with the answers will the office-bearers hand over the enrolment form. The housing society is only for Brahmins. No non-Brahmin is entertained. If a Brahmin fails to reply to the questions, he is not accepted as a member. Once a member, the Brahmin is entitled to buy a piece of land being sold by the housing society at throw-away prices. But the scrutiny is thorough. There can be no cheating. No one can fake it because the questions asked are such that only a Brahmin, a practising one at that, will know the answers (Prasad, 1993:7).

The housing society, 'The Brundavana Nagara Socio-Economic and Cultural Development Trust', like the 'capitation fee colleges' where a particular community sets up an educational establishment, admission to which is restricted, are examples of new economic organisations based on social bonds. The powerful Lingayat (worshippers of Lord Shiva) and Vokkaliga (land-holding caste) communities have already formed associations and societies which are funding educational institutions, cooperative societies and housing groups – only for their own communities (Kaul, 1993).

Once they are set up, the economic organisations develop a multiplicity of functions. Thus, the leaders of the Trust have shown considerable skill in recruiting the religious leaders of various sects of Karnataka Brahmins, who, though they 'seldom agree on any one issue, supported the Trust and promoted it.' The Trust next identified the shortage of accommodation as an area on which to concentrate. Its plans to provide subsidised land to members has been the first successful step in the direction of bigger ventures of this kind. The Trust intends to 'start a school for training *archaks'*, pujaris who work in temples. Formal training and reasonable career prospects, the Trust hopes, will attract more young Brahmins to the priesthood than is currently the case. Training will be given by noted Sanskrit scholars. To keep the heads of various religious *mutts* happy, the Trust will give them one acre to build temples. This temple complex will be unique in the sense that it will have temples of different sects standing side by side. A matrimonial bureau will be opened to encourage marriages of young widows. A novel feature of the planned township will be medical and engineering colleges.

Caste, community and modern politics

Two significant points emerge from the account of the Housing Trust discussed above. In the first place, though the Trust is composed of social units that perceive themselves in traditional, social mode, it is itself a new creation with no prior recorded existence in the sacred texts. The Trust is aimed at all Brahmins from the Karnataka region. It has made an attempt to overcome the *jati*-based division into quarrelling sects of Brahmins. Provided that the members meet the specific requirement of the knowledge of the Gayatri mantra, the mystical, pan-Indian totem of Brahminness, the members will be treated equally in the dispensation of the resources. Secondly, the growth of this community, created for the specific purpose of defending the interests of Brahmins facing the threat of competition from other, better-organised, communities is resented by others, as would be clear from the sarcastic undertone of the conclusion to the media report on it: 'The allotment of sites would start in October this year, on a first-come-first-served basis. But they will first have to recite the Gayatri Mantra and know their *gotra*. Without that, no site' (Prasad, 1993).

The environment within which the Trust and its detractors operate is by no means unique to Karnataka. Formation of communities is the predictable outcome of the new atmosphere of competitive, modern politics where the logic of numbers and scarce resources are increasingly clear to social groups trying to acquire new privileges or to hold on to what once appeared securely theirs but is now coveted by other groups as Washbrook's analysis of Tamil Nadu makes clear. The politics of community formation can be presented in terms of an analytical scheme. (Table 2) Unlike 'modern' or 'traditional' organisations, a community is a necessarily liminal structure, with a vernacular face turned towards local society, to which it appeals in terms recognisable to the local arena, and a universal, associational face turned towards the modern state and the market. The caste association is the most frequent but not the only type of community one is likely to come across in contemporary Indian politics.

Table 2 *The politics of community formation*

	Identity	Area	Strategy
caste (*jati*)	'thick'	insular	close
community (*sampradaya*)	'thin'	broad	open

Seen as communities, castes are uniquely Indian in form but universal in content. Under the impact of four decades of electoral competition and social legislation, new economic opportunities and new political linkages have developed. Castes, as the analysis undertaken here has attempted to show, have never been the rigid, timeless essence of an unchanging India. The introduction of competitive politics and democratic institutions have quickened the pace of change in the social and political organisation of castes, increasingly perceived as communities in which people come together to promote collective interest. Castes are now perceived not as rigid but flexible by their members who treat them more as vehicles of self-promotion rather than a structure of domination by the powerful and self-censorship by the powerless. 'Scholars' as Inden argues, kept India 'eternally ancient' by attributing to her various 'essences, most notably that of caste' (Inden, 1990:1). A new perspective which can depict India's institutions and political discourse as instruments through which her people seek to influence the course of their history therefore should start with a re-evaluation of caste.

Conclusion

Though castes are omnipresent and have been the subject of extensive field research, this general interest in caste is not matched by a general and parsimonious theory of its resilience.

Communities drawing on the solidarity of caste networks are increasingly present in Indian politics where modern institutions compete for space with the traditional. This chapter has attempted to provide the groundwork for an explanation for these characters in search of an author, by first questioning the established view of caste as the essence of rigid, ageless India; and, then, formulating a conjecture that relates the resilience of caste to the search for identity, power and material benefits in India's competitive politics.

Whether one looks at the role of caste in elections, or its involvement with social and economic life in contemporary India, it becomes quite clear that the empirical complexity of caste is out of sync with its ontological perception by many educated Indians. Whereas the former points towards a social institution of enormous vitality, the latter dismisses it as a vestige of the past whose disappearance is a pre-condition for the great leap into the brave new world of modernity. The continuation of this essentialist perception of caste, this chapter has argued, serves only to drive a wedge between the state and society. This intellectual stigma prevents law, bureaucracy and the media from doing precisely those things that would help transform caste from being an instrument of political oppression, hierarchy and social closure to a social organisation available for the creation of a plural and multi-cultural nation. 'A modern state, especially one as richly diverse as India, cannot be a collection of decommunalised individual atoms. It is and cannot but be a community of communities. Unless they are exclusively and politically divisive, corporate identities including healthier and suitable redefined caste identities are conducive to rather than hinder India's political integrity' (Parekh & Mitra, 1990:107).

The analysis presented here seeks to describe the evolution of India's society and state in terms of a scheme that lays the baseline of analysis in the segmentary state whose dispersed authority structure was ensconced within a fragmentary society where the *jati* formed the basic social unit (Mitra, 1991). The pan-Indian *varna* scheme provided a structure of ideological integration and social cohesion to these local *jatis* and regional *varna* schemes (Fox, 1969:27–44). The relative power, status and rank of these social units was mediated by the 'enticing but enigmatic figure of the king'. Authority within the Indian state tradition was the result of mutual legitimation of the raja and the Brahmin, although the specific nature of the balance of power depended on the local context (Shulman, 1985:15). The flux that characterised the system and, in many parts of India, survived the arrival of Muslim rule (Annecharlott, Kulke & Tripathi, 1986) went into suspended animation once the British gained complete political supremacy. On their part, the British, after the bitter experience of the Mutiny, refrained from direct intervention in Indian society. The colonial prejudices against the ability of Indian society to be self–governing were complemented by the essentialist constructions of caste and Indian religion.

The arrival of independence and universal franchise greatly accelerated the competition for social status that had already started under British rule thanks to the slow extension of popular representation. The discussion of caste and competitive politics has shown how caste consciousness and multi-caste factions served to challenge the domination of traditional social notables. This dialectic of castes and democracy has produced communities that have emerged as the most vital link between the traditional society and the modern state and its economic institutions.

Liberal democratic theory and the constitution of India consider the free interplay of voluntary associations as a legitimate method for the promotion of collective interest. In fact, the constitution, which is deeply committed to individual interest and representation, also makes symbolic overtures towards traditional values. Thus the constitution itself introduces the dialectic between the individual and the society as the basis of nation and state formation in India. It is therefore difficult to understand the venom with which *jatis* and communities are greeted by India's secular intellectuals except to attribute it to a new form of orientalism in Indian guise. Clearly, the solution against the abuses of caste solidarity, in the case of the Brahmin Housing Trust and others of its kind, is not to ban them or to question their bona fides but to produce the political and institutional conditions under which they can function as legitimate social associations. The judicial and administrative institutions of the state should make sure that the organisation is accountable to the state and to its members, and that, within the parameters laid down by its legal constitution (under the Societies Registration Act), the Trust provides equal access to all its members. The political and moral acceptability of the premises on which the Trust is based are negotiable in the high politics of the state and judiciary. The Indian Constitution and Supreme Court provide the necessary institutional basis for this. There is still plenty of as yet unexplored potential for further social development within the ambit of India's social institutions for the creation of an endogenous modernity through which the society and state can be sure to gain mutual cognitive access.

In the final analysis, the two faces of caste are a part of the grain of Indian society. Permeated by the values of individual rights and dignity, they find themselves in a flux. In the process, they are constantly adding new layers of complexity to Indian identity. These several Indian identities are not mutually exclusive. In order to come to a full measure of understanding of Indian society and politics, it is indispensable for social theory to comprehend this complexity rather than presenting it in simple, dichotomous forms derived out of nineteenth century European constructions of non-western societies in terms of fixed, immutable essences.

Notes

1 Parekh talks about the efforts of India's modernist leadership, particularly Nehru, which 'condemned caste, "casteism" and "caste-mindedness" but did not know how to slay these demons.' See Bhikhu Parekh, 'Caste Wars', *The Times Higher Educational Supplement* 15.2.1991, p. 13.
2 Derrett quoted Coomarswamy to suggest the complementarity of sacred and secular power as follows: 'The king says to the priest: "Turn thou unto me so that we may unite . . . I assign to you the precedence: quickened by thee I shall perform deeds".' (Ananda Coomarswamy, *Spiritual Authority and Temporal Power in the Indian Theory of Government*, New Delhi: Munsiram Manoharlal, 1978, p. 8.)

References

Berreman, G., (1968), 'The concept of caste', in *International Encyclopedia of the Social Sciences*, New York, Macmillan and Free Press.
Berreman, G., (1973), *Caste in the Modern World*, Morristown, N.J.: General Learning Press.
Béteille, A., (1983), *The Idea of Natural Inequality and Other Essays*, Delhi: OUP.
Chambers, E., (1951), *Encyclopaedia*, London:
Derrett, D. and O'Flaherty, W.D., (1978), *The concept of duty in South Asia*, India: Vikas.
Dumont, L., (1980) [1966], *Homo Hierarchicus: The Caste System and its Implications*, Complete revised English edition, Chicago: The University of Chicago Press.
Eschman, A., Kulke, H., and Tripathi, G.C., (eds), (1986), *The Cult of Jagannath and Regional Tradition of Orissa*, Delhi: Manohar.

Fox, R., (1969), 'Varna Schemes and Ideological Integration in Indian Society', *Comparative Studies in Society and History*, Vol. 11.

Fox, R., (1970), 'The Avatars of Indian Research', *Comparative Studies in Society and History*, Vol. 12.

Frankel, F. and M.S. Rao (eds), (1989), *Dominance and State Power in Modern India: Decline of a Social Order*, Delhi: OUP.

Gould, H., (1990), *The Hindu Caste System*, 3 volumes, Delhi: Chanakya.

Haynes, D. and Prakash, G., (1991), (eds), *Contesting Power: Resistance and Everyday Relations in South Asia*, Berkeley: University of California Press.

Hocart, A.M., (1950)[1938], *Caste: A Comparative Study*, London: Methuen.

Hutton, J.H., (1951), *Caste in India*, Cambridge: Cambridge University Press.

Inden, R., (1990), *Imagining India*, Oxford: Basil Blackwell.

Kaul, R., (1993), *Caste, Class and Education: Politics of the Capitation Fee Phenomenon in Karnataka*, Delhi: Sage.

Kroeber, A.L., (1930), 'Caste', in *Encyclopedia of the Social Sciences* Vol. 3, New York: Macmillan.

Madan, T.N. *et al.*, (1971), 'On the Nature of Caste in India: A Review Symposium of Dumont's *Homo Hierarchicus* in *Contributions to Indian Sociology*', N.S. 5. 1–8.

Mitra, S., (1982), 'Caste, Class and Conflict: Organization and Ideological Change in an Orissa Village', *Purusartha* 6 (1982), 97–133.

Mitra, S., (ed.), (1990), *Politics of Positive Discrimination: A Cross National Perspective*, Bombay: Popular.

Mitra, S., (1991), (ed.), *The Post-Colonial State in Asia*, Milton Keynes: Harvester.

Nandy, A., (1980), 'The making and unmaking of political cultures in India' in A. Nandy, *At the Edge of Psychology: Essays in Politics and Culture*, Delhi: Oxford University Press.

Parekh, B., (1989), *Colonialism, Tradition and Reform*, Delhi: Sage.

Parekh, B. and Mitra, S., (1990), 'The Logic of Anti-Reservation Discourse in India', in Mitra, S., (ed.), *Politics of Positive Discrimination: A Cross National Perspective*, Bombay: Popular.

Parekh, B., (1991), 'Caste Wars', *The Times Higher Educational Supplement*, 15, 2.

Prasad, R., (1993), 'Land prices a filip to the twice-born', *The Statesman Weekly* (Overseas Edition), August 7, p. 7.

Quigley, D., (1993), *The Interpretation of Caste*, Oxford: Clarendon Press.

Robinson, M., (1988), *Local Politics: The Law of the Fishes – Development through Political Change in Medak District, Andhra Pradesh (South India)*, Delhi: OUP.

Rudolph, L. and Rudolph, S., (1967), *The Modernity of Tradition*, Chicago: Chicago University Press.

Scott, J., (1985), *Weapons of the Weak: Everyday Forms of Peasant Resistance*, New York and London: Yale University Press.

Sheth, D.L., (1979), 'Caste and Politics: A Survey of Literature' in Gopal Krishna, ed., *Contributions to South Asian Studies* vol 1, Delhi: OUP.

Shulman, D., (1985), *The King and Clown in South Indian Myth and Poetry*, Princeton, N.J.: Princeton University Press.

Washbrook, D.A., (1989), 'Caste, Class and Dominance in Modern Tamilnadu: Non-Brahmanism, Dravidianism and Tamil Nationalism', in Frankel and Rao, Vol. 1.

Berreman revisited; caste and the comparative method

Ursula Sharma

Abstract

In a series of articles and books published in the '60s and '70s, Gerald Berreman argued that the institution of caste is not confined to Hindu India. In particular he drew attention to the similarities between caste in India and race in the United States of America, and drew specific attention to the processes by which deference was exacted by high caste/whites and by which untouchables/blacks devised ways of dealing with demands for deference. The dominant trend in the ethnography of caste (and in 'Indianist' ethnography in general) is away from comparison, towards a Dumontian emphasis on the *sui generis* nature of Hindu society. This is in line with a tendency in western anthropology to stress the specific and incommensurable nature of particular cultures.

It is argued that despite this fragmenting trend, comparison is nonetheless a useful tool. While we may reject Berreman's grand *schema* for classifying different kinds of social inequality as representing a totalising enterprise which anthropologists have rightly discarded, his use of comparison is valuable on two counts:

a) it permits sociological generalisation about the micro processes by which domination is both attempted and resisted,
b) it acts as valuable rhetorical device (used by 'modernists' and 'post modernists' alike) through which juxtaposition of the unexpected can surprise the reader into examining the implicit preconceptions and values which they bring to the analysis of other cultures.

Introduction

In this chapter I wish to re-examine some of Gerald Berreman's arguments regarding the significance of caste in Indian society. I

do not intend to assess his entire *oeuvre*; I am concerned princi-
pally with his assertion that caste may be and should be compared to other kinds of status inequality, specifically with
black/white relations in the United States of America, drawing
on work first published in the '60s and early '70s. I shall use use
this as an opportunity to discuss some more general issues
regarding the usefulness or legitimacy of comparison in social
anthropology which are pertinent at the juncture at which both
sociology and social anthropology find themselves in the '90s.
These issues are important in view of a) the tendency of many
anthropologists, following Dumont, to treat Hindu society (effectively if not explicitly) as *sui generis*, culturally distinct to the
extent that it is exempt from comparison with other societies,
and b) a widespread tendency (which I personally find very problematic) in contemporary anthropology to emphasise 'difference'
and the incommensurability of cultures.

I shall argue that Berreman's comparisons between Hindu
caste and American 'race' are instructive in that they encourage
us to think about general interactional processes through which
domination is achieved and resistance expressed. While critical of
some aspects of Berreman's work, I shall defend his general project of considering caste in terms of the exercise of power and
will argue against an anthropology which sees its role as the exegesis of 'unique' and 'incommensurable' cultures, whether in
South Asia or anywhere else. There is surely some space between
a thorough-going cultural particularism and a naive universalism
for provocative comparisons which are more than mere illustra-
tions of difference. In the course of this argument I shall raise a
number of issues relating to value freedom and the stance of the
observer/anthropologist in relation to those whom he or she
observes.

Caste, race and 'inequality'

Gerald Berreman conducted fieldwork for his doctorate in a village (which he called Sirkanda) in a mountainous area of Uttar
Pradesh and published a monograph entitled *Hindus of the
Himalayas* on this fieldwork in 1963. This book covered various
aspects of village society ('the economic context', 'the supernat-
ural', etc) and did not focus on caste exclusively. However in the
'50s and '60s he also published a series of papers, collected in the

volume *Caste and other Inequities* which address a limited number of common theoretical themes.

It is interesting that Berreman conducted his field research in an area of India which is not noted for the intensity or complexity of its intercaste relations. Nonetheless, Berreman argues, caste relations between the two main blocs of castes – the Brahmans and Rajputs on the one hand (who either separately or in alliance with each other form the locally dominant land owning groups) and the unclean artisan castes on the other – must be described as exploitative. The artisans are fragmented in terms of caste membership and own an insignificant proportion of the land available for cultivation. Their economic dependence on the local land-owning castes enables the latter to exact deference and to extract labour of various kinds on pain of economic or physical sanctions (Berreman, 1979:19ff; Berreman, 1963:57ff). In the essays of *Caste and other Inequities* Berreman shows a greater interest in the actual ways in which deference is exacted, and the ways in which the low castes deal with their powerless and stigmatized position than in the underlying economic conditions which favour dominance.[1]

It is this quality of interpersonal relations rather than any particular event or structural feature which struck me most vividly, forcefully and surprisingly as similar in Alabama and India when I first experienced them for over a year each within a period of five years. (Berreman, 1979:201).

Low caste people, he asserts again and again, do not accept the unclean and demeaning status to which they are assigned. They have diverse notions of their own as to how and why the caste system developed, most of which refer to the superior power of the high castes rather than their superior purity. They have no option however but to defer to local high caste persons unless they wish to be beaten or deprived of their livelihood.

How do they live with this contradiction? Berreman draws heavily on Goffman's work on stigma to make sense of this social psychological problem. The low castes are not passive recipients of their fate, he argues, and cope with it in various ways. They may make their life tolerable by simply avoiding interaction with high castes or keeping such encounters to the minimum or by sullen resignation. They may elaborate their own myths and ideologies in which their own caste 'really' is entitled to high status but, usually through the deceit of high castes or sheer misfortune, has come down in the world. Individuals may make fun of the high castes behind their backs, and some simply leave the village for the town where they remain poor but are less likely to be obliged to demonstrate deference at every social encounter. In this respect Berreman's project is comparable to that of more recent feminists (though he says little about untouchable women) and black writers who have striven to rescue the notions of agency and resistance for oppressed groups, even where their resistance has not lead to open revolt or successful revolution.[2]

Berreman explicitly compares caste to race in the United States (Berreman, 1979:1ff), though he was not the first to do so. While caste in India has many features which are not shared by other systems of inequality, eg the particular form of religious justification for hierarchy, the particular complexity of the divisions involved, in essential respects it is not at all unlike the racial divisions of the USA. In each case group membership is defined by birth. Just as whites exact deference from blacks in the USA, so do the high castes exact deference from the lower castes in India. The fact that the latter justify their superiority in terms of a specific notion of ritual purity whilst whites in the USA use quite other ideologies is less relevant than the similarities in the modes of interaction and the fact that sexual and other contacts which imply equality between superior and inferior persons are regarded as contaminating by the former and may be punished. In both societies the dominance of the subordinate groups is upheld by an ideology which the subordinate group must seem to subscribe to in 'front stage interactions' (to use Goffman's term) but which they may reject in backstage discourse among themselves. At this point Berreman is engaged in a polemic not with Indianists but with American sociologists such as Simpson and Yinger (1953) and O. C. Cox (1948), who argued that the Indian caste system is essentially unlike other systems of inequality in as much as it is informed by a hierarchical ideology to which *all* its members subscribe and is therefore less inherently unstable than western forms of inequality, where inegalitarian practice confronts egalitarian ideology. Berreman in general draws on and reacts to various contemporary influences in American sociology. Significantly the article on 'Caste in India and the United States' appeared for the first time in *The American Journal of Sociology* in 1960, and not in an anthropological context. However the debate about whether caste in India is *sui generis* or simply an extreme instance of a form of stratification which can be found in various parts of the world, was also addressed by anthropologists engaged in South Asian studies at around the same time, so that it is not surprising that in the footnotes of this article we also find references to Leach, who thought that caste society was fundamentally different from class society (Leach, 1971) and Bailey who opted for a more comparative approach (Bailey, 1959).

What did Berreman want to do with the comparison between Indian caste and caste outside India? He did not in fact write much about Japan and the despised group of Burakamin beyond asserting in a number of contexts that the comparison between Burakamin and untouchables is a legitimate one (1979:91). Nor did he write in more detail about race in the United States than in the original 1960 article. What is quite clear is that he wanted to establish the legitimacy of such comparisons to assert the possibility of a global and humanistic (in both the current senses of the term) analysis of social forms, though he does not actually use the term humanism. He assumes unselfconsciously that the various cultural differences among the groups he defines as having caste in some sense or another pose no problem to generalising about how people deal with caste, react to it, how it frames their affect, in short that inequality in general is among other things, 'an existential phenomenon' (1979:289). This kind of approach is of course very unfashionable now among anthropologists who, if they are concerned about inequality at all concern themselves more with the inequality between observer and observed than those among the observed. Strathern's lesson that it is problematic to translate 'native' difference into inequality and subordination as those terms are understood in western societies (Strathern, 1987:279ff) has been influential. Berreman however is concerned with sociological analysis rather than cultural translation, and in any case finds his own political and ethical rejection of inequality echoes in what Sirkanda low castes have to say on the matter, so does not recognise this as a problem.

In spite of having written a text which is often offered to students as an example of the fact that fieldwork cannot be done without engaging directly with the agendas of those who are to be studied (*Behind Many Masks* 1962), Berreman in fact holds to what would now be regarded as a rather outmoded and ethnocentric concern with cross cultural comparison and the generation of broad based social scientific theories. However the broad theories he develops with most insight and originality are not structural ones about the conditions in which caste systems develop, but represent a convergence of sociology and social psychology. He is interested in how subordination works in terms of interpersonal interactions, how people cope with it psychologically, how deference is regularly exacted and sometimes resisted. High castes in Sirkanda expect to be accorded honorific greetings, a form of respect which is 'enforced if it is not volunteered'.

> The rules are known by everyone, but a misjudgement can lead to a rebuke or physical punishment. When a Rajput asked me the time, using an honorific form of address, a low caste man made bold to look at his tattoo watch (a common form of male adornment) and say "4.30 by my watch". The questioner shot back edgily "Watches sometimes get broken". (Berreman, 1963:251).

Low castes seat themselves below high castes when in their presence, whereas high caste people can enter low caste dwellings when they wish and demand that members of low castes perform small services on demand. Equally, Berreman tells us much about how demands for subordination are parried in conditions where they cannot be enforced. Almost as many of his ethnographic anecdotes refer to the ways in which low caste people can occasionally manipulate high castes as to demands for deference. Berreman is also interested in the conditions under which demand can be resisted.

> A young Rajput man of a large household known by village artisans as a bad credit risk and not a particularly desirable client, came to the blacksmith with an axe he wanted sharpened. The blacksmith, who was listening to the anthropologist's radio, took the age, inspected it with evident distaste and announced "This axe is worth eight annas (ten cents). My file is worth 15 rupees (three dollars). It would spoil my valuable file to sharpen this worthless axe. Go find a flat rock and sharpen it yourself". (Berreman, 1963:236)

Cheek can be risked where the high caste recipient is not materially powerful or personally influential.

Berreman and Dumont

With the publication of Dumont's *Homo Hierarchicus* in 1966 and its translation into English in 1970, anthropological work on caste took a definitive turn. The limits of caste were no longer a matter of empirical comparison (how different does a system of stratification have to be from that which we find in Hindu India before we must cease to call it a caste system?) but a matter of methodology (Can we talk in terms of comparing a system of stratification in a global sense at all without imposing inappropriate western notions upon Hindu social reality?).

Berreman contributed to an issue of the journal *Contributions to Indian Sociology* devoted to reviews of *Homo Hierarchicus* by a range of well known anthropologists, both western and Indian. His reaction was one which was perhaps predictable in terms of his particular interest in the caste system, namely that Dumont had been listening to Brahmans too intently to hear the voices from other regions of the hierarchy. The ideological celebration of hierarchy based on principles of purity and pollution which Dumont regarded as essential to Indian society was not shared by the low castes who had their own definitions of the situation. Why should anthropologists, or anyone else for that matter, regard these views as less significant than those of the literati of Hindu India, the Brahmans? His first line of criticism of Dumont was at one level therefore an empiricist one; Dumont does not attend to

> the extensive empirical literature on village India and on caste in India which has emerged during the post Independence era . . . It is a view which conforms rather closely to the high-caste ideal of what the caste system of Hindu India ought to be like according to those who value it positively; it conforms well to the theory of caste purveyed in learned Brahmanical tracts. But it bears little relationship to the experience of caste in the lives of many millions who live it in India, or to the feeble reflections of those lives that have made their way into the ethnographical, biographical and novelistic literature. And this is, I insist, a travesty. A frank talk with an untouchable who knows and trusts one would be enough to make this clear. (Berreman, 1979:162)

Many of Berreman's empirical misgivings about Dumont's arguments were shared by other critics, in view of which it is interesting that it has nonetheless been Dumont's ideas more than anyone else's which have formed the fulcrum of debates about the nature of Indian society among western social scientists. However Berreman showed that there were also more theoretical issues at stake – about how fieldwork is done, and about whose version of a local reality should be privileged.

With the modern, or post-modern, concern with reflexivity the accusation that Dumont listened to Brahmans might seem less self-evidently a methodological crime than it did when Berreman made it. Many have rejected the notion of the anthropologist as detached observer, associating it with what is now widely represented as an outmoded positivist paradigm. Engagement with the person or the group who forms the object of the study is now seen as less problematic and there is considerable experimentation that blurs insider/outsider boundaries in much recent ethnography writing (Marcus and Fischer, 1986:69ff).

Problems arise with this approach however where (as is always the case) there are different versions of social reality to choose from. With whom should we engage? and how should we justify our choice if not in terms of some hegemonising intellectual or moral *schema*?

Let me however argue as devil's advocate for a moment. If there are problems with listening exclusively to Brahmans, may one not ask why it would be any better to listen to untouchables' versions of Hindu reality, especially given the undoubted influence of the Brahmans? If, as Burghart suggests, the Brahmans as 'privileged native spokespersons' are the 'local counterpart' of the western ethnographer (Burghart, 1990:277) then if we engage with anyone in Hindu society it ought presumably to be with Brahmans. To Burghart the problem with this project is not (as for Berreman) its political or moral suspectness, but its tendency to produce redundancy;

> . . . why become a European Brahman when there are so many Indian ones? (Burghart, 1990:277)[3]

To Berreman, the need to listen to the untouchables' story is effectively a political choice, in line with Becker's privileging of the story of the underdog; when we study a hierarchical situation, argues Becker, we must always look at the situation from somebody's point of view and the choice as to whose point of view we privilege is a political one. If we take the point of view of the superordinate we are, most likely, only reproducing a picture of the world which is already well known in the society in question because it has a dominant place in the 'hierarchy of credibility' (Becker, 1967).

Berreman does not just reject Dumont's claim that Hindu India is a unique social reality, but aims to produce *global* comparisons. Not only does he assert that caste can be compared with other forms of inherited ranking in West Africa, Japan etc. but, in an article entitled 'Social inequality: a cross-cultural typology', written in 1978 and reprinted in *Caste and other Inequities* (Berreman, 1979:288ff), he devises a schema for classifying diverse kinds of inequality – class, caste, estate, ethnicity, also sex and age. Re-reading this article I find it rather dry, based on a distinction between extrinsic and intrinsic criteria for ascription to social strata which would be difficult to maintain today in the face of modern work on the complexities of ethnic and other identities.

Class and similar distinctions are made on the basis of extrinsic criteria – extrinsic to the individuals who are so distinguished that is, such as income, occupation, etc. Institutions like caste are based on intrinsic criteria – that is, individuals are regarded as being different from each other by virtue of some intrinsic differential worth. My main problem with this distinction is that it is hard to find a form of inequality or indeed social classification of any kind in which those who benefit from the order thus established do not attribute intrinsic worth to themselves or deny it to others.

Nor am I convinced by Berreman's claim that this kind of cross-cultural comparison will help us to identify alternatives to social stratification and the damaging effects of inequality. The study of specific social movements, social experiments and historical political processes will be more instructive here, if indeed such issues are ever settled in the academy. But it is in the nature of typologies to have a short shelf life in social sciences. As Leach taught us many years ago, schemes of classification take place within a frame of reference which implicitly or explicitly defines what is relevant to analysis (Leach, 1961). The Dumontian problematic (and other schemes which place India in a category of its own and contrast it to class societies, societies based on individualism, etc) suggests to us that the frame of reference which we should adopt is that of culture and ideology. The cross-cultural comparisons which Berreman proposes instruct us to look for structural similarities which may exist in spite of profound cultural diversity.

This, I think, is a lesson worth remembering, but based on an opposition between culture and structure which is surely an artificial one. The particular insight which anthropologists can bring to the study of inequality derives from observing the micro situations in which the superior and subordinate interact. Here 'cultural' notions about the basis of inequality may now be used to justify action, now ignored. Structural sources of inequality may have less effect in some encounters than personal and situational factors, as Berreman's field material shows (see examples above). My own view is that Berreman's insight that the ways in which Brahmans dominate untouchables is similar to the way in which whites dominate blacks in the USA is worth any number of general typologies or holistic accounts.

Comparison in anthropology

Nonetheless, much contemporary ethnography sees itself as concerned with *cultures* rather than *social structures* and these cultures are effectively treated as *sui generis* albeit displaying regional similarities. The kind of classification of cultures favoured by Ruth Benedict has been rejected and the comparative scheme which Berreman attempted would be rejected by many out of hand as example of outmoded positivism. Many would reject Goody's suggestion that the function of comparison is to

find out which elements of behaviour are given in 'human nature' and which man himself (sic) creates. (Goody, 1969:9)

though working through this problematic was a necessary foundation for much feminist anthropology in the recent past. What anthropology has had to say about human nature has usually been fairly trite, whilst what it has had to say about what men and women create for themselves on the basis of their common nature has proved extremely interesting, so perhaps we may as well start from the proposition that it is this created world which concerns our discipline.

In this climate what becomes of the comparative method, once hailed as the hallmark of social anthropology? If we have already decided that that which is common to all humans is either uninteresting or beyond the scope of our discipline, if cultures are to be regarded as 'arbitrary codes' (Schweder, 1984:45) what possible role can comparison have in this sea of 'difference'? Parkin's suggestion that we may more fruitfully pursue cultural transformations at a regional level rather than attempt generalisations through global comparisons would probably meet with the approval of a good number of contemporary anthropologists (Parkin, 1987:56ff). In practice it is certainly true that anthropology has generated a number of regional traditions (Fardon, 1990) although the South Asianists are probably the most insistent on the specificity of their concerns. These regional traditions seem to me to have as much to do with the growth of social anthropology as a profession with its own sub-groups and specialisms as anything else. South Asianists do not need to assert that caste is not comparable to class societies or to the egalitarian societies of the west any more; even if they (like Berreman) know something of Alabama from their personal experience they will probably have learned their anthropology in an academic setting in which it was quite unnecessary for them to read any ethnographic work on Alabama or anywhere like it in order to qualify. Those anthropologists such as Mary Douglas and Jack Goody who use comparison to develop broad classifications of social forms across these regionalisms tend, significantly, to have more intellectual influence outside the discipline of anthropology at the present time.

In effect, however, comparison across widely different cultures is far from dead in anthropology in general, notwithstanding the trends just referred to. Those who write in theoretical vein are happy to compare examples from almost any society with almost any other society. Let me take an example from the work of Marilyn Strathern. In the second chapter of *After Nature* (Strathern, 1962) Strathern starts off by building up a picture of English conceptions of kinship, and the characteristic way in which the English have thought of the birth of the child as producing a totally new individual person rather than as reproducing social relations, which belong to the sphere of 'culture' and therefore have to be tacked on to the 'natural' products of physical procreation. In the course of this discussion she refers to the way in which conception and birth (including births which are the product of various forms of reproductive technology) are made to demonstrate notions about the person and the ways in which new persons are made. In this chapter, the English are constantly compared with other societies, mostly Melanesian. Thus Strathern uses Nancy Munn's ethnography of the Gawa, juxtaposing the English capacity to imagine the foetus as a new person (which can nowadays not only be conceived outside the body in the literal sense, but 'conceived' as a distinct entity from the mother who carried it through the means of scientific photography, amniocentesis and other devices for making the hidden foetus manifest) with the Gawa analogy between the mother's body and a canoe carrying, not a particular new person, but future members of a clan. Further exegesis take place of work on the Trobriands by Weiner and on the Baruya by Godelier. If Gawa ways of imagining conception and the creation of persons is so different from that of the English, what is the point of comparison? Strathern constantly appeals to notions like 'counter view', 'counter instance'. Presumably this contrastive effort is required because she expects the reader to be so imbued with these notions him/herself as to find it difficult to perceive them for what they are, as very particular and historically situated cultural constructions. And this turns out to be exactly the case, for the chapter ends with a brief critique of Gellner, another social scientist and, to boot, professor of anthropology at the University which Strathern was later to join. Gellner is (implicitly) criticised for his assumption that kinship simply imposes a cultural form upon facts which are essentially 'natural', demonstrating the way in which the 'English' notions of individual and person are thus embedded in much anthropological discourse. The work which Strathern's comparisons are made to do in this chapter are not to help construct any kind of typology about the conditions in which particular notions of the person develop and flourish, but to surprise the reader by showing the very relative nature of the assumptions which s/he may be supposed to hold (if a professor of anthropology is unaware of their very cultural construction, how much more may other readers require this shock).

What of Berreman's comparisons, who after all is explicitly striving to establish *similarities* rather than set us loose (free?) on a relativistic ocean? Like Strathern, Berreman is aiming to surprise us. He implicitly assumes that the reader does not think that Hindu Brahmans and whites in Alabama are like each other. The surprise may work in two ways. It may jolt the complacency of the modernist westerner who cannot identify with the 'archaism' of Hindu caste society, who believes himself or herself to live in a different world with different values, even if these (egalitarian) values are not always achieved. Nowadays Berreman's comparison between caste and race may jolt the reader out of another set of attitudes, namely the sense that we must be careful not to apply our own ethnocentric attitudes to the people we study. We are given permission to challenge caste, to call a spade a spade and, *contra* Dumont, to recognise 'hierarchy' for another form of stratification, indeed oppression.

In either case comparison serves a rhetorical rather than classificatory function. We are meant to be surprised. Both forms of comparison set out to make juxtapositions which lie far outside the comparisons legitimated by folk classifications of societies (primitive/modern societies, east/west, etc). In both cases the comparison has a moral function, for the reader is cut loose from familiar moorings whether into the shallow seas of total relativism or (as in the case of caste) the deeper and much more dangerous waters in which we find ourselves when we attempt to marry awareness of the relativity of cultural notions to a need to make political judgements (which are the waters which applied anthropologists and anthropologists who take any kind of political commitment into the field inevitably find themselves sailing in, whatever their philosophical positions).

If the useful role of comparison is a didactic one then, *pace* Parkin and contrary to the practice of modern South Asianists, I do not see why we should not compare any society with any other society, according to the point we are trying to get across, the preconceptions we are trying to challenge. However I would argue that in the case of Berreman comparison does serve a valuable analytic function as well, namely of focusing our attention on process – in this case the processes by which group domination is enacted, lately rather eclipsed by the concern with the construction of identity. The micro enactment of domination, the strategies of deference, the implicit forms of inclusion and exclusion which it involves, the muting of direct conflict in everyday interaction, are surely of great interest to anthropologists and indeed there are many examples of the ways in which they have studied them. Examples might include Jeffery, Jeffery and Lyon's study of ways in which Indian village women in labour are silenced by the practices of 'modern' medicine in local hospitals (Jeffrey, Jeffrey and Lyon, 1989:116ff), or Hastings Donnan's study of inter-ethnic joking in a London factory (Donnan, 1976). These instances demonstrate the special (though not unique) competence of the anthropologist in revealing the micro-processes by which hegemony is locally achieved, and frequently also disguised. Inasmuch as power has come to be understood as pervasive, exercised through many agencies and in many contexts, with the coming of 'global' society we cannot say in advance that any particular ethnographic comparison of these processes is inadmissible.

Multivocal cultures

The value of Berreman's reminder that the kind of account we produce depends on whom we listen to is its insistence that (cultural) texts have authors. We might say that Berreman does not do a particularly sophisticated deconstruction job on either Brahmanical or untouchable representations of Hindu society, but perhaps the way in which Hindu society is represented is of less interest to him that the way it is experienced. However he can be seen as one of the anthropologists whose work stimulated the debate about the degree to which India is in fact a plural society. As against Dumontian monism, by which I mean the idea that ideologically India is essentially one culture regardless of local variations or empirical deviations, Berreman suggests that we need assume no such unity or continuity. Obviously untouchables and Brahmans share some terms or conventions or communication of any kind would be impossible, though as Levinson has shown linguistic deference as shown in use of honorifics to members of another caste need not be accompanied by admission of superiority in eg ritual practice (Levinson, 1982). 'Objectively' anthropologists who did their fieldwork around the same time as Berreman's Sirkanda research found various differences in practice as between high and low castes with respect to eg marriage and divorce, patterns of household composition, ritual forms etc. Did these represent local warping of a common cultural pattern, which low caste people would have conformed to were it possible for them to do so, but which local economic and political conditions made impossible for them to realise? The recognition of Sanskritisation as a project for attempting upward mobility suggested that the low caste themselves recognised cultural values which if not universally celebrated were of very widespread currency and validity. Some studies of low castes revealed much adherence to the hierarchical values proposed by Dumont

85

(Moffatt, 1979) whilst others have suggested that these castes had their own cultural understandings of the world, that they might positively value some features of their practice or ideology which were contrary to Brahmanical notions, not seeing them as simply concessions to circumstance of one kind or another (Searle-Chatterjee, 1981; Deliège, 1993).

To Berreman the issue of cultural divergence was not a great problem. Using the notions of M. G. Smith he described India as a culturally plural society, pinned together by the exercise power on the part of those who held economic and political control.

The plural society is held together by power rather than consensus. (Berreman, 1979:77).

Some cultural features are shared amongst Hindus of different castes of course – there must be some areas of consensus – but there is quite a high degree of divergence. Difference in life experience and situation generates different interpretations of the natural and social order, noted by Weber. In addition castes are relatively self-contained units (socially, though not economically), ideal breeding ground for differentiation.

One might argue that since Berreman wrote this piece, anthropologists have developed more sophisticated concepts for analysing the relationship among different cultures or subcultures which co-exist within the same socio-political environment. He could have made good use of Ardener's notion of muted groups (Ardener, 1978) to analyse the way in which untouchable views of the social world develop from their experience yet do not reach explicit articulation in the public realm. Saifullah Khan's analysis of the ways in which the culture of the Pakistani minority in Britain is encapsulated within a hegemonic British culture (Saifullah Khan, 1982) might also provide an exemplar for the analysis of cultural divergence in South Asia. And there is plenty of evidence from Hindu society itself that universally recognised notions like 'karma' are in fact used situationally (Sharma, 1973). Theories of cultural articulation are not as well developed as one would expect within anthropology, a discipline which nowadays claims special competence in the analysis of cultures, yet we ought surely to agree with Berreman that the presence of diverse definitions of key values within Hindu society should not surprise us, and we may well feel that modern 'Indianists' have made rather heavy weather of the whole issue. Possibly it is just because discourse on South Asian society has been so cut off from general social science discourse that few have thought of applying general sociological or anthropological theories about the articulation of subcultures to this debate.

At the most general level, Deliège reminds us that we have no reason to suppose that people in general are always consistent in their beliefs or practices. If we are familiar with the idea of high caste people subscribing to communism and practising hierarchy, Christians who practise caste, why expect any more uniformity or consistency among low castes? (Deliège, 1992). I think that Berreman's field material not only bears this out but illustrates the fact that it is in the nature of oppressive systems that the subordinated are doomed to live out contradictions which the powerful and prestigious can often glide over or avoid. Feminist scholars are very familiar with the fact that women in many societies participate in the dominant values of their societies which define women as *inferior*, less competent, etc whilst being obliged to exemplify in their own lives *superior* self control, resilience, social competence, etc. Women depend on men and are publicly defined as dependents, yet may also participate in a muted female discourse about the fragility of male character, men's incompetence and uselessness as providers, etc. More practically, women may have to choose between acknowledging dependence on male patrons in order to achieve personal material success or expressing solidarity with other women in order to achieve more general benefits. There are no end to the contradictions which the disempowered or culturally undervalued may have to work out in their own lives, and Berreman's work demonstrates that this is often accomplished at considerable practical and psychological cost to the individual. It is the privilege of the powerful not to have to constantly face and tackle such contradictions, although we might argue that in the case of South Asia high castes do face the tension between ritual and political superiority. The Brahman who by virtue of his fitness as a Brahman accepts gifts from the king or members of the locally powerful ruling group eats their sin and the king who accepts the ministrations of the Brahman by doing so recognises the latter's ritual hegemony (Burghart, 1983). However these are contradictions with which ordinary princes and priests usually find means of accommodating without the compromise of personal dignity to which the untouchable is doomed if s/he is to survive.

Political commitment

Berreman does not claim to be politically neutral in his work and sometimes has used fairly strong language to refer to claims to neutrality which effectively condone the effects of inequality ('Brain damage and the defense of inequality' is the title of one critical paper). His work on caste shows an explicit commitment to a universal humanist egalitarianism and generates a critique of both western and Indian society which I find sympathetic, if rather repetitive at times. *Caste and other Inequities* demonstrates the passionate political commitment which was manifest in a good deal of debate among anthropologists and other social scientists in the '60s and early '70s. This produced radical works like Hymes's *Reinventing Anthropology* (Hymes, 1974) and stimulated the debate about anthropology's relationship with colonialism. In keeping with the spirit of this period Berreman has no hesitation whatsoever in applying 'western' notions like equality to Hindu society.

More fundamentally for modern anthropology, his work challenges the assumption that in studying 'exotic' societies or 'other cultures' we are engaged in a confrontation between the self and the 'Other' except in the mundane sense that the social scientist must objectify anything to a certain degree in order to study it. As Spiro (1992:67) and others have argued, we can only study 'other' cultures at all because they are not actually totally incommensurate with our own culture; if it were otherwise we could not begin to say anything about them. There must be something therefore which is *not* alien to the observer who studies another culture, whether we choose to see this as a continuity in 'human nature' or as I prefer to think, in the fact that in spite of huge cultural diversity, societies exhibit many common features and the anthropologist will find many familiar processes at work beneath the diversity of language and ideology. If we concentrate on the content of representations and ideologies we shall probably not see these continuities; if we concentrate on process then we may do so. Berreman is not of course saying that Sirkanda is just the same as Alabama but he does show that there is sufficient similarity in the processes of subordination and oppression at work for us to claim the right to be as questioning of the power of the high castes in Sirkanda as we are of the high castes in Alabama. But unless we had made the comparison we might not have reached that point.

In terms of its value judgements we must assess Berreman's work as we would anything else, according to our own political and moral convictions, whatever these may be. Intellectually we can judge his commitment as a positive factor in his work in as much as it encourages us to make juxtapositions, jumps of relevance, connections which call into question the assumption of profound difference between Hindu and all other societies. It enables us to look at the tired old 'ethnographic facts' of Hindu village life in a new light, a light which retains its freshness and clarity still.

Notes

1 I shall refer to those of Berreman's articles which were re-published in *Caste and other Inequities* as they appear in the latter, and not as they appear in their original sites of publication.
2 In this literature 'resistance' is a concept which embraces all the actions and cultural forms through which oppression is questioned or subverted, explicitly or implicitly, or simply survived. See Guru's work on Asian women in Britain (Guru, 1987), and a wide literature on slavery in the United States (eg Russell, 1982).
3 However Burghart comes to a similar conclusion to Berreman in the end, though coming further philosophically and working from a less naive methodological viewpoint, namely that having spent a good deal of effort in dialogue with their 'local counterparts' in South Asia

> it is time for South Asianists to look outward and pursue an intertextual dialogue with their colleagues. (Burghart, 1990:277)

References

Appadurai, A., (1992), 'Putting Hierarchy in its Place', pp. 34–47 in G.E. Marcus (ed.), *Rereading Cultural Anthropology*, London: Duke University Press.
Ardener, S., (1978), 'Introduction: The Nature of Women in Society', pp. 9–48 in S. Ardener (ed.), *Defining Females. The Nature of Women in Society*, London: Croom Helm.
Bailey, F.G., (1959), 'For a sociology of India?' *Contributions to Indian Sociology*, 3:88–101.
Becker, H., (1967), 'Whose side are we on?' *Social Problems*, 14 (Winter) pp. 239–247.
Berreman, G., (1962), *Behind Many Masks. Ethnography and Impression Management in a Himalayan Village*, Bobbs-Merrill Reprint Series.
Berreman, G., (1963), *Hindus of the Himalayas*, Berkeley and Los Angeles: University of California Press.
Berreman, G., (1979), *Caste and other inequities. Essays on Inequality*, Meerut: Folklore Institute.

Burghart, R., (1983), 'For a sociology of Indias; an intracultural approach to the study of "Hindu Society"', *Contributions to Indian Sociology*, 17 (2):275–299.

Burghart, R., (1990), 'Ethnographers and their local counterparts in India', in R. Fardon (ed.), *Localizing Strategies. Regional Traditions of Ethnographic Writing*, Edinburgh: Scottish Academic Press.

Cox, O.C., (1948), *Caste. Class and Race*, New York: Doubleday and Co.

Delìege, R., (1992), 'Replication and consensus; untouchability, caste and ideology in India', *Man* 27:155–73.

Delìege, R., (1993), 'The myths of origin of the Indian untouchables', *Man* 28(3):531–549.

Donnan, H., (1976), 'Inter-ethnic Friendship, Joking and Rules of Interaction in a London Factory', pp. 81–99 in L. Holy (ed.), *Knowledge and Behaviour*, Queen's University Papers in Social Anthropology Volume 1, Belfast: Queen's University.

Dumont, L., (1970), *Homo Hierarchicus. The Caste System and its Implications*, Chicago and London: University of Chicago Press.

Fardon, R., (ed.), (1990), *Localizing Strategies. Regional Traditions of Ethnographic Writing*, Edinburgh: Scottish Academic Press.

Goody, J., (1969), *Comparative Studies in Kinship*, London: Routledge and Kegan Paul.

Guru, S., (1987), *Struggle and Resistance. Punjabi Women in Birmingham*, PhD thesis, University of Keele.

Hymes, D., (1974), *Reinventing Anthropology*, New York: Vintage Books.

Jeffrey, P., Jeffrey, R. and Lyon, A., (1989), *Labour Pains and Labour Power*, London: Zed Press.

Leach, E., (1961), *Rethinking Anthropology*, London: Athlone Press.

Leach, E., (1971), 'What should we mean by caste?', pp. 1–10 in E. Leach (ed.), *Aspects of Caste in India, Ceylon and North-west Pakistan*, Cambridge: Cambridge University Press.

Levinson, S.C., (1982), 'Caste rank and verbal interaction in western Tamilnadu', pp. 98–203 in D. McGilvray (ed.), *Caste Ideology and Interaction*, Cambridge: Cambridge University Press.

Marcus, G.E. and Fischer, M.J., (1986), *Anthropology as Cultural Critique. An Experimental Moment in the Human Sciences*, Chicago and London: University of Chicago Press.

McGilvray, D., (1982), 'Mukkuvar vannimai: Tamil caste and matriclan ideology', pp. 34–97 in D. McGilvray (ed.), *Caste Ideology and Interaction*, Cambridge: Cambridge University Press.

Moffatt, M., (1979), *An Untouchable Community in South India: Structure and Consensus*, Princeton: Princeton University Press.

Parkin, D., (1987), 'Comparison as the search for continuity', in L. Holy (ed.), *Comparative Anthropology*, Oxford: Blackwell.

Russell, M., (1982), 'Slave codes and liner notes', pp. 129–140 in Gloria Hull, Patricia Bell Scott and Barbara Smith (eds), *But Some of Us Are Brave. Black Women's Studies*, New York: Feminist Press.

Saifullah Khan, V., (1982), 'The role of the culture of dominance in structuring the experience of ethnic minorities', pp. 197–215 in C. Husband (ed.), *'Race' in Britain. Continuity and Change*, London: Hutchinson.

Schweder, R.A., (1984), 'Anthropology's romantic rebellion against the enlightenment, or there's more to thinking than reason and evidence', pp. 27–66 in

R.A. Schweder and R.A. Levine (eds), *Culture Theory. Essays on Mind, Self and Emotion*, Cambridge: Cambridge University Press.

Searle-Chatterjee, M., (1981), *Reversible Sex Roles. The Special Case of Benares Sweepers*, Oxford: Pergamon Press.

Sharma, U., (1973), 'Theodicy and the doctrine of karma', *Man* 8 (3):347–264.

Simpson, G.E. and Yinger, J.M., (1953), *Racial and Cultural Minorities*, New York: Harper and Bros.

Spiro, M., (1992), *Anthropological Other or Burmese Brother? Studies in cultural Anthropology*, New Brunswick: Transaction Publishers.

Strathern, M., (1992), *After Nature. English Kinship in the Late Twentieth Century*, Cambridge: Cambridge University Press.

Strathern, M., (1987), 'Conclusion', pp. 279–302 in M. Strathern (ed.), *Dealing with Inequality*, Cambridge: Cambridge University Press.

Girasias and the politics of difference in Rajasthan: 'caste', kinship and gender in a marginalised society

Maya Unnithan

Abstract

Anthropologists have often contrasted 'caste' and 'tribe' as forms of social organisation based on opposite principles (eg 'castes' are based on hierarchy, 'tribal' society is undifferentiated and egalitarian). The concept of 'caste' is both an imposed one, a product of colonial governmental and academic exercises, and one which has political realities. However, whilst such national and regional formulations of caste are important, they do not always reflect the social categories which are central to the organisation of people's lives at the local level.

The Girasias (generally held to be a 'tribe' by others) live in Rajasthan in proximity to the Rajputs (generally held to be a 'caste'; Girasias themselves claim to be a branch of the Rajput caste). On many points the way in which a group categorises itself does not correspond with the way in which it is categorised by members of other groups. In practice the Girasias share many social, economic and religious institutions with the other 'caste' communities in the region as also with the 'tribal Bhils. This does not mean that these groups are indistinguishable, but 'Rajput' and 'Bhil' stereotypes were used within the Girasia group to express differences, identifications and evaluations. However the tribe/caste distinction and the corresponding division of labour between anthropologists and sociologists in India is thereby called into question.

To the Girasias, patrilineal kinship and territory play a central role in their sense of 'caste' identity, unlike other communities (the Rajputs and Bhils are exceptions) for whom caste is a more dispersed, agnatic and affinal group. Descent is crucial. Although their kinship ideology emphasises a sense of separation rather than hierarchy, Girasia kin divisions present members with equal opportunities to be unequal. Lineal kinship provides the paradigm for talking about all relationships whether or not based on actual biological ties. Equally, gender provides an idiom for the construction of difference. Descent groups are differentiated according to the evaluation of groups from which they have been able to obtain wives. Both Girasias and outsiders use the attire and the behaviour of women and perceived gender roles to distinguish between themselves. Despite the local complexity of Girasia kinship and gender relations which cannot be expressed in the language of caste and tribe, outsiders (other castes, classes, government officials, academics) continue to regard the Girasias as tribal as a result of the politics of caste and gender at the local, regional and national levels.

Introduction

In this chapter, I use material on the Girasias, a so-called tribal group in southern Rajasthan to question the use of tribe and in turn, of caste, as useful analytic categories in the study of Indian social organisation.[1] I suggest that more useful insights are gained by a consideration of the concept of kinship in India which allows for the study of both similarities and differences which exist between social categories such as caste and tribe, without necessarily seeing them as opposed social entities. I do not propose that caste and tribe do not exist or are unimportant, but that because they are complex categories, embedded in wider social, political and economic contexts, they are less likely to serve as rigorous analytical tools in themselves, especially in the study of communities, such as the Girasias, where the boundaries between caste and tribe are unclear.

The notion of caste is analytically complex as it is at once an imposed category, a product of colonial, governmental and academic exercises, and also one which has practical realities. Caste is at the same time both an ideological classification (*varna*) and a social grouping (*jati*). It is centrally linked to Hindu religion and at the same time an Indian concept which can be found to influence other religious, social and economic categories in the region. Caste has, moreover, provided the basis for the formulation of other, opposed social constructs such as 'tribe'. Thus in India, tribe is what caste is not. While a caste unit has been defined as relating its members through birth, endogamy, a hierarchy of occupations and a restricted commensality (Dumont, 1980; Marriott and Inden, 1985), the word tribe has been used to denote social organisations with less complex social, economic and religious institutions as compared to caste groups. The preoccupation with hierarchy amongst caste members is considered to be replaced by tribal egalitarianism. For example, the unconcern with social ranking is supposed to explain tribal clan exogamy and fewer restrictions on women as a means to preserve the purity of the group. In the economic sphere, the absence of social ranking is considered to be reflected in a greater sharing of resources and no internal division of labour, compared to the hierarchical nature of inter-caste service transactions. In the religious sphere, tribal groups are believed to be unconcerned with ritual purity, without use for ritual experts and practising animism.

The different forms and contexts in which caste and tribe have been used and conceptualised have, until recently, not been seen as problematic. The uneasy fit between the academic categories, such as caste, and everyday processes has been evident, both to 'field-workers' in India and Indologists (see Inden, 1988) yet, as far as I am aware, no suitable perspectives have been developed which focus on kin-type categories other than caste, or study the diverse constructions, individual, collective, historical and contemporary, of social categories, including caste. There has, furthermore, been little work which considers tribes as other than non-caste (Bailey, 1960; Chauhan, 1978; Béteille, 1978, 1984; Trautman, 1981 are some notable exceptions). The study of tribes has particularly lacked a historical perspective thereby making it especially difficult to conceive of more permeable and shifting boundaries between social categories in India. For example, the category of tribe in Indian government and academic accounts was rarely seen as a product of historical processes, such as those of disempowerment. In the case of the Girasias, I found that their increasingly tribal identity was linked to the community's weakening hold over the political, economic and symbolic resources of the region.

In my own work on the Girasias I suggest that they have a similar social organisation, particularly in terms of their kinship institutions, ideologies and practices, to other castes, such as the Rajput, as well as to other 'tribal' groups such as the Bhil in Rajasthan. Despite the similarities in kinship organisation and processes, the Girasia, Rajput and Bhil communities saw each other as distinct and unequal social groups. The Rajputs saw the Girasias and Bhils as lower (less 'pure') than them and the Girasias similarly saw the Bhils as lower than them in social standing. Kinship was the commonly used idiom than express the differences of identity and status amongst these groups. Furthermore, I found that social boundaries were constructed using kinship not only at the level of caste and tribe but also within these categories, at the levels of smaller groups and individuals. Kinship organisation and ideologies were particularly important in understanding the shifting nature of group dynamics and political action for the Girasias and Rajputs.

I use kinship in two senses. Firstly, kinship refers to the relationships formed through both descent and marriage. Secondly, and in a more abstract sense, I refer to kinship as a set of physical relations which provides a paradigm for conceptualising all other social relations (following Gellner, 1985). Furthermore, I take kinship to be communicative of more general, underlying concerns in any society (like Lévi-Strauss, 1949, 1967).

Gender analyses complemented the study of kinship in Rajasthan in important ways. The ways in which the members of the various communities talked about other communities was often with reference to the very different attire, attitudes and social institutions relating to women from these communities. Women were thus used as metaphors of the perceived social distances both between communities and within kin groups. Furthermore, a study of gender politics within and across the Girasia, Rajput and Bhil communities provided a pertinent understanding of the implications of their kinship ideologies. Unlike some gender theorists (Collier and Yanagisako, 1989 for example), I do not suggest that gender determines or constitutes kinship. Instead, I believe that gender is another way of speaking about social organisations and processes which is both related to and distinct from kinship analysis. I, therefore, see the combined analysis of kinship and gender as contributing to the search for analytically pertinent perspectives on Indian social organisation which are sensitive to historical and contemporary local ideologies, institutions and practices.

I use empirical material on the Girasias to develop an argument about gender and kinship which I see as overcoming some of the problems (discussed in the rest of this section) in the existing theories of caste and tribe. In Section 2, on 'Women, Men and Girasia Kinship', I describe the Girasias, with particular reference to the use of kinship and gender as political tools within their community. In Section 3, I compare the Girasias to two other social groups in the region, the Rajputs and the Bhils. I show that these groups, 'caste' and 'tribe', share a common 'language' and strategic use of kinship, despite their apparently contrasting social organisations. In conclusion, I look at the changing use and meaning of kinship for the Girasias and the Rajputs, in the context of the shifting politics of the region.

Maya Unnithan

Theoretical context: The anthropology of kinship and studies of Indian society

To a large extent the popularity of caste as an analytical tool and, in turn, the specific and fixed view of tribe, is a consequence of a relatively recent academic division of labour. After Indian independence, Indian social organisation and especially caste became the subject matter of sociologists. Social anthropology was largely regarded as synonymous with the colonial study of tribes, kinship and what was perceived as static and unchanging in Indian culture (Béteille, 1974; Madan, 1982). The study of caste, on the other hand, enabled the study of systems of stratification and therein concerns which followed American scholarship at the time (Béteille, *ibid.*). The lines which were drawn between castes and tribes, considered to be opposed social systems, became the divisions between the disciplines of sociology and anthropology in India.

The academic divisions in the Indian social sciences were further reinforced by the agenda for development set by the newly-formed government of independent India (Dhangare, 1985).

In this agenda sociology was seen as more capable than anthropology in providing the large scale information and evaluation of data required by the machinery of development economics (Dhanagre, *ibid.*). Sociology was thus regarded as more central to the progress of independent India compared to anthropology which in turn enabled sociologists to gain more funds for research. It is therefore, not surprising to find, following Padel (1988), that, 'Victorian anthropologists' representations persist in modern India and Indian anthropology remains deeply evolutionist in its tribal studies'.

Kinship has been of central concern within social anthropology since its conception as an academic discipline in the early part of the twentieth century. However, the approaches to kinship, especially in Britain and France, have shifted considerably with time and in general, have reflected the changing nature of the wider theoretical perspectives in the discipline. The theoretical work of the French structural anthropologist Claude Lévi-Strauss (1949, 1967), marked a distinct turn in the discipline that was in part connected to academic scholarship on South Asian societies. Previous knowledge in anthropology had so far been based on models of African societies which were descent-based and more visibly egalitarian. Studies of South Asian societies revealed the importance of marriage, in contrast to descent, in what was seen as a central preoccupation with the status and ranking of social groups and individuals. Lévi-Strauss first suggested that both descent and marriage should be seen as equally important components of the social structure and should be studied as such.[2]

These ideas have been developed in the workers of Dumont (1960, 1977) and also by Tambiah (1976) who emphasised the importance of both marriage and descent in the study of hierarchy and social ranking in Indian society. Among the important observations by Dumont, and relevant for the purposes of this paper, was the idea that marriage as well as descent were important vantage points from which to study the closure of social groups. For Dumont the different criteria for marriage distinguished caste from tribe in that tribes tolerated marriages outside the group as compared to castes who permitted marriages only within the group.[3] However, material on communities in southern Rajasthan showed that both caste and tribe had clans, emphasised patrilineal descent as well as endogamous marriages within a group of clans (which I saw as caste). It was, therefore, not possible to claim, like Dumont, that a caste was a closed group at only one level (ie, versus tribe), as its closure varied from level to level within each caste community.

Dumont's thoughts on tribes must be regarded in terms of his much wider project to explain the axiomatic principles underlying the caste system as a whole, of which marriage and descent were surface manifestations. Dumont showed caste to be a product of the underlying religious principles of purity and pollution which were most clearly reflected in an occupational hierarchy in which the Brahmin priests, because of the nature of their occupation, were considered to be the purest and therefore the highest caste. By extension, tribal groups who fell outside the network of an intercaste exchange of services, were not governed by the same rules of purity and pollution and not part of the caste system. Dumont's focus on the underlying values of purity and pollution as structuring the caste system presented a somewhat homeostatic picture of caste which has been subject to much criticism (Kolenda, 1978; Tambiah, 1973; Barnett, 1977; Raheja, 1986; Daniel, 1984).[4]

With regard to the relation between caste and tribe, I find the earlier work of Lévi-Strauss much closer to my own observations. For Lévi-Strauss, unlike for Dumont, there was a common ideological basis for the social organisation of caste and tribe in India (*The Savage Mind*, 1966). According to him, castes could be seen as transformed variants of totemic (ie, tribal) systems, especially evident in the manner in which they distinguished between social groups.[5] Lévi-Strauss also illustrated how caste and totemic systems were both exo-practising, in that they marked difference by the outward exchange of objects (women in the case of totemic systems and food and services in the case of caste societies), despite '. . . the superficial differences of endogamy and exogamy between the two' (*ibid.*, 122). Thus, for Lévi-Strauss, 'Totemism . . . could at the cost of a very simple transformation equally well be expressed in the language of the regime of caste, which is quite the reverse of primitive' (*ibid.*, 129).

Dumont's emphasis on caste as a distinct unit of social analysis was a novel approach for the time, especially as it facilitated the move away from an earlier village studies era (Fuller and Spencer, 1991) which saw the political economy of the villages as unconnected to studies on the ideology of caste and patterns of regional stratification. But it is in the micro-level connections between religious, social and political activities that Dumont's work has been weak. It is in this context that I find material on the political aspects of social organisation, such as in the earlier work of Hocart on caste (1950), more useful (also see Inden, 1986).

Hocart, like Dumont, sought universal explanations for caste and saw caste as manifested through an occupational hierarchy. However, for Hocart, unlike Dumont, caste was a product of divine kinship and the king as patron and chief sacrificer of Hindu rituals occupied the apex position in the occupational hierarchy. All other caste groups had their social positions ranked according to the nature of their services to the king. Hocart acknowledged that social ranking could change by acts of heroism, loyalty or other kinds of services to the king, thereby allowing for the principles of heroism as well as ritual hierarchy in structuring the social system.[6] The concept of the heroic study, in contrast to a society organised along the lines of brahmanic caste principles, presented a view of the social system which was more fluid as it acknowledged individual endeavour outside the organically (functionally) oriented caste rules of action and gave place to achievement alongside ascription. This perspective is particularly relevant to the study of Indian regions where rulers (of the *kshatriya varna*), such as the Rajputs in Rajasthan, were politically dominant and the state was kin based and lineage centred, unlike other communities and regions where caste was a dispersed agnatic and affinal group (also see Fox, 1975). Furthermore, status and power amongst Rajput kin was determined not only by a genealogical distance from the ruling lineage but through loyalty and service which allowed distant kin a privileged proximity and access to economic, political and social resources. The different structures and processes of Rajput kinship and politics compared to other caste communities opens up an altogether new and interesting way of thinking about caste, which at the same time collapsed the analytic boundaries between caste and tribe as in the case of communities such as the Girasia.

The theories of both Dumont and Hocart have been relatively top-down theories of caste in that they presented perspectives of the top two groups in the *varna* (ideological) hierarchy, the priest and the ruler. In the 1980s, important insights to the study of social organisations in India came from the subaltern school of Indian historians. The subaltern approach (following Gramsci's use of the word subaltern to mean 'peasant') developed in response to the historiography of colonial South Asia. Focusing on lower class and caste communities, these historians undertook to rewrite Indian history through a study of peasant protest (Guha, 1982). The subaltern historians particularly emphasised the need to understand subaltern politics, its method and nature of mobilisation, and separate its connections with the elite in the colonial period. The subaltern studies group (Amin, Arnold, Chatterjee, Guha, Hardiman, Pandey are some of its prominent figures) moves beyond social structures to consider the processes of subaltern solidarity, which according to them was based on the common experiences of domination and a shared desire to present resistance to such domination. Within the subalternist perspective there was emphasis on considering the effects of historical experiences on the consciousness of individuals and communities, which have both been, to my mind, critically weak areas of anthropological investigation.

Among the main points to emerge from subaltern analyses and especially useful for social anthropology have been firstly, the stress on the historical analysis of violence and spontaneity as a way into understanding community organisation and mobilisations (Das, 1987). Focusing on the popular leaders of subaltern protests also allows for the consideration of individual action within the community frame. I find this approach particularly useful in conceptualising social change in India (see last section of this chapter). Secondly, the subalternist project has brought back the importance of kin and territory structures as significant units of social analysis. There are two important areas in which, however, the subalternist approach could be strengthened. Firstly, in order to recapture a peasant history, such as that of the Girasias, which is passive, rather than visible through violence, it needs to go beyond the violent moments and into everyday life (generally acknowledged by Guha and Das, *ibid.*). Secondly, gender issues are not centrally addressed, although some recent work tends to overcome this shortcoming (for example, see O'Hanlon, 1988).

The concern with gender perspectives in the anthropology of South Asia has been relatively recent. As elsewhere, the question has essentially been one of representation rather than on the absence of empirical material (H. Moore, 1988). In Lévi-Strauss's work in the 'Elementary Structures of Kinship', while anthropology moved away from an emphasis on descent to focus on marriage alliances, marriages continued to be seen from the perspective of men in society rather than women. Material on women in the studies of caste, in pre- or post-independent India until the 1970s, did not question the structural view of caste women as passive, subordinate and mainly invisible members of their social groups. More recent, pertinent work in the field of kinship studies has been influenced by feminist scholarship concerned with developing appropriate tools to express women's experiences, mainly through the social and cultural analysis of gender roles and relations. Feminist studies are particularly important, I believe, because gender is not only about women but more generally about structural subordination.

Most of the feminist-oriented work on India has been concerned with the dialectical relationship between cultural ideologies and the control over resources in everyday practices in caste and class communities (for example, Sharma, 1980; Standing, 1992; Afshar and Agarwal, 1989; Dube and Leacock, 1986). In my own work I considered in what ways these ideas could be extended to 'tribal' women who are seen to have a much more favourable relation to resources and consequently a stronger position in their relationship with men and their communities in general, compared to middle or upper caste women. One of the conclusions I reached was that although there were differences between caste and tribal women in the access to economic resources, even more profound ideological similarities existed which rendered these differences superficial. The differences between women across and within castes and tribes were, however, central to the ways in which members of these communities described themselves and others. Gender perspectives thus enabled an understanding of how kinship based categories such as caste and tribe, despite their underlying ideological similarities were constructed as mutually opposed. Here, I found work on changing symbolic representation of women in the context of community and state politics (for example, Chhachhi, Kandiyoti; discussed in Section 3 below), particularly useful.

In the following section, I use both archival and ethnographic material on the Girasias, based on my stay in 1986–87, to illustrate how kinship and gender are important conceptual tools in the study of communities and persons in India.

2 Women, men and Girasia kinship

In Rajasthan the Girasia community lived in mainly three southern districts of Sirohi (58,191 people according to the 1981 census figures), Udaipur (38,257 people) and Pali (20,198 people). Most of the Girasias in Sirohi, where I stayed, were settled in the hilly and forested region of the district. They were a community of poor farmers who preferred to live by themselves in the more rugged and inaccessible parts of the Aravalli hill region. The nearest local farmer, artisan and service populations lived in multicaste villages which were linked to the railway town of Abu Road. Abu Road was close to the state border with Gujarat and hence an important trade centre.

The Girasias described themselves to non-Girasias, as members of Rajput (caste) lineages of Girasias. However, the local residents of the surrounding villages and Abu Road referred to the Girasias as tribal, forest people, who came to the village or town markets to sell bundles of wood or other forest produce. These outside descriptions invariably included a reference to 'tribal' Girasia women who wore colourful skirts, wraps and jewellery and whose behaviour in the market was uninhibited when compared with the girls and women of other castes and communities. Even journal articles, academic accounts and government documents referred to the Girasia as tribal and discounted any possibilities of the suggestion that they were Rajputs. The Girasia claims to Rajput identity were largely regarded in the region as an indication of the process of social emulation (referred to as sanskritisation by Srinivas, 1972) whereby lower sections of people claimed higher status for the purposes of social, political and economic mobility. If it had not been for my field and archival work, I would have probably believed such views.

The Girasia descriptions of themselves as a caste to outsiders and the non-Girasia perception of them as a tribe was only one, albeit the most encompassing, of a series of us/them, or insider/outsider categories. Girasia notions of kinship, especially of birth and lineal seniority, on the other hand, played a central role in the construction of difference between Girasia and non-Girasia communities, and groups and persons within Girasia communities (see Section (i) below). While the Girasias used kinship as an idiom to express their ideal of agnatic solidarity to non-Girasias, at the same time, kin ties symbolised the differences between members within the community. In this sense, Girasia kinship was about difference and often inequality as much as about sameness and equality.

Notions of exclusion and inclusion of kin also served to illustrate how gender functioned as a category of belonging and at the same time one of alienation. For example, although Girasia kinship was about descent and marriage, the relationships through descent were considered more central, by both Girasia men and women, to group identity than the kinship ties based on marriage. The preferential status given to being related through descent over marriage was particularly important in understanding the material and ideological differences between Girasia women and men. The privilege accorded to descent was reflected in the genealogies which recorded only male members of the patrilineage and functioned as a male social mapping over a region and through history. Reinforcing the significance of male kinship traced through descent, were the rules of transmission of immovable property, according male kin groups rights over territory and shares in the land and water resources.

(i) The Lineage in Girasia Kinship

The Girasias had no commonly used word for village but referred to it as the (space occupied by the) patrilineage (*Jath*). The Girasia *Jath* consisted of members who were descended from a common lineage ancestor. The village I stayed in belonged to the Taivar patrilineage who traced descent from an ancestor named Tava (hence Taivar, literally 'of Tava'). In general, the Taivar Girasias believed they were descended from the Parmar clan of Rajputs, who were, according to archival sources, the Rajput rulers in the region of Sirohi until the fourteenth century A.D. According to the elders in the village, their ancestors had been granted land in the hills (Bhakar) approximately a hundred and fifty years ago by the chief (Thakur) of the Chauchan clan of Rajputs who had ruled the area since the fourteenth century until Indian independence. The Taivar ancestors had earlier lived in a village of Parmar Rajput Girasias close to the Gujarat border, but had been forced to leave as a result of disputes over land.

The lineage was central to the economic and political organisation of Girasia life. Within the Taivar Girasia village, the patrilineage (*Jath*) was referred to as the place of, and dealing with matters of, the 'kaka-baba' or father's younger and elder brothers. Based on the ties of male siblingship, the *Jath* was conceptualised in terms of a 'brotherhood'. *Jath* membership was further qualified by patrilineal descent and divided into sublineages whose members were directly descended from the same 'son of Tava' up to four generations. These kin groups were referred to as the *hojvan* (which were sub-lineages). In the Taivar Girasia village, there were eight sublineages (*hojvan*), the smallest consisting of six households and the largest with fifty one households.) In total, there were a hundred and seventy eight Taivar households. The *hojvan* was the post powerful, restraining and prescriptive institution in the village. Each *hojvan* had its own set of ritual mediators (*bhopa*) and political arbiters (*patel*). There was a ranking of *hojvans* in the village based on lineal seniority. The distinctions between these sub-lineages was reflected in the territorial divisions of the village, with the older lineages occupying the lower portions of the village (*Nichalli phalli*), and land which they first settled. The more junior lineages lived in the middle (*Beechali*) and upper (*Upali*) sections of the village, thus dividing the territory occupied by the lineage into older (more senior) and newer (more junior) portions which were to the Northwest and Southeast of the village respectively.

Conceptually, we find, that whereas the lineage (*jath*) was a brotherhood based on classificatory kinship ties (ie, the aggregation of individuals to a category, in this case based on the relationship between brothers), the sublineage (*hojvan*) was a smaller brotherhood of stronger links, based on more immediate blood ties. Therefore, within the 'us' category of lineage members, some were more 'us' than others. There was a further differentiation between blood brothers of a sublineage (*hojvan*) into those who were *haga* or 'true' brothers versus those who were not. The use of the word 'true' referred to sons who had been born 'of the same stomach', or those who shared the same mother, in contrast to those who had different mothers. The difference between sons of the same mother and the sons of stepmothers (*mahi*, literally mother's sisters) was a common operative distinction among the Girasias because more often than not, a man's father had more than one wife in his lifetime. The smallest unit of the brotherhood was this relation between men born of the same mother. The importance of this unit could be seen in terms of the spatial and economic organisation of Girasia kin. Often, 'true' brothers and their families would live in adjoining huts. Adjoining households were separated in the daily production and consumption of food, in men's control over the labour of women and in the distribution of money income earned by individual members of the household. However, 'true' brothers would form distinct units for economic activities related to the provisioning for subsistence such as ploughing fields, watering and harvesting crops. More generally, sublineage brothers would get together for long term provisioning such as the building of wells in which the *Haga* ('true' brother) units would have shares. The division of shares in land and water took place within the household and were inherited by a man's sons. Here the individual household head had the immediate decision making powers but the *hojvan* elders had the ultimate control. For example, household heads could not allocate even the nonproductive land to their affinal relations for purposes of residence without consent from other members of the sublineage. Usually such land was provided to the '*ghar jamai*' or resident sons-in-law who could only farm their father-in-law's land so long as he was alive.[7]

The Girasia household which had no special term, it seemed to me, was downplayed as a significant unit of Girasia life for two interrelated reasons. Firstly, because it represented the 'dilution' of male kinship by the presence of women from other patrilineages whereby the authority of the patrilineage could potentially be challenged by 'outsiders' (women as wives). Secondly, because of the lineal organisation of the Girasia economy, the household presented the potential for economic differentiation to arise between brothers within the lineage.

Despite the organisational and mainly gender-related measures to ensure the equality of members of the Taivar Girasia patrilineage, in reality there were continuous and longstanding conflicts between 'brothers', related to social status and ranking in the lineage. These conflicts surfaced particularly around institutions and processes in which women were centrally involved, bringing questions of gender much more to the fore in an analysis of kinship, as illustrated in the following lines.

(ii) Marriage and Girasia gender roles and ideologies

The centrality of the patrilineage had very different implications for Girasia men and women. There was a very real difference between husbands and wives in terms of their access to resources, food, and relations with members of different generations in the village. For women these differences became most tangible after marriage. The relatively restricted life of adult Girasia women in their husband's household and village was explained to me as resulting from the fact that married women belonged to a different patrilineage than their husband and therefore could not expect to have any rights over the property of his kin group. So we find that while on the one hand, the Taivar Girasias claimed they married partners from equal Rajput Girasia patrilineages (*Jaths*), on the other hand, the inferiority of the wife's patrilineage was continually stressed in the day to day activities in the village.

Wives could not participate in the *Jath Panchayatis* or village councils because it was . . . 'a matter for the husband's *Jath* only'. Even other women, sisters and daughters, were excluded from these councils because of the fact that they eventually would become wives, move away to other villages and never own the land and water shares of the *Jath*. In their husband's village, generally women in their early and later married life did not, unlike women in other castes, gain increasing control over some of the household resources despite the fact that some women were more influential than others in the village. Women could also not command the labour of their husband or his kin so, for example, wives could only eat if they cooked for themselves, while their husbands on the other hand could eat at their parent's or brothers' places.

New brides especially, were supposed to eat in separate vessels (*vadku* and *lota*) which they brought with them from their parent's house. Wives were further proscribed in their daily activities, for example, Girasia wives would not sit on rope beds in the presence of affinal men because to do so would be to state the equality of their *Jath* with the *Jath* of the husband. Furthermore, Girasia women had to cover their heads and faces before certain categories of male related affines (the father-in-law, husband's elder brother, husband's elder and younger sister's husband, husband's sister's sons, but not for the mother-in-law, husband's younger brother or husband's sister).

In the village, Taivar Girasia wives, I found, were not all lumped together as a category of outsiders, but in fact were differentiated according to their (father's) patrilineage. Ideally all Taivar Girasia men married women from upper ('purer' in kin terms) or Rajput type Girasia lineages. (There were fourteen such marriageable patrilineages in 1987 which were to the west, east and south of the village). In reality, Taivar Girasia men also married women from what they described as 'lower' or Bhil type Girasia lineages. Thus I found, that even those marriageable patrilineages which were considered equal were differentiated along a scale of purity, with the 'better' wives coming from caste (Rajput) type Girasia lineages and the 'worse' wives from tribal (Bhil) type Girasia lineages. In fact, in 1986–87, the smallest Taivar Girasia sublineage in the village was considered a fallen sublineage by the numerically dominant sublineages because some of its men had married 'lower', impure Bhil type Girasia women. The lower sublineage in turn was constantly trying to increase its status vis-a-vis the other sublineages by organising feasts for other lineage members (a shared commensality was regarded as an indication of the equality of the brotherhood).

The different lineal affiliations of the married women created differences at the level of individuals, between husbands and wives and also at the level of groups, between the sublineages in a lineage. The differences that arose between the sublineages in the Taivar patrilineage were especially manifest in their different preferences in marriage. So while men of a Taivar Girasia sublineage could marry women from any one of fourteen prescribed Girasia patrilineages, certain sublineages tended to prefer women from a select group of patrilineages, while men of other sublineages had different preferences although there was an extent to which there was an overlap. Thus Taivar Girasia men would most often marry women from their 'true' father's brother's wife's patrilineage and their sons would marry women from their paternal grandmother's patrilineage.[8] Taivar Girasia marriages were thus seen to reinforce the genealogical connections between closer kin. However, there were other cultural notions regarding kinship which worked to prevent potential hierarchical divisions from being realised. For example, several women told me that for a man to have two wives from the same patrilineage was not 'proper' (*hau-ne/theek-ne/khoti*) and that it was inconceivable for two 'sisters' to share a husband. This unstated preference, along with the tendency for men to have more than one wife, meant that although certain affinal categories were preferred, at the level of the *hojvan* or sublineage, these various preferences balanced out. Thus while marriages at the level of the sublineage and 'true' brothers tended to differentiate amongst Taivar Girasia kin, at the level of the patrilineage, Taivar Girasia men were seen to be diversifying rather than consolidating their affinal links within the wider Girasia community. So here we find that marriages distinguished between the sublineages in Girasia patrilineage yet at the same time worked to maintain an equality among the sublineages.

Marriages were occasions for gender differences to be manifest, for example, in the institution of Girasia marriage payments (Unnithan, 1992). Girasia brideprice was paid in cash by men and was the largest sum of money to be transacted among the Girasias. (It was usually given in two or three instalments over a fixed period such as a year). The differences in brideprice amounts depended on the distinction between 'better' and 'worse' wives, based upon both the rank and status of the wife's patrilineage as well as her physical fitness and reproductive capacity. Better wives commanded a higher brideprice than worse wives. The loss or gain of brideprice sums provided a real incentive for Girasia men to strategise to improve their financial position, especially as most households were to some extent in debt given the uncertainty and generally low level of agricultural productivity in the area. Often jewellery was pawned as a means to provide the brideprice for a son. It was also essential for Girasia men and women to have money to be able to terminate their marriages. While divorce was easy and women could ideally leave their husbands whenever they chose, their subsequent marriage, essential for any access to resources, was dependent on the provision of the bridepiece amount by the second husband (with an added 'compensation' fee for the first husband), or in the absence of another suitor of the return of the brideprice including the additional compensation for the husband, by the wife's male kin.

In this section we have seen what it means to be related in Girasia terms and how the Girasia ideas of high and low social status, of 'good' and 'bad' wives, were centrally connected to and expressed through their notions of kinship. The centrality of patrilineal kinship and the use of women as markers of kinship differences were not unique Girasia practices. They were in fact part of a common 'language' shared across the range of communities in the region. Following Gellner (1985), I would suggest that kinship conceptualised in terms of biological relationships, provided the paradigm for talking about all relationships which may or may not be based on actual physical ties. The following section considers the manner in which a kinship perspective is helpful in understanding not only the conceptions and action of the Girasias but also how these were related to two apparently contrasting social categories in Rajasthan – the Rajput caste and Bhil tribe.

3 Girasias, Rajputs and Bhils: the politics of representation and the changing meanings of kinship

The Rajput caste and Bhil tribe are popularly regarded as representing two ends of the social spectrum of communities in Rajasthan. There is very little documentation on the number of social groups and communities in the state. One recent estimate is that there are two hundred different groups in Rajasthan (Mathur, 1986). In terms of size, the largest groups are the Jat (agricultural), Chamar ('untouchable'), Bhil ('tribal'), Rajput (feudal), Mahajan (trading), Mina ('tribal'), Gujar (pastoral), Mahi (horticultural).

The Rajput and Bhil categories are important for a study of the Girasias for two reasons. Firstly, while the Girasias were labelled tribal, like the Bhils, by the non-Girasias, Girasia kinship was organised along the lines of the Rajput (lineage) caste system. Secondly, the various Girasia lineages used the Rajput and Bhil categories to denote a purity and impurity of kinship respectively, to differentiate within their community.

The Rajputs have historically been amongst the dominant, wealthy and landed, ruling elite in the erstwhile Rajput states of

Rajasthan. The specific Rajput customs and styles of dress are still emulated by other communities in the region who continue to distinguish amongst themselves according to their historical association with the Rajputs. Rajasthan is known as the land of the Rajputs and popular folklore and ballads revolve around the brave and glorious military achievements of the Rajputs kings and chiefs.

In south Rajasthan, the Bhil were frequently described as *Jungali*. In its literal sense, the word *Jungali* referred to life in the forest or jungle. However, *Jungali* was also a term used in Hindi to refer to a primitive, wild or savage state. This primitiveness was seen by the non Bhils to be particularly reflected in the apparent Bhil preference for beef which is proscribed for Hindus. The stereotyped image of the Bhils associated them with 'impurity' or inappropriateness not only in their food habits but also in their social customs, such as in the easy exchange of wives, frequent divorce and brideprice payments which in the hierarchy of marriage payments described in Brahmanical Hindu texts, ranked at the bottom of a decreasing scale of appropriate practices. The derogatory image of the Bhil was, however, accompanied by an unstated admiration for Bhil life as hardy, chivalrous and representing all that was secretly desired in caste society, from the eating of forbidden food to sex with many women.

In many ways the Rajputs and Bhils had common stereotypes attached to them in such labels as hardy, warrior-like and meat-eating. Generally it was believed that the Rajputs had won Bhil land in battle. Their common tie to the land was marked by a ritual at the coronation ceremony of a Rajput king, where a Bhil had to anoint the forehead of the ruler with the blood from his finger, thereby blessing the king and promising allegiance (Carstairs, 1974). These shared experiences did nothing to detract from what was regarded by the other castes as the social inferiority of the Bhils.

I will only mention two features of Rajput social organisation which I consider significant for the purposes of this chapter. Firstly, the most important characteristic of the Rajput community, as reflected in its historical, political organisation, was the fact that it was kin based and lineage centred. For Ziegler (1978), the key features of Rajput identity were the Rajput relations of the brotherhood (*bhaibamdh*) and relations by marriage (*saga*). The *bhaibamdh* was a unit of patrilineal descent represented by the clan (*vams/kul*) and branch (*sakha*). While the clan and branches were spread over various territories in and around Rajasthan, the functionally corporate units were the small brotherhoods (*khamp* or twig) of three to six generations. Genealogical proximity to the ruling lineage, determined the amount of status and political power of members in the community. For Fox (1975) the kin based competition for power led to the rise and fall of certain lineages over time in a cyclic pattern such that there was always the likelihood that lineages out of power would regain power. Due to the possibility of regaining status and power, the Rajputs had a more fluid social structure than generally attributed to caste communities.

The second feature of the Rajputs was their notion of kinship as providing an ideological solidarity which linked the local lineage to the dispersed caste (Fox, *ibid.*). The ideological solidarity was not based on actual genealogical ties but on the status attached to membership of the Rajput kin system. Such status concerns were particularly relevant at the wider, regional level where Rajputs defined their status *vis-à-vis* non-Rajputs. While genealogical ties and the lineage were important in claims to the membership of the minimal Rajput unit at the local level, at the regional level it was important to articulate a symbolic kinship.

The difference between ideological kinship and physical kinship has important implications for the nature of the relationship between caste and lineage in the Rajput state. Fox suggests that Rajputs thought in terms of local lineages, rather than in terms of caste as a dispersed agnatic and affinal group. The Taivar Girasias shared this lineage centred view of caste with other Rajputs. Even the Bhils, who were portrayed as 'lower' in Girasia social ranking were lineage oriented in their social institutions. According to Deliège (1985), the Bhils were a loose cluster of dispersed lineages within which there were territorial kin groups.

The Girasias, Bhils and other Rajput lineages and clans all emphasised patrilineal descent as well as endogamous marriages within a group of lineages or clan (which I see as caste). Their lineage centred view of caste did not detract from the fact that there could be caste type hierarchical differences within the lineage, much in the same manner as illustrated by Parry in his study of the Rajputs of Kangra (1979). The main difference between the upper and lower sections of a Kangra lineage lay in their tendency for opposite marriage practices. The upper Kangra clans had the ideal of hypergamous marriages (men married women of their own brotherhood (*biradari*) or from a *biradari* inferior to them) and had the custom of dowry payments. Men from the lower clans, in contrast, married hypogamously (where wives came from the husband's own or upper status clans) and exchanged brideprice. These different practices lead Parry to suggest there was a 'caste like barrier' (*ibid.*, 233) within the same Rajput lineage.

The Girasias were both a lower caste (Rajput) and a lower class in the region. Institutions such as brideprice, divorce and other kin related practices which they shared with the lower Rajputs and Bhils were common to the lower class communities more generally, irrespective of the divisions of caste and tribe. For example, there was a stated equality of marrying groups and a certain extent of individual choice in the selection of marriage partners. In both communities, as with the lower Rajputs, there were hierarchical relations between affinal groups in actual practice, but these were more fluid and less permanent distinctions between the marrying groups (as emphasised by Parry for the Rathi sublineage of Kangra Rajputs, and Deliège for the Bhils).

Three main issues emerge from the observations made so far in this section. Firstly, while social groups in Sirohi and the surrounding region were continually stressing kin based status differences amongst themselves, most forcefully conveyed by the use of labels such as caste and tribe, there were in reality many underlying similarities as was evident from their kinship ideologies, organisation and processes. Secondly, the examples used in this section and the previous one indicate that the groups shared a common kinship and gendered form in which their assertions of difference were made. Thus underlying the framework of caste was the shared language of kinship and gender used to describe oneself and others. Thirdly, the wider social principle to emerge was that any group considered those lower than it to have less strict boundaries than it did itself. On the contrary, I found that all groups were equally concerned to keep the boundaries of their group fairly impermeable, although in reality deviations from the social ideal occurred across the groups (also see for example, Tambiah in Goody, 1976; Madan, 1964).

While the agenda of this section has been to show the social similarities between groups in the region despite their discriminating use of categories such as caste and tribe, I did not see the emphasis on differences made by the Girasia, Rajput and Bhil communities, as unimportant. The assertion of social differences is centrally related to the politics of the representation of social identities. As Cohen (1985) has observed, the maintenance of difference lies at the heart of questions of identity and, '. . . community derives its sense of self from contrasting itself to others, but further from its juxtaposition with others in a larger relationship' (*ibid.*, 116). My focus on social similarities, on the other hand, is mainly addressed to academics and administrators who are concerned with the politics of community identities, yet who often unwittingly participate in the processes of social discrimination as is clear in the case of the Girasias, outlined below.

Administrators, Academics and Popular Stereotypes

One of the striking points to emerge from archival material on the Girasias was the increasing reference to them as 'tribal', particularly in the later period of British colonial rule and the early part of the administration of newly independent India. Academic and administrative accounts and classifications have contributed to reinforcing rather than dispelling the popular stereotypes of the divisions between communities in the region. An unintended consequence of these interventions has been to strengthen the divisions in favour of those on top, ie, a section of elite Rajputs.

The British paramountcy, like the Mughal empire before it, curtailed the possibility of territorial expansion of the Rajput states. This had a significant impact on the social mobility of the Rajput lineages as the fixing of the political map froze the Rajput hierarchy in favour of those in positions of power at the time (Stokes, 1978). It became impossible for the politically marginalised Rajput lineages and clans who had fewer landholding rights to expand these rights by a conquest over land. As land became a fixed commodity and unattainable outside claims to heredity, we find there was an escalation in the claims to kinship status as a means to ensure landholding rights in the British period. The poorer Rajput communities, such as the Girasia, were the worst affected by the freeze on land acquisition which in turn led not only to their economic and political marginalisation but also to a position of cultural inferiority.

Tod (1832, 1920), Sherring (1881), Baden-Powell (1892) were some of the early British writers to comment on the organisation of the Rajput states in western India. In their accounts, the Girasias were fallen Rajput lineages, who were marginal to the state (but not 'tribal') at the time of the British presence in India.

However, the extent of their marginality varied from state to state. Baden Powell's study particularly notes that the Girasia were dispossessed Rajput chiefs and the Girasia title in the British period denoted a cash allowance, although the Girasia also had claims to alienated land. Copland (1982) observes that the Girasias in Kathiawar in Gujarat were already somewhat 'debased' by other Rajputs in the 18th century because of the favour they gained with the Mughal rulers.

The shift from being marginal members of the Rajput state to being tribal and outside the state, at least for the Taivar Girasias, was also in large part a consequence of the British forest policies. Their previous form of shifting agriculture (*walra*) was prohibited (Erskine, 1908) and their use of forest products was legally restricted. Subsequent periods of meagre rainfall and resulting drought had impoverished a number of Taivar Girasia households. Because of their association with the forest, made inevitable by the British land and forest policies, the image of the Taivar Girasias as tribal was further reinforced for the non-Girasias.

Census classifications by the government of independent India have conclusively reinforced the tribal identity of the Taivar Girasias. Central to the notion of development and progress formulated by the Indian government in the late 1940s and early 1950s was the idea of selected 'underprivileged' sections of society to receive government fund and benefits. Two schedules or lists of social groups, one for castes and the other for tribes, were drawn up for this purpose. The classification of communities along the lines of caste/tribe to receive state funds had a tremendous impact on the relations between social groups as well as on the way castes were conceptualised. For the first time, claims to a lower social status brought rewards and potential social mobility, in contrast to a previous social degradation. Some communities asserted 'lower' caste positions in the census to claim government benefits, especially to get into the employment quotas. Other communities found the marginal positions assigned to them in the census unjust. The result of an escalation of claims to social identity made accurate classification impossible (also see Béteille, *ibid.*, 299). While the Girasias in Rajasthan appear under the list of scheduled tribes (Rajput Girasias are mentioned to be omitted from the list but do not appear anywhere else in the census), the Girasias in Gujarat are classed as members of the 'Other Backward Classes' (considered a rank above the scheduled tribe).

Most of the Government surveys relied on the work of anthropologists and sociologists who themselves worked with certain preconceived assumptions and imaginings. The anthropologists accounts of the Girasias and the Bhils suggest two separate approaches. One approach regarded the Girasias as tribal and denied all Rajput-Girasias connections (Meherda, 1985; or Sinha for the tribals of Chhota Nagpur). In this view, all Girasia customs, even if similar to the Rajput, were a deliberate emulation of Rajput lifestyles. Meherda, for example, even denies Tod's observation that Girasias were children of unions between Rajput men and Bhil women by asserting that the offspring should have been either Rajputs or Bhils (Dave, 1960 has a more measured perspective). The second approach saw the Bhil and Girasia communities as 'tribalised' in their customs and institutions as a result of the fall in their status as Bhils and Girasias rather than Rajput (Nath, 1954; Navalkha, 1959; Chauhan, 1978). The second approach is more useful in terms of its analysis of social identifies in terms of the processes of disempowerment. However, it is difficult to accept the idea that disempowerment led to a completely new set of 'tribal' customs. On the contrary, the Girasia material suggests that the Girasias were able to continue their customary practices precisely because of their social distance from the other communities.

To whatever extent the exercises of classification in the British and nascent Indian states distorted the social realities, for the first time caste as an institution became nationally defined and gained a new-found importance as a means of economic achievement. Caste also began to play an important part in the political processes at the national level where votes determined the 'visibility' and power of a community. In this context, we find kinship politics taking on a new and wider dimension. Among the Rajputs and in contrast to the emphasis on lineage-based kinship in the Rajput state, the ideological basis of kinship has become more important than ties based on physical kinship as a means to forge stronger political alliances in the modern state. This is nowhere better reflected than in the more recent preoccupations within groups of the Rajput community where there is a strong move to build a monolithic identity on the basis of a selective resurrection of Rajput 'custom'. Occasions provided by the relatively recent incidents of *sati* (immolation of wives on the funeral pyres of their husbands, especially the Deorala incident in 1987) have been used by Rajput leaders and politicians to resurrect a

Rajput status in order to exhibit their strength and solidarity to the electorate. While *sati* in the traditional context was a result of politics within the household and signified honour for the male lineage, in Rajasthan today, *sati* is a powerful means of political action at the national level.

In the recent representations of Rajput identity, around the issue of *sati* for example, we find that the focus has moved away from an emphasis in lineages which in the Rajput state determined the status of the community, to a wider brotherhood, a more dispersed caste-type identity. Two issues emerge from a study of Rajput caste oriented polities in a context where especially the upper Rajputs move further and further away from their glorious past. First, following Kothari (1970) the Rajput community is another example of a caste community adjusting to democracy. Kothari believes that for any political system to be stabilised in the Indian context, it is necessary that its earlier procedures and symbols are both traditionalised and internalised. The second point concerns the growing creation of communal identities in contemporary Indian politics and following Chhachhi (1990) the use of women as symbolic representations in the making of fundamentalist communities. Chhachhi emphasises that 'tradition' is reconstituted in a selective manner by the fundamentalist elements, both men and women, of the respective communities. Chhachhi sees the call for a return to 'tradition' in *sati*, and other communal action, as a means by certain sections in the communities to combat a perceived threat from the state to undermine the patriarchal authority embedded in their customary institutions.

The shift in the basis of Rajput identity from the lineage centred to the wider symbolic form which as we saw was related to the change in the nature of Rajput politics in the nation state, has particularly weakened the claims to Rajputness by the Girasias. The Taivar Girasias did not actively seek to represent themselves as Rajputs in the region and were uninvolved in the national politics of the Rajputs in Sirohi and Rajasthan more generally. They only saw themselves as Rajputs in relation to the past when they were the most prosperous in terms of their economy with low tax rates granted by the local Rajput chief, and also in terms of their social prestige. In fact, the Bhils and the Girasias in Gujarat, where the Rajput rule had been more dispersed and terminated with the advent of the British, had a much higher social status in independent India (see for example, Nath,

1945; Lal, 1979) as compared to the Girasias and Bhils in Rajasthan.

Without use for the national and politicised Rajput identity, at least till 1987, of greater importance to the Taivar Girasias in terms of the political relations within the Girasia community was the use of Rajput and Bhil categories as idioms of pure/impure kinship. In terms of identity, there was in fact a distinct move by some of the Girasias to forge class-type links with other lower castes and communities in the region and create an identity separate from the upper castes. A section of the Taivar Girasias, for example, were members of the Anop Mandal, a semi-religious and political organisation of lower castes and classes in southern Rajasthan and Gujarat. The Anop Mandal was the only politicised organisation in the region which had been able to draw in Girasias as members. The Anop Mandal was especially successful because it was able to address the very real economic hardships and control over resources faced by the poorer communities in a language based on local understandings of history and social relations. The moneylending community were seen as the main exploiters of the poor. As I suggest elsewhere (1991), the Girasia members of the Mandal had the implicit support of their kin despite the fact that Mandal required its members to abstain from meat, worship its founder and give up certain customs central to Girasia life. The most important observation in relation to the concerns of this paper is that membership of the Mandal followed along the lines of Girasia kinship within the patrilineage and reinforced the kinship divisions within the Taivar Girasia community. It was because Girasia notions and practices of kinship were so firmly connected to their economy, territory, identity and way of life that we find links with other communities to be encompassed and accommodated with existing kin ties. As a consequence, unlike the predictions of social theorists like Srinivas (1972) for whom social change results from the hierachisation of kin ties, social change among the Taivar Girasias resulted in an extension of their notions of kinship as a means to accommodate the changed circumstances.

In conclusion, the example of the Girasias used in this chapter has shown that even the so-called marginalised or 'tribal' communities share significant ties, in the form of kinship institutions and a shared political history, with other groups, caste and tribe in the region, which makes it difficult to use caste to describe some groups in Rajasthan and tribe to describe others.

Furthermore, the chapter has shown how processes which separate (or unite) communities in the region must be seen in relation to the politics of identities at the wider level, such of the Rajput state and the Indian nation, on the one hand, and equally must consider the local interpretations of identity, on the other. In the case of the Rajputs we find that with a different form of state politics, the meaning of caste shifted to emphasise symbolic rather than physical ties of kinship. Because their notions of caste were based on physical kinship, particular lower Rajput communities, such as the Girasias, were further marginalised from the emerging form of caste politics. The small minority of Girasias who sought to form class-type links in the region were careful not to disrupt their ties of physical kinship. This points to the continuing importance of kinship in the study of local and community based action in Rajasthan and possibly elsewhere.

Notes

1 I would like to thank Ursula Sharma and Mary Searle-Chatterjee for their helpful comments and an anonymous referee for suggestions.
2 For Lévi-Strauss, social structure like language was a system of communication consisting of a set of elements, none of which had intrinsic meaning apart from the meaning derived from the relations to surrounding elements. Furthermore, the structure was deep, underlying and abstract rather than simply manifest at the surface. Kinship was thus not about lineages, groups or networks of people – these were just the surface manifestations, like speech. Kinship was a communicative code which conveyed the general, underlying structural ways of thinking.
3 For Dumont, castes were 'endo-recruiting' (*ibid.*, 112) in the sense that both marriage (endogamy) and the transmission of group membership (descent through both parties) were within the group.
4 Daniel and Raheja's work is informed by the recent transactionalist approach spearheaded by Marriott (1976). For Marriott, caste was essentially transaction-based and caste hierarchy was the result of the maintenance of subordination through transaction. The transactionalist approach was stimulated by the more recent theoretical concerns in social anthropology, particularly in America, to understand social categories through people's own meanings, in this case as Hindu constructs of relatedness (Fuller and Spencer, 1990). A resulting major drawback of such ethnosociology, according to Fuller and Spencer, lies in the assumption of an exaggerated cultural unity of Indian society (Fuller and Spencer, *ibis.*). The transactionalist approach has nevertheless contributed important perspectives on caste which attempt to transcend the dualities in western thought and also place the individual rather than the community in the forefront of analysis. Furthermore, the approach has encouraged work which emphasises the multidimensional and shifting aspects of caste

interaction which point to the importance of values other than those of hierarchy (Raheja, 1986) or of prescribed occupation (Barnett, 1977).

5 While totemic groups used animals or plants to distinguish between social groups, castes used occupation and manufactured objects to achieve the same objective. Lévi-Strauss showed how the Bhil tribe in western India and the Munda tribe in eastern India used animals, plants as well as manufactured objects as clan names. This in-between position wherein a tribe used both caste (manufactured objects) and totemic insignia (natural objects) reinforced for Lévi-Strauss the notion that castes and totems were variants of each other.

6 Sahlins (1985), for example, finds Hocart's model of divine kingship close to his own model of the hierarchic heroic society. Using historical material from Hawaii, Fiji and New Zealand, Sahlins showed how tribal egalitarianism and solidarity based on bonds of kinship and the relation to ancestral lands could be undercut by a loyalty and subordination to the ruler (manifesting what for Sahlins was a solidarity based on subordination).

7 Forty-seven out of a total of two hundred and twenty-five household units in the village were those of affinally related men who did not own land in the village.

8 The stated rules of marriage prohibited marriages of men with women from their mother's patrilineage, although daughters could marry men from their mother's patrilineage. For men this excluded their mother's brother's daughter as wives. A man could marry his mother's sister's daughter, however (provided the mother's sister was not married into his patrilineage), as the mother's sister's children are not considered members of the mother's patrilineage. A man could take a wife from his paternal or maternal grandmother's patrilineage. These marriage rules, I argue elsewhere (Unnithan, 1991), show characteristics of both North and South Indian marriage patterns as described by Dumont (1966).

References

Agarwal, B. and Afshar, H., (1989), *Women, Poverty and Ideology in South Asia*,

Baden-Powell, B.H., (19892), *Land Systems in India*, Oxford: Clarendon Press.

Barnett, S., (1977), 'Identity Choice and Caste Ideology in South India', in David, K., (ed.), *The New Wind: Changing Identities in South Asia*,

Bailey, F., (1960), *Tribe, Caste and Nation*, Manchester: Manchester University Press.

Béteille, A., (1974), *Six Essays in Comparative Sociology*, Delhi: Oxford University Press.

Béteille, A., (1984), *Individualism and the Persistence of Collective Identities*, Colchester: University of Essex.

Béteille, A., (1986), 'The Concept of Tribe with Special Reference to India', *Arch. Europe. Sociol.*, Vol. XXVII, 297–318.

Carstairs, G.M., (1974), 'Bhils of Kotra Bhomat', in K. Mathur and C. Agarwal (eds), *Tribe, Caste and Peasantry*, Lucknow: Ethnographic and Folk Culture Society.

Chhachi, A., (1990), *Forced Identities: Communalism, Fundamentalism, Women and the State in India*, paper prepared at the ISS, the Hague.

Chakrabarty, D., (1991), 'History as Critique and Critique(s) of History', *Economic and Political Weekly*, 37, Sept. 14.

Chauhan, B.R., (1978), 'Tribalisation', in Vyas, N.N., Mann, R.B., and Chaudhry, N.D. (eds.), *Rajasthan Bhils*, Udaipur, India: MLV Tribal Research Institute, Social Welfare Department, Government of Rajasthan.

Cohn, B., (1987), *An Anthropologist among the Historians and Other Essays*, Delhi: Oxford University Press.

Collier, J.F. and Yanagisako, S.J., (eds), (1987), *Gender and Kinship: Essays towards a Unified Analysis*, Stanford, California: Stanford University Press.

Copland, I., (1982), *The British Raj and the Indian Princes: Paramountcy in Western India, 1857–1930*, Bombay: Orient Longman.

Das, V., (1987), 'Subaltern as Perspective', in R. Guha (ed.), *Subaltern Studies*, Vol. VI, Delhi: Oxford University Press.

Dave, P.C., (1960), *The Girasias*, Delhi: Bharatiya Adimjati Sevak Singh.

Deliège, R., (1985), *Bhils of Western India: Some Empirical and Theoretical Issues in Anthropology in India*, National Publishers.

Deliège, R., (1992), 'Replication and Consensus; Untouchability, Caste and Ideology in India', *Man* (n.s.), 27, 155–173.

Dhanagre, D.N., (1985), 'Sociology and Social Anthropology in India, in Atal, Y., (ed.), *Sociology and Social Anthropology in Asia and the Pacific*, Paris: Wiley Eastern Limited and UNESCO.

Dube, L., Leacock, E., and Ardener, S., (eds.), (1986), *Visibility and Power: Essays on Women in Society and Development*, Delhi: Oxford University Press.

Dumont, L., (1966), 'Marriage in India: The Present State of the Question III. North India in relation to South India', in *Contributions to Indian Sociology*, Old Series, Vol. 9, 90–114.

Dumont, L., (1980), *Homo-Hierarchicus: The Caste System and Its Implications*. Complete Revised Edition, translated by Sainsbury, M. *et al*, Chicago: University of Chicago Press.

Erskine, K.D., compiled, (1908), *The Imperial Gazetteer of India, Provincial Series*, Calcutta: Government Printing Press.

Fox, R.G., (1967), 'Varna Schemes and Ideological Integration in Indian Society', *Comparative Studies in Society and History*, Vol. 11, no. 1, 1969.

Fox, R.G., (1971), *Kin, Clan, Raja and Rule: State Hinterland Relations in Pre-Industrial India*, Berkeley: University of California Press.

Fuller, C. and Spencer, J., (1990), 'South Asian Anthropology in the 1980s', *South Asia Research*, Vol. 10, No. 2, November.

Gellner, E., (1985), *The Concept of Kinship: and Other Essays on Anthropological Method and Explanation*, Oxford: Blackwell.

Guha, R., (1982), *Subaltern Studies*, Vol. I, Delhi: Oxford University Press.

Hocart, A.M., (1950), *Caste: A Comparative Study*, London: Methuen and Company.

Inden, R.B., (1986), 'Orientalist Constructions of India', *Modern Asian Studies*, 20, 3.

Kandiyoti, D., (1992), *Women, Islam and the State*, London:

Kolenda, P., (1978), *Caste in Contemporary India: Beyond Organic Solidarity*, California: Benjamin/Cummings.

Kothari, R., (1970), *Caste in Indian Politics*, New York: Orient Longman.

Lal, R., (1979), *Sons of the Aravallis. The Garasia*, Ahmedabad: Gujarat Vidyapeeth Publication.

Lévi-Strauss, C., (1966), *The Savage Mind*, London: Weidenfeld and Nicholson.

Lévi-Strauss, C., (1969), *The Elementary Structures of Kinship*, Boston: Beacon Press.

Lynch, O., (1969), *The Politics of Untouchability*, New York: Columbia University Press.

Madan, T.N., (1982), 'Anthropology as a Mutual Interpretation of Cultures: Indian Perspective', in *Indigenous Anthropology of Non-Western Countries*, Fahim, H., (ed.), Durham, N.C.: Carolina Academic Press.

Marriott, M. and Inden, R.B., (1985), 'Social Stratification: Caste', in *Encyclopaedia Britannica*, 15th edition, vol. 27, pp. 348–356, Chicago: The University of Chicago Press.

Mathur, U.B., (1986), *Folkways in Rajasthan*, Jaipur: The Folklorists.

Meherda, B.I., (1985), *History and Culture of the Girasias*, Jaipur: Adi Prakashan.

Moore, H., (1988), *Feminism and Anthropology*, London: Polity Press.

Nath, Y.V.S., (1954), 'Bhils of Ratanmail: Lineage and Local Community', in *The Economic Weekly*, VI 49, pp. 1355–1360.

Navalkha, S.A., (1959), 'The Authority Structure among the Bhumij and the Bhil: A Study of Historical Connections, in *The Eastern Anthropologist*, Vol. 13, No. 1, pp. 27–40, Lucknow: Ethnographic and Folk Culture Society.

O'Hanlon, R., (1988), 'Recovering the Subject: Subaltern Studies and Histories of Resistance in South Asia', in *Modern Asian Studies*, 22 (1):189–224, Cambridge: Cambridge University Press.

Padel, F., (1988), *Anthropologists of Tribal India: Merchants of Knowledge?* Paper presented at the South Asian Social Anthropologists meeting on Orientalism and the History of Social Anthropology of South Asia.,

Parry, J., (1979), *Caste and Kinship in Kangra*, London, Henley and Boston: Routledge and Kegan Paul.

Quigley, D., (1988), 'Is Caste a Pure Figment, the Invention of Orientalists for their own Glorification?', *Cambridge Anthropology*, 13 (1).

Quigley, D., (1988), *Kings and Priests: Hocart's Theory of Caste*, Pacific Viewpoint: New Zealand.

Raheja, G.G., (1988), *The Poison in the Gift: Ritual, Prestation and the Dominant Caste in a North Indian Village*, Chicago: University of Chicago Press.

Rudolph, S. and Rudolph, L., (1984), *Essays on Rajputana: Reflections on History, Culture and Administration*, New Delhi: Concept.

Sahlins, M.D., (1985), *Islands of History*, London and New York: Tavistock.

Sharma, U., (1980), *Women, Work and Property in Northwest India*, London: Tavistock.

Standing, H., (1992), *Autonomy and Dependence*, London: Routledge.

Srinivas, M.N., (1972), *Social Change in Modern India*, Bombay: Orient Longman.

Tambiah, S.J., (1973), 'From Varna to Caste through Mixed Unions', in J. Goody, (ed.), *The Character of Kinship*, Cambridge: Cambridge University Press.

Trautman, T., (1981), *Dravidian Kinship*, Cambridge: Cambridge University Press.

Unnithan, M., (1991), *Constructive Difference: Social Categories and Girahya Women, Kinship and Resources in Rajasthan*, unpublished PhD, University of Cambridge.

Unnithan, M., (1992), 'The Politics of Marriage Payments in South Rajasthan', in *South Asia Research*, London, May 1992.

Ziegler, N., (1978), 'Some Notes on Rajput Loyalties during the Mughal Period', in Richards, J.F., (ed.), *Kingship and Authority in South Asia*, Madison: University of Wisconsin Publication Series.

Caste without a system. A study of South Indian Harijans

Robert Deliège

Abstract

According to Dumont, caste can be understood as the institutionalisation of hierarchy, and the principle of hierarchy permeates all relations within Indian society. So understood, caste ideology is uniform
throughout the society. This point has been contested by several
ethnographers, especially those working among untouchables whom
they often described as more 'egalitarian'. This chapter aims to discuss
the concepts of hierarchy and equality among the Paraiyar caste in a
Tamil Nadu village. It will show that in spite of a basic acceptance of
the value of caste, the Paraiyar espouse a strongly egalitarian ethic so
far as relations among themselves are concerned; while there are forms
of differentiation within the village, these cannot be conceived according to a hierarchical model. There is a general resistance to any form
of internal leadership or domination, to which constant disputes, jeal-
ousies and accusations of theft bear witness. Gender roles are not as
sharply demarcated as is generally expected in the subcontinent and
the relations between affines are not conceived hierarchically.

Although hierarchy can be taken as an intellectual device to grasp
the foundations of Indian society, it cannot account for all the social
relations within that society, which require theorisation of a different
kind. It is a mistake to think that people are either egalitarian or hierarchical.

Introduction

The village of Valghira Manickam is, in many ways, atypical: it
is, for instance, a rural but mostly non-cultivating entity and
above all it is chiefly inhabited by Harijans.[1] There is here no
trace of castes exchanging services and foodgrains in some sort of
organic solidarity. It has been said, most notoriously by Dumont,

that caste does not exist outside a system. The reference to a system to explain caste is actually an important heuristic and theoretical device but its actualisation is more problematic. Classical anthropological studies report cases of well–balanced villages where a great number of castes depend on each other by exchanging services and bunches of grains on the threshing floor at harvest. Such villages undoubtedly exist, but many others do not include a wide range of different castes which are organically linked. Valghira Manickam is such a village and it is therefore a good place to see what happens to caste when there is little trace of a system. We shall see that caste and untouchability clearly survive in the absence of organic links between various castes. The first aim of this chapter is thus to sketch out the working of caste and caste values in a contemporary South Indian village.

India's traditional social organisation has also been seen as an 'institutionalisation of hierarchy'. The very title on the most influential book on the caste system, *Homo Hierarchicus* (Dumont, 1966), suggests that hierarchical values have permeated the whole of Indian society and shape the minds of its members. Dumont did not content himself with asserting that the ideological foundations of the system were hierarchical (which is globally acceptable) but he also claimed that all social relations within Indian society were hierarchical and that what happened within the caste was also regulated by the principles of the system as a whole (for instance Dumont, 1957:III). As Toffin rightly pointed out in a recent study (1993:29), in *Homo Hierarchicus*, Dumont constantly passes from the sphere of values to that of social practices, and he is therefore sometimes inclined to suggest that hierarchy is the only thing Indians actually care about. In any case, he draws a very sharp distinction between the egalitarian West and the fundamentally hierarchical India. The danger of such a view is to over-emphasise the distance between East and West. Yet modern India has been able to adapt very well to a democratic parliamentary system and has developed a deep democratic political culture among its inhabitants.

It is not my aim to argue that caste society is profoundly egalitarian nor even to deny the importance of hierarchy as an explanatory factor of Indian society. What seems to me more arguable is the claim that 'all' social relations within Indian society are marked by hierarchy. Parry's statement that 'The "encompassing" ideology of hierarchy permeates every sphere of social life' (1979:6) clearly does not apply here. Besides, the same author argued elsewhere (1974) that egalitarian values do exist within a hierarchical society and I will thus try to single out various manifestations of those egalitarian values from the study of a small Tamil village. The fact that this village is mainly inhabited by low caste people probably reinforces the stress on equality but the difference between them and higher castes is mostly a question of degree, and most of the observations made below could be made among higher peasant castes: the isogamous nature of marriages, for instance, is a well-established fact of South Indian ethnography. There are some spheres of social life in which low caste people are more liable to experience social equality than higher castes: this is for example the case of gender relations (Searle-Chatterjee, 1981), but the point to be made here is that egalitarian values exist among all castes and that the *homo hierarchicus* only exists at a theoretical, abstract level. It will also be clear that the existence of egalitarian values does not emanate from the recent changes which India has undergone and they cannot therefore be reduced to a consequence of modern political values. In a convincing study, Rajni Kothari has even argued that tradition and culture have a great relevance to the acquisition and stability of a democratic polity in India, and that most if not all the threats to democracy in India come from the modern sector (1990:155).

In recent years, it has become increasingly fashionable to argue that caste was something like a 'colonial construct'. As Kuper has recently argued, such a thesis can be formulated in a strong or a weak form: 'Generally,' he goes on, 'in its strong form it is interesting but obviously wrong, in its weak form, rather obvious but sometimes right' (Kuper, 1992:58). This is also true of the discussion on caste: the 'soft' view was expressed long ago by anthropologists like Béteille who wrote, for instance: 'Detailed studies of caste at the local level have greatly enriched our understanding of social life in contemporary India. But too great a preoccupation with this problem has also led the social anthropologist to develop his own conception of Indian society, a conception which many have criticized as being narrow and one-sided' (1974:23). This is generally correct; it amounts to saying that the importance of caste is less overwhelming than some anthropologists tried to make us believe. The 'strong form', on the other hand, is more problematic; it is expressed by Inden who goes as far as saying that 'the idea of an India . . . divided into castes is not an isolate based on empirical research' (1990:49).

Inden is sometimes not far from asserting that caste is the pure product of the ethnographers' imagination and he suggests that caste mainly exists in the mind of Western observers. Put in such a way, this view is totally unacceptable; a great deal of Inden's demonstration derives from a discussion of Victorian scholars such as Vincent Smith while ignoring most of contemporary ethnographers. It often looks as if we ought to feel some sense of guilt for the rather partial views of our nineteenth century forefathers (Quigley, 1993:13ff.) such as Risley, who has recently become the target of much criticism. As Gellner has argued, the final meaning of the operation is a refusal to countenance any objective facts, and therefore 'It is also unclear why, given that universities already employ people to explain why knowledge is impossible (in philosophy departments), anthropology should reduplicate this task, in somewhat amateurish fashion' (Gellner, 1992:29). If caste is a pure colonial or academic construct, it is hard to understand why people get killed, even today, on the mere ground that they are Harijans. Similarly it is no academic invention that the problem of the Backward Classes has recently contributed to the fall of a government. As the most influential theoretician of caste, Dumont has been accused of all sorts of evils. Some, such as Mencher or Berreman, reproached him for presenting a high caste view of caste while, more recently, other writers have stigmatised his theory as typical of a colonial construction of the 'other'. Both criticisms are obviously fairly contradictory. The first one might contain some truth but the second one, I reckon, is totally unjustified and unfair. It may be old-fashioned but I do think that caste actually 'exists' and is held to be fundamental by the Indians themselves, especially by those among whom I worked.

The ethnographic setting

The village of Valghira Manickam, where fieldwork was conducted, is located in the Ramnad region of Tamil Nadu (South India). It is close to the small town of Devakottai and its inhabitants belong to two communities of an untouchable caste, the Paraiyars. The Paraiyars of Valghira Manickam are divided into a Roman Catholic section which represents two thirds of the village total population, and a Hindu Paraiyar section which comprises the remaining third of the village population.

Both communities are very close to each other but do not inter-marry.

Economically, the villagers are poor. The vast majority of them are landless. There are a few who cultivate some land on lease from the Kallars of the neighbouring village but these are dry, quite unproductive lands. The main occupation of the villagers is brickmaking, coolie work and agricultural labour; these are not exclusive. There is no shortage of work in the village but the income people get from it is very little. People thus only just manage to make ends meet. They eat mainly rice and rice water (*kanji*) with only a few vegetables. They eat very little meat but collect various types of food from the fields: fishes, insects, and snails are regularly caught and eaten. I have no evidence of people eating carrion but they do eat beef when available. People live mainly in precarious huts. A few pots are sufficient to start a family and most people never succeed in owning much more in the rest of their lives. Infant mortality is high: I was not able to collect systematic data on the subject but most married women had had some children (up to five) who had died in early infancy. There are other symptoms of poverty and malnutrition among the villagers: leprosy, tuberculosis, temporary blindness, and skin diseases are endemic.

A significant number of villagers have left the traditional sector of the economy to engage in more modern occupations: these however remain largely manual. There are only two white-collar workers among the villagers but a good number of people are employed in the organised sector and work as municipal scavengers, workers for the Electricity Board, for example. Finally, several people are self-employed and work as masons, bullock cart drivers, brick kiln owners, and so on. There is thus some increasing internal differentiation among the people.

Intercaste Relations

The spatial isolation of Valghira Manickam does mean that its inhabitants are socially independent. It is true that some of them are now engaged in caste-free occupations but at the same time caste remains highly significant for a great deal of their interactions. It is worth noting that the Brahmans are almost completely absent from this area. There are a few priests working in neighbouring temples, or a few professionals working in Devakottai town but they do not behave as a caste group and certainly do not play, as a caste, a significant role in the region. The Paraiyars of Valghira Manickam would certainly not consider them as the main source of their oppression. They would rank the Brahmins (Iyers) as the 'highest caste' but they have almost no contact with them and this superiority is little relevant to them. It must be pointed out that the Brahmans of the region do not play a significant role on the rural scene. For instance, a Brahman would have very little chance to be elected to the legislative assembly from this area. This very weak presence of Brahmans does not entail a weakening of untouchability. If Brahmans and untouchables are linked together as the projection of purity and impurity on the social scale (Dumont, 1966:77), this is only true for the intellectual perception of caste. In actual fact, the middle peasant castes are more often than not the main upholders of untouchability.

Two castes or caste groups dominate the region: economically, the Chettiars constitute the strongest caste of the Devakottai-Karaikudi region which they used to dominate politically as well since it was called Chettinad or 'country of the Chettiars'. The zamindar of Devakottai was a Chettiar. Many of them have migrated to South-East Asia and have become prosperous merchants and businessmen. The immense houses which they built in the local towns testify to their splendour which is sometimes said to be declining. As a mainly urban caste, their contact with the Paraiyars is limited. There is a very wide socio-economic gap between both castes and they rarely come into contact with one another; in any case, the Chettiars rarely intervene in rural life.

The Kallars are the other important caste of the region. One can argue that, in recent years, their power has been considerably reinforced. They are typical of those agricultural castes which have taken advantage of recent political changes to increase their position within the local society. Their ritual status is traditionally low, they were even considered as a criminal caste by the British. The very word *kallan* means thief in Tamil, and they remain a quite fierce people, with an ethos of fighters. If, for instance, someone touches them in a market, they may warn: 'Beware, I am a Kallar'. People know what this means and the Kallars are indeed involved in all sorts of violence; they are also the most anti-Harijan caste of the region and are ready to kill in order to preserve their alleged superiority. This happened many times and a very spectacular riot took place in a neighbouring village a few months before my arrival. The Pallars of Oonjanai are relatively wealthy and they decided to ask for a greater participation in the village festival. Their main demand was the right to use the temple horse. The District Collector came to settle an agreement: it was decided that the Kallars would hold their procession in the beginning of June while the Pallars would celebrate their own feast at the beginning of July. The Kallars conducted their festival as planned but on June 27, 1979, a very wide group, perhaps a thousand, of Kallars had assembled in Oonjanai and at 8.30 a.m., they attacked the Pallar hamlet, burning the huts, stealing the cattle, wounding many people and killing five. Such violence is not a rare occurrence in the region. It always remains unpunished and it is largely believed that it was instrumental in bringing many Pallars of the area to convert to Islam. In any case, Harijans know what they should expect if they oppose the Kallars too openly. I find it hard to see how one could speak of caste as a 'colonial construction' in such a context which shows how deep the gap between caste groups has remained and how persistent untouchability remains in modern India.

In recent decades, the Kallars have taken advantage of their numerical strength to increase their power. They dominate the local *panchayats*, and local Members of the Legislative Assembly are mostly Kallars. They control many organisations in the town. Furthermore, they consider themselves the owners of the land. It would be impossible to dig a reservoir or a waterpond without asking their permission. Although a separate entity, Valghira Manickam has no right to the land. Some Kallars even claim that they own the house plots of the villagers; they have no legal document to prove this right on the land (*patta*); yet they continue to lease out land to the Harijans. Kallars have relatives in the local police, they control the ration shops and the *panchayats*. On top of this, they often lend money to the Paraiyars who then become very dependent upon them. Even when they are free, the Paraiyars fear the Kallars very much and would not dare to oppose them openly, I believe quite rightly so. When they work as agricultural labourers for the Kanda Devi Kallars, they do it for lower wages. A young man told me that a Kallar threatened to cut his hands if he did not come immediately to work for him.

The festival of the Kanda Devi temple is the stage of a very significant ritual. On the day of the procession, the Kallar 'leaders of the four *nadus*', i.e. four neighbouring villages, accompanied by a band and the Kallar males of their village, proceed to

Kanda Devi. Their arrival is celebrated by noisy crackers and music. Each village is entitled to pull one of the four huge ropes of the carts upon which the image of the god is placed. The enormous wooden cart is then pulled by the Kallars around the temple. It is the political integration of the Kallars which is here stressed. Although there is a great variety of castes in Kanda Devi, only Kallars are entitled to pull the cart along. They are joined by other Kallars from allied neighbouring villages whereas the rest of the villagers remain passive.

The inhabitants of Valghira Manickam come to watch the procession, but typically they remain outside the village. They are not actually welcome into Kanda Devi. There is no formal interdiction which prevents them from entering the village; but they know that without a specific reason, they should not walk into its streets. There is a Harijan community in Kanda Devi and Valghira Manickam is thus formally independent of that village. Yet, there are many ways through which some kind of dependence has been perpetuated and untouchability maintained: as stressed above, the Kallars lend money to the Paraiyars, they lease them out some land to cultivate, they control most political decisions, and may, occasionally, help them to solve some problems. They also consider the Paraiyars as absolutely inferior and would not allow them to behave towards them on an equal basis. This is quite clear in daily life: when approaching a Kallar, a Paraiyar would remain shy, stand aside to let him go, speak with humility, etc. Kallars, on the other hand, do not hesitate to threaten the Harijans. Thus the absence of organic links between both castes has not proved sufficient to eliminate untouchability.

The relationship between Pallars and Paraiyars

Valghira Manickam is not exactly an independent territorial unit. It is in fact attached to another hamlet which is inhabited by another untouchable caste, the Pallars who are all Hindus. The Pallar hamlet is named Pani Pulan Vayal, and typically there is no name to designate the whole agglomeration. This is not so surprising when one considers that Pallars and Paraiyars have little contact. The proximity of their respective settlements encourages some informal relations and even a few cases of friendship; but they have no institution whatsoever in common. They live side by side without any sense of community. Each community has its own temple and manages its own affairs. During the catholic village festival of Arockiyai Mary, the statue of the Virgin is taken around Valghira Manickam but does not enter Pani Pulan Vayal. The Paraiyars have a well and the Pallars a hand pump. There is no ritual taboo forbidding the members of one caste from taking water at the other caste's waterpoint, and I have indeed seen Paraiyar women at the Pallar pump. But usually, as water is scarce, people feel that each community should take water in its own hamlet. It is also interesting to note that, for administrative purposes, Pani Pulan Vayal belongs to the Devakottai panchayat whereas Valghira Manickam is part of the Kanda Devi Panchayat. Although they are contiguous, the two hamlets are thus socially separated. There is here no village spirit which transcends caste frontiers.

Traditionally, the Pallars are held to be superior to the Paraiyars. In the present context, however, they have almost no opportunity to express this alleged superiority. They just happen to live side by side, without many relationships. They sometimes work in the same fields or on the same construction sites, but tend to keep separate, especially as communities. Cases of friendship across the two castes occur and thus show that there is no formal taboo which keeps them separate, but they tend to be rare and individual. As a matter of fact, Pani Pulan Vayal, seems to be a world of its own. Some Pallars claim to be superior to the Paraiyars but this claim is most of the time not supported by facts. For instance, I remember a Pallar woman who claimed that she would not accept water from Paraiyars but a few days later, I saw the same woman drinking a glass of water within the house of a Paraiyar family. Others claimed that they could not take food from Paraiyars; I pointed out to them that every day their own small children ate food cooked by Paraiyars at the local *Balwadi* school (kindergarten); they replied that the pan was only used for the school and not in Paraiyar houses, but this argument was rather unconvincing since it is the status of the cook which matters in such cases; in any case, most Pallars agreed that they do not mind eating food cooked by Paraiyars, which they actually do when they are invited to a feast.

One could hardly speak of a true inequality between Pallars and Paraiyars. Individual cases of friendship also occurred, but as such both communities remained strongly separated, if not hostile. As a matter of fact, some tension permanently divides them and the slightest spark suffices to poison the relations.

There had been several disputes dividing both communities in previous years. During the fieldwork, there was some bitterness due to the Pallars' opposition to the construction of a road connecting the agglomeration to Devakottai. The Block Development Office (BDO) of Devakottai had granted 68,000 rupees to realise the work, and the parish priest had been put in charge of the project. The Pallars objected to this appointment and wanted the project for themselves. Due to this quarrel, the road was never constructed. The Paraiyars refrained from getting too much involved but there was some resentment towards the Pallars and people tended to avoid each other. It must be pointed out that the Pallars were the principal victims of their uncompromisingness: quite a few of them are bullock cart drivers who would have greatly benefited from the construction of such a road. Sowrymuttu, one of the Pallars, wanted the contract for himself and had taken the lead in the opposition: he turned the whole thing into a caste problem and the bullockcart drivers were therefore unable to oppose him. This incident is typical of the way through which personal problems can be made into caste problems which then become very difficult to solve. For a Pallar, to oppose Sowrymuttu would have amounted to being a traitor, who goes against his family interests. The gap between the different castes thus remains wide, sometimes unbridgeable even when they are structurally very close as is the case here.

The Paraiyar caste

Whereas the relations between the Paraiyars and other castes are marked by inequality or distance, this is clearly not the case of the social relations within the caste. The structural implication according to which 'what happens without the caste also happens within the caste' clearly does not hold true for the Paraiyars, and presumably for most of the other local castes. Internal relations are marked strongly by equality.

The Paraiyars, as well as the Pallars, belong to one of the largest castes of Tamil Nadu which comprises several million members. Among them, the Catholics are much less numerous but they include tens of thousands of people distributed all over Tamil Nadu. Given the numeric importance of the caste, it is divided into local sections which are more or less endogamous. The Pallar subcastes are socially better defined, with two main groups, namely the Atta and Amma Pallars which are endogamous. The status of these two groups, however, is not unequal. Some people even told me that they could not marry members of the other subcaste because they considered the latter as *pankalis* (ie blood relatives). This surely is not very coherent but it shows that the two groups do not consider each other as fundamentally different. If the Paraiyars are also divided into numerous subcastes, my informants were very vague about the latter. Some people could name a few of them but most of the people did not even know to which group they belonged, and I wondered whether some of these groups existed at all. Some Catholics claimed to be Nesavukara Paraiyars or 'weaving' Paraiyars and said they knew of one other subdivision, the Tootti Paraiyars or 'scavenging' Paraiyars without, however, being able to tell me where the latter could be found. The Hindu Paraiyars were even vaguer; most of them had never heard of such endogamous subdivisions; some thought they belonged to the Putchikara Paraiyars but again knew of no other subdivisions. Both Christians and Hindus pointed out to me, in any case, that they could marry all Paraiyars. This was, besides, more than a theoretical possibility since some people had already prospected for marriage in relatively distant regions. This is particularly the case for the better off or better educated people who had to venture further away to find a partner who could match their wealth or qualifications. This was particularly true of educated girls who cannot marry a boy less educated than themselves. I once discussed with the cross-cousin of a girl who had studied up to SSLC[2] whereas he himself had only studied to 10th standard; he could not even imagine marrying that girl and there had never been question of it; as we shall see, there is some equality between man and woman among the Paraiyars, it does not follow that men would accept a clear inferiority to their wife.

An obstinate anthropologist could manage to find some Hindus or Catholics who claimed that they were superior to the other community. For the majority of members of both communities, however, there is a total equality between both communities. This is, furthermore, reinforced by the numerous observations which can be made in the daily village life. Both Hindu and Catholic Paraiyars live in the same streets, mix together, and both men and women meet at various places in the village. The children play together all the time and it would not be an exaggeration to say that both communities live in perfect harmony. 'The only thing', people comment, 'is that we do not intermarry, otherwise, we are like brothers'. People use kinship terms to refer to each other and they can, for example, introduce a member of the other community as a 'brother', 'brother-in-law' or 'maternal uncle'. It occurs that sexual liaisons cut across caste, and people more frequently go to each other's houses, drink from the same wells, wash in the same pond and eat one another's food, whether cooked or not.

One could argue that this equality is restricted to the internal relations of the caste. This is correct but it is nonetheless quite significant. As said above, the Paraiyars do form a very large group and most of their social relations take place within the caste itself. Their relatives, their in-laws, their friends, and even their colleagues mostly belong to that caste, and a very great deal of their time is spent with people of their own caste. It could be said that most of their daily interactions concern people of the same caste. The Paraiyars strongly reject the possibility of marriages with higher castes for precisely the same reason: they resent the deep inequality which would result from such marriages.

Kinship and Affinity

If intra-caste relations are basically egalitarian, this is even more true of kin and affinal relations. Within the family, this emphasis on equality results in the prominence of the nuclear family. In the absence of land or property, brothers are little inclined to live together and tend to split as soon as possible. The pattern of marriage tends to be as follows: in the absence of a male heir or in some other circumstances, uxorilocal residence is fairly frequent but it is not the rule, and most generally, after the wedding, the young couple come to live within the boy's family. I never came across a young couple who immediately settled independently and this is quite strange since it is normally expected that the young couple would not stay too long with the boy's family. It must be pointed out that the young couple often earn as much (in truth as little) money as the boy's parents and the young woman soon resents seeing their incomes '*wasted*' (sic) by her in-laws. Tension soon arises within the family: the young daughter-in-law might be accused of giving big portions of food to her husband at the expense of the other members of the family, and she will soon have words with her in-laws, most often her mother-in-law or brothers-in-law. If she becomes 'rude' or 'disrespectful', her husband will side with his own family and beat her if needed. But when things get worse and as time goes by (sometimes a mere few months, rarely more than one or two years), he will back his wife and the quarrel will then lead to a splitting of the family. In the first stages, the young couple might simply cook on a separate stove (a rudimentary construction made of a few bricks); they might take a few coconut leaves to build a separate and precarious shed outside the house; ultimately they will build a separate hut and form a completely independent household. Basically all families have gone through such a scenario. Once the young couple live separately, the relationship with the boy's family tends to return to normal. But by now the young couple form a separate unit, they cook for themselves and manage their own money.

Within the family, there is thus little emphasis on seniority and old age. The father is neither a *'patriarch'* nor given much respect. Younger men, given their physical strength and their ability to work harder, are often more prominent. When growing old, hard–working manual labourers become less fit than the younger men and employers may prefer more productive younger men. Within a family, old people may thus rely on their sons who become the real heads of the family. This is true of village matters as well: young people are often described as the 'future of the village' and they are more involved in the various village affairs than the older people. The village festival, for instance, is mainly organised by the middle aged men while young unmarried men also play a good part in the organisation. Younger men are also more 'sanskritised', better educated, more politically conscious. They are less ready to adopt the obsequious attitudes traditionally expected from Harijans; they dress better and a good number of them do not depend in any way on the higher castes. These recent changes thus further reinforce the importance of younger people among the Paraiyars. Socially their lineages are shallow, people do not know the names of their great-grandfathers, and they have of course no family names.

If the authority of the father is often contested, this is even more true of the elder brother's. There is little emphasis upon primogeniture among Paraiyars. Given the settlement pattern explained above, it is normally the youngest son who stays last with the parents. By the time he gets married, his brothers have already left the parental home. Normally the property would be divided equally between the brothers. Usually this amounts to very little indeed. If there is something (for instance a large housing plot or some agricultural land), they may organise a drawing of lots to decide the distribution of the different shares. This equality between brothers is source of considerable problems, and disputes among them, as we shall see, are extremely frequent. Tamil kinship terminology divides people according to relative age but this distinction has little practical effect among the Paraiyars.

The affinal tie is also marked by a strong emphasis on equality. Tamil marriage unites people of equal status and the practice of cross-cousin marriage strongly reinforces this tendency. The Paraiyars explain the practice of cross-cousin marriage through the importance of reciprocity: a girl 'given', they comment, must be 'returned'. 'If I give one of my daughters to my relative's son', further explains a man, 'I am short of a girl and he must return me one in the next generation'. This is only a principle for, in practice, people do not actually count the number of girls given and received from another family; furthermore, it is nuclear families and not lineages or clans which exchange girls; yet they try to ensure that a girl given is returned so that a link can be maintained between two families. This reciprocity is clearly a sign of the equality between families related by marriage. When it is not possible to maintain the reciprocity, one nevertheless tries to perpetuate the affinal link, for instance by giving a second daughter. Husbands and wives often try to marry their children on their sides: the father will insist on keeping links with his sisters' families whereas the mother will try to arrange something with her brothers'. While a brother is likely to become a rival, an affine is more of an ally. When a quarrel occurs within a family, a man will call upon his sister's husband to support him.

The ideal marriage for a Paraiyar is that which unites a boy to his *attai makkal* (FZD), that is to say the patrilateral cross-cousin marriage. This marriage makes sure that a girl given in one generation is returned in the next generation. As Needham pointed out, such a system prevents the formation of corporate groups since a unit is both wife-giver and wife-taker *vis-à-vis* one partner (1962:115). This system thus entails a 'structural weakness' and fits in better with an absence of authority and social hierarchy (see Deliège, 1988:180). Thus the marriage system of the Paraiyars is particularly consistent with an absence of internal differentiation and a sense of equality. Preferential unions *sensu stricto* (uniting first or second degree cousins) account for about 40 per cent of all marriages. The other marriages concern people of equal status. If one gives a daughter to an *aniyan* (non-related person), one will try to receive a daughter in return and therefore a new alliance is then created. The reciprocity between both families is exemplified in the wedding ceremony which sees the young couple travelling between the two families. Dowry here is extremely reduced: many people say that the do not give anything to their daughters apart from a few pots.

If arranged marriage is on the whole the rule, 'love' marriages are extremely common. It was difficult to list them all because people know that they are despised by the neighbouring castes and they sometimes try to conceal them. Nevertheless, people insist that one must take the young people's advice into account, and that when a youth has 'someone in his head', one cannot go against it; on the whole they are thus very indulgent towards eloping couples. Besides, a good number of marriages were love marriages and every family has been touched by the phenomenon. This is clearly no recent phenomenon since many older people were often married in such a way. The pattern is more or less always the same. A boy and a girl love each other; they may swear to be faithful to each other in front of friends (which makes marriage with another person rather difficult) and then one day they elope to some mysterious place and ask the blessing of a priest. I suspect that they do not go very far and even that they might be hiding somewhere in the village. Nevertheless when they reappear, they go to the boy's place and are considered as husband and wife. The girl's family will be angry and some negotiation will be undertaken; after some time, things will return to normal; the girl's *taymaman* (maternal uncle), who is normally responsible for arranging her marriage, might be the last one to accept the new union. We may suppose that 20 per cent of marriages are 'love' marriages of this kind. This is particularly interesting from the material point of view since it does not entail any expense at all. Catholics may claim that they will get married 'properly' (in front of a priest) later on, but in most cases, they do not bother and things remain as such. It must be pointed out that all these marriages are intra-caste. 'Love' marriages with members of other castes are extremely rare and not favoured. In such rare occurrences, the families are integrated into the village and the children are considered as Paraiyars.

We thus see that the whole institution of marriage among Paraiyars is marked by a strict equality between the families. Little emphasis is put on the group as such and much freedom is left to the individual.

The position of women

In a study among the Benares sweepers, Searle-Chatterjee has argued that the untouchable women have a 'great deal of independence and freedom', and enjoy a strong position in their community (1981:2). The data of Valghira Manickam largely confirm her comments.

When a woman is pregnant, Indian people usually prefer a boy to a girl. This is to some extent also true for the Paraiyars, but the latter very often say that to them it matters little and they welcome a girl as well as a boy. They love children very much and being childless is a misfortune for them. A man who has only daughters is not pitied. Daughters are very much loved. A father especially stresses the fact that his daughter will be going one day and that therefore she should be given much love. She will consequently be very much attached to her family and in case of marital problems she has always the possibility of coming back to 'her' home. Her brothers are expected to defend her and shelter her in case of emergency. Girls will be given more household duties than boys. At the age of five or six, they will be expected to look after younger children, especially when both parents work. They will be sent to school when there is no work at home. Girls are always to be seen carrying babies on their hip. They will also help their mothers but generally speaking their childhood is free and happy.

The ceremony of first menstruation (*manjal nirattu villa*) is very important here. It announces the marriageability of the girl. She is then secluded for eight days in the verandah of the house where she is hidden behind palm leaves. On the ninth day, the main ceremony is performed: guests will bring presents and her *taymaman* should bring cooking vessels, saris, rice, turmeric powder and so on. His wife ritually washes the girl who then puts on the sari; she is now ready to be married. From now onwards, her *taymaman* is supposed to participate in the negotiations or to let the parents know that he wants her to marry his own son. But we have seen that the girl may decide otherwise. It is interesting to note that during the adolescence there is little coquetry about the girls whereas the boys wear nice trendy shirts, have fashionable haircuts, and go to great lengths to look very smart.

We have already described the early stage of the woman's married life. People often say that women are troublesome and that their presence inevitably leads to dispute. In fact, the Paraiyar women are able to assert their personality within the family and are not ready to tolerate the domination of their in-laws. A husband is thus expected to support her after some time. A husband has the right to beat his wife. Women themselves agree with this; but they also point out that the beatings should neither be too heavy nor too frequent. In such cases, a woman may always return to her natal home and there are many of them who actually do. People even say that it is not so good to marry within the village (even though 50 per cent of all marriages are intra-village), because then the wife keeps returning to her parents; when her village is more distant, it is less easy for her to return home. Once she goes home, the husband is expected to fetch her and he might have to beg her to return and promise to behave in a more acceptable way. His wife may permanently refuse to resume the relationship but in such cases her situation is more precarious since she will have to rely upon her brothers for a living unless she 'marries' someone else. A woman has thus the potential to end an unbearable relationship. A widow is also allowed to remarry although her marriage will normally not be arranged and if she is too old she will find it rather difficult to seduce someone. Celibacy is here, as elsewhere in India, a rare occurrence. Women living alone (either celibate or divorced) may have some ritual powers; they may be possessed by the goddess Mariyamman and dance to cure people affected by smallpox and the various forms of *ammai*. Divorces are frequent even among Catholics who nevertheless claim that they do not allow it. It is initiated by men as well as by women. Adultery is said to be rampant but people always quoted the same well-known examples when I expressed my surprise. Young men of other castes also claimed that all Valghira Manickam women are prostitutes (*tevadiyar*) but I am not sure these accusations were not directed towards women who simply speak publicly to men. Some unmarried girls, however, were known for having affairs with several men and therefore 'spoiling the village name'. I was once told by an Indian friend that many Harijan women prostitute themselves during the night, but I do not know whether this was the case of the women from Valghira Manickam.

The behaviour of Harijan women is on the whole quite different from that of high caste women. They go to the town unaccompanied, talk to men, publicly contradict their husbands, shout and swear. They are expected to be respectful towards their husbands but they are often quite bold. The practice of teknonymy is followed and a woman never pronounces the name of her husband. 'One should not pronounce the name of God and her husband is like a God to her' comments a man. The smiles on the women's faces, however, make it clear that they do not really consider that ordinary little man like a god! This practice is purely formal and reflects inaccurately the actual relationship between husband and wife. In a similar vein, I remember a woman who refused to sit down next to her son-in-law, because she should respect him. But in the conversation which followed, this woman talked much more than he did, and generally speaking women are talkative, pleasant and sociable. One day, a man asked to be photographed with his cow. On hearing this, his wife came out of the house and shouted that all men want to be taken with their family and he only thought of his cow. This is a very typical way to intervene in conversations and shows the character of women.

Women also play an important role in daily matters. They often do the shopping themselves and keep some money to run the family. It should be noted, as we shall see below, that almost all women work for a living and their incomes are generally essential to the survival of the family. There are even some men who give their daily wages to their wives; actually this seems to be the rule and Den Ouden reports that, in Konkunad, the wages of labourers are paid to their wives (Den Ouden, 1977:96); in practice, however, most men keep a part of their income for their own expenses, mainly alcohol, tea and snacks in 'hotels'.

Women's labour

As among other sections of the Indian population, Paraiyar women do most of the housework but on top of this most of them also work for wages. Coolie work, agricultural labour and brickmaking are the main occupations of women who therefore fulfil essential economic functions; their income is essential to the survival of the family and there is no family of daily wage labourers which can make both ends meet without the incomes of women. Yet it is also remarkable to notice that when the husband has a good salaried job, his wife often gives up working or works very occasionally. Coolie work is considered as demeaning, hard and poorly paid. People for instance imagine hell as a 'place where one has to carry stones on one's head' and they sometimes add that this work is hell for them. Most men want to escape it and find a 'proper job', if possible in the organised sector. Women, less mobile (they could not go working far away unaccompanied) and more involved in the housework, are therefore more attached to the various manual tasks which are easily found around the village.

The importance of women's work finds a remarkable expression in a body technique which is peculiar to them. While working, they keep their legs stretched and lean the trunk forward; this gives them more mobility and more speed; it is particularly useful in their traditional agricultural tasks such as weeding or transplanting rice. Men are unable to work in such a position for a long time and mainly work squatting. This difference is very noticeable in brickmaking where the teamwork is often composed of a couple; the picture on the front page of my book *Les Paraiyars du Tamil Nadu* illustrates these various techniques.

If women work hard and fast, they do it for much less money than men. In brickmaking, people are paid by the piece and thus women can get as much as men but this is not true of coolie work and agricultural labour for which women receive wages inferior to men. Usually, a woman's wage is 50 to 60 per cent of a man's: in 1981, women received 4 to 5 rupees per day whereas men got 8 to 10 rupees. This difference has clearly no economic justification, for women can be as productive as men; the latter, it is true, can fulfil tasks which require more physical strength, but even when they do the same job as a woman they get a higher wage. I often expressed my surprise at such a wide gap but people seemed to consider it as a matter of fact. Yet they all agreed that it was not justified by a difference of productivity.

Although it is essential, women's work also appears as supplementary; people think that men ought to provide the major part of the household incomes, and that is why men try hard to leave the unorganised sector to find a salaried job or to engage in a self-employed job as a mason, bullock cart driver or small contractor. Many males have thus left the traditional sector of the economy and once they earn a reasonable amount of money, their wives tend to stop working. That is why families with a member earning a salary, such as a municipal scavenger, are not much better off than those labourers who can count on at least two sources of income. If the economic activities of the Valghira Manickam Paraiyars have considerably diversified, the women are not very evident in the more modern occupations; yet by their work, they often allow their husbands to try to find a better job.

My first impression that women earned as much money as their husbands engaged in the traditional occupations was not confirmed by the data which I collected. An inspection of the economic activities of four married couples of labourers during one month showed that in all cases males earned much more money than their wives; this is not only due to the higher wages they receive since they also worked more days than the females (see Deliège, 1988:73). As for brickmaking, the workteams are often composed of husband and wife and it is difficult, if not impossible, to estimate their relative part; I went through the accounts of a brick factory which employed seven teams of workers; one of them was composed of two women but their income was much below the average. Almost all jobs in the organised sector are held by men and therefore it is clear that men account for the major part of the village incomes; yet people could not afford to lose the wages of women which are essential since it should be remembered that most villagers live from hand to mouth in a state of dire poverty. It is equally clear that the position of women in the society is somewhat reinforced because of their economic importance. If the burden of housework mainly rests upon their shoulders, their husbands can be more involved in it than in some other sections of the Indian population: it sometimes happens that a man goes fetching water; he can also look after the children and certainly entertain them. The cooking, however, largely remains in the women's hands.

Authority

Kathleen Gough has written elsewhere that the Harijans displayed a 'fanatical emphasis upon equality' (1960:44). The formula is, no doubt, somewhat extreme, yet it is not completely foreign to the situation of Valghira Manickam. When interviewed about the leadership, villagers often reply: 'In this village, every man is a leader' which amounts to saying that they do not recognise any leader at all. One could almost say that they even resent anyone among them who tries to rise above the rest of the population. Traditionally, they were very much dependent upon higher castes and were engaged in some sort of vertical solidarity. Kallars could also be called upon to settle their internal disputes and there was nobody among them who enjoyed much authority. This last remark still holds true today.

Before I decided to study this village, outsiders tried to discourage me from doing so by describing the people as hopeless and always engaged in some sort of dispute. Although I never had to regret my decision to ignore their warning, I must say that there is a good deal of truth in it: bitter jealousy, everlasting accusations of theft or fraud, and unceasing quarrels are commonplace, and one could draw a map of the network of disputes within the village. Brothers were particularly prone to dispute: there were several cases of brothers living with their families on a tiny plot of land who had not spoken to each other for years. When a man can earn some money on a particular undertaking, he is likely to meet stiff opposition from fellow villagers; several development projects were completely ruined for this reason. Every office is bound to arouse suspicion and bickering from others. This is for instance the case of the catechist, whose function is rather repellent and certainly unprofitable but which nevertheless attracts the curses and threats of the other villagers. There is of course no official leader (*talaiyari*) among villagers, no official village council; and the elder people, as we have seen, are given very little respect.

Jealousy is absolutely rampant. Once the NGO One Thousand Wells allowed one of its workers, born in another village but married into Valghira Manickam, to build a hut on its compound. This favour immediately entailed bitter quarrels, every worker then claiming a housesite. The poor catechist who was affected with leprosy is regularly reminded that his illness is owing to a mishandling of the parish money, a cruel and totally unfounded accusation. Every family has a good number of enemies within the village. Usually the quarrels start with minor problems but could easily lead to a complete break in the social relations between the families concerned. More often than not, the quarrels were even transmitted to the next generation. Usually families in dispute do not talk to each other and behave as if the others did not exist; from time to time, however, the fighting may resume for one reason or another. People then start shouting and threatening each other. Women are not the least involved, and insult the other party as much as they can. In such circumstances, all the villagers rush to the spot to watch the quarrel without getting involved; it is quite remarkable that there is so little actual violence.

The use of black magic clearly intervenes in this context of jealousy. My data on the subject are rather piecemeal but all cases I was able to collect were intra-familial and occurred to harm a successful member of the family. This is for example what happened to Sowryamman, a lady who had a job as municipal scavenger; she was then 'rich' and happy and her family could not bear this; one day, while she was asleep under the verandah, one person whom she could not recognise approached her and sprinkled a white powder over her body. All at once, Sowryamman was paralysed; she wanted to scream but the words would not come out of her mouth. She remained in this state of lethargy for several days and was ill for several months. As she was thereafter unable to work, her nephew took her job at the municipality. She thinks that her brothers were jealous of her success and used black magic to make her lose her job. This story is quite typical of black magic accusations. I wonder, however, as Epstein argued (1967), whether it is mainly directed towards women. It seems however that people who have a good job, who lead a happy life, who are successful in life are the main victims of black magic while it is someone fairly close to the victim who is mostly accused of being responsible for the curse.

Conclusions

Valghira Manickam does not constitute a unit by itself. It belongs to a wider world and the Paraiyars do not form a self-contained society. They are included within a social organisation which is fundamentally hierarchical; it would thus be wrong to represent them as fundamentally unaffected by the hierarchical values of caste. Yet what this article attempted to show is that a good deal of the Paraiyar's life and values is not permeated by caste ideology. Egalitarian values exist, and most probably have always existed, among them.

The picture drawn above is most probably not the effect of recent social changes. We have enough evidence to believe that the rules of cross-cousin marriage, the relative importance of women, and the absence of hierarchical divisions within the caste are not recent phenomena. It is of course difficult to know what the Paraiyars thought and believed one or several centuries ago. Their oral literature, however, suggests that they already had some sense of equality in a more remote past: this is the case of the well-known Paraiyar myths of origin which I have analysed earlier and which stress the original equality between Brahmans and Paraiyars (see Deliège, 1989). Similarly Trawick suggested that the Paraiyar songs protest against the social hierarchy of the village (1987:197).

In recent decades, however, modern values have permeated the life of the Paraiyars; the ideals of social equality and democracy have become very widespread among them and people are even less ready than they might have been before to bear the burden of exploitation and social discrimination. They not only take an active part in the election process but some of them also get involved in various movements asserting the rights of the 'downtrodden'. It is thus certain that egalitarian values are much more evident today than they might have been in the past.

Caste, however, has preserved its importance for the Paraiyars. Usually, they prefer to move with people from their own community; most of their friends and acquaintances belong to their own caste, and they cannot even think of inter-caste marriage. Yet the ideology underlying caste is weak: the questions of purity and pollution are not essential elements of their understanding of caste; municipal scavengers are, for instance, considered as lucky to have a good job and their task is little demeaning. More generally, people refuse to consider their own caste as intrinsically impure and claim some equality with other castes. That is why they send their children to school and hope for better jobs for them. I often heard people saying that untouchability is merely a question of money and power; this is surely a simplification of reality, yet their main preoccupation is now with their material welfare while their ritual status has increasingly become an irrelevant issue. Caste thus tends to transform itself into an ethnic group which competes with other such groups.

The paradox of this modern transformation is that while the different caste groups become increasingly alike and are in competition with each other, there is a greater differentiation within each group: in the past, most members of a caste of barbers worked as barbers and enjoyed a similar socio-economic status. This is no longer the case today and there is a wide range of occupations within each caste. This is also true among the

Paraiyars of Valghira Manickam among whom one can find a school teacher, a clerk, several 'wiremen' of the Electricity board or a few brickmaking entrepreneurs who enjoy considerably higher incomes than the coolies and labourers who form the majority of the village population. The interests of a brick factory owner are clearly different from those of his workers. Yet one cannot speak of the development of class groups within the village population. People who enjoy a higher income cannot dissociate themselves from the rest of the population; they do not form a sufficiently important community to constitute a subgroup within the caste and they continue to marry in the traditional way. It is true that some parents, whose sons have a good job or who can afford some dowry for their daughters, can look for a partner outside the traditional circle of marriage but these attempts are not yet widespread and not always successful. Finally, there is no class consciousness within the village: bullock cart drivers, salaried workers, masons, coolies and brickmakers have the feeling of belonging to the same community (ie to be Paraiyars), and this feeling is little eroded as yet by diverging class interests.

Notes

1 Although the term 'Harijan', like the term 'untouchable', is unacceptable to many of the people now classified by the Government of India as 'scheduled caste', it is used here because it is the word most common among my informants.
2 Secondary School Leaving Certificate.

References

Béteille, A., (1974), *Studies in Agrarian Social Structure*, Delhi: Oxford University Press.
Caplan, L., (1980), 'Caste and Castelessness Among South Indian Christians', *Contributions to Indian Sociology* (n.s.), 14, 213–238.
Deliège, R., (1988), *Les Paraiyars du Tamil Nadu*, Nettetal: Steyler Verlag.
Deliège, R., (1989), 'Les mythes d'origine chez les Paraiyar (Inde du sud)', *L'Homme*, 29, 107–116.
Deliège, R., (1992), 'Replication and Consensus: untouchability, caste and ideology in India', *Man* (n.s.), 27, 155–173.
Deliège, R., (1993), *Le système des castes*, Paris: Presses Universitaires de France.
Den Ouden, J., (1977), *De Onaanraakbaren van Konkunad: een onderzoek naar de positieverandering van de Scheduled Castes in een dorp van het district*

Coimbatore, India, Wageningen: Vakgroep Agrarisch Sociologie van de Niet-Westerse Gebieden.

Dumont, L., (1957), *Une sous-caste de l'Inde du sud: organisation sociale des Pramalai Kallar*, Paris: Mouton.

Dumont, L., (1966), *Homo Hierarchicus: essai sur le système des castes*, Paris: Gallimard.

Epstein, S., (1967), 'A Sociological Analysis of Witch Beliefs in a Mysore Village', in *Magic, Witchcraft and Curing*, J. Middleton (ed.), Austin: University of Texas Press, 135–154.

Gellner, E., (1992), *Postmodernism, Reason and Religion*, London: Routledge.

Gough, K., (1960), 'Caste in a Tanjore Village', in E. Leach, (ed.), *Aspects of Caste in South India, Ceylon and North-West Pakistan*, Cambridge: Cambridge University Press.

Inden, R., (1990), *Imagining India*, Oxford: Blackwell.

Kothari, R., (1990), *State Against Democracy: in Search of Human Governance*, London: Aspects Publications.

Kuper, A., (1992), 'Post-Modernism, Cambridge and the great Kalahari Debate', *Anthropologie sociale*, 1, 57–71.

Lévi-Strauss, C., (1967), *Les structures élémentaires de la parenté*, Paris: Mouton.

Molund, S., (1988), *First We Are People . . ., the Koris of Kanpur Between Caste and Class*, Stockholm: Stockholm Studies in Social Anthropology.

Needham, R., (1966), *Structure and Sentiment: a Test Case in Social Anthropology*, Chicago: University of Chicago Press.

Parry, J., (1974), 'Egalitarian Values in a Hierarchical Society', *South Asian Review*, 7, 95–124.

Parry, J., (1979), *Caste and Kinship in Kangra*, London: Routledge & Kegan Paul.

Quigley, D., (1993), *The Interpretation of Caste*, Oxford: Clarendon Press.

Searle-Chatterjee, M., (1981), *Reversible Sex Roles: the Special Case of the Benares Sweepers*, Oxford: Pergamon Press.

Toffin, G., (1993), *Le palais et le temple: la fonction royale dans la vallée du Népal*, Paris: CNRS Editions.

Trawick, M., (1987), 'Spirits and Voices in Tamil Songs', *American Ethnology*, 14, 193–215.

Caste, religion and other identities

Mary Searle-Chatterjee

Abstract

Religion is one of the many principles of social identification in India. It is becoming increasingly important – although, very often, what appears to be mobilisation on a religious basis can just as adequately, indeed more satisfactorily, be described in terms of caste, class or regional affiliations. Vested interests may encourage the reification of religions, and academics overseas, especially in Religious Studies departments, may, unwittingly, provide them support. This chapter examines the link between caste and religion, particularly in the case of the very lowest status groups. It suggests that both caste and religion mean very different things at different levels of the hierarchy. It then proceeds to look at the distinctive characteristics of religious identities in India. The discussion is related to wider debates about ethnic and racial identities and issues. Should class or interest group membership and allegiances be prioritised over other cultural identities, whether ascribed or acquired? It is argued that it is mistaken to reduce any one of these to another. Searle-Chatterjee draws on a range of historical and sociological/anthropological literature and also makes use of her own research in Varanasi (Banaras).

Introduction

Caste and kin-based networks are but one, albeit very important, of many principles of social identification and solidarity in India. A complex range of identities intersect in an ever-changing variety of ways, sometimes cross-cutting, sometimes overlapping. It is mistaken to attempt to privilege any one of these, or to reduce any one to another. In this chapter I shall attempt to indicate some of this variety. Particular attention will be placed on the relationship between caste, class and religion in the context of wider debates about ethnic and racial issues. Should we, for example, prioritise class or interest group membership and allegiances over other cultural identities, whether ascribed or acquired?

Anthropologists have focused on caste as the central institution in Indian society yet at this moment it is not caste but religious 'community' which is the social issue most in the public eye. Indeed, it is significant that whenever the English words 'community' and 'communal' are used in India, as they often are, they almost always refer to religion, rather than caste. For many Indians, especially in urban areas, it is religious, rather than caste, affiliation which is fast becoming the most prominent aspect of personal identity. *Jati* is the term conventionally translated as caste even though the word has always been used more widely to refer to group, type or species.[1] The Jan Sangh, a rightwing Hindu chauvinist party, and its successor, the Bharatiya Janata Party, sometimes refer to Hindus as 'one *jat*'. As far as these organisations are concerned, Muslims have now become the other main group in a multi-group or even two-group system, in which Hindus would, in the natural state of affairs, be the dominant group with others being in a client relationship. This 'natural' state of affairs does not always occur because the 'alien' origin of the 'other' religions indicates a lack of respect for the ancestors and the traditions of the past, and a certain subversiveness towards the *status quo* and the rightful social order.

Both caste and religious affiliations may have many positive functions for the individual's sense of identity as well as for social support and integration. Whereas in villages it is membership of a caste which is generally more salient in peoples' lives, in town specific religious identities may be more important. In expanding, anonymous urban areas, religious sects and cults, as well as caste and regional associations, may function like ethnicity in American cities. They may add to the social work performed by more traditional institutions such as neighbourhood mosques and temples (see Mitra in this volume). Monastic orders such as Bharat Seva Sangh and sectarian organisations, such as the Jamia Salfia, not only provide a resource for the formation of networks but may also engage in philanthropic work. Very often, creative and aesthetic activities, too, find a focus in religious centres and occasions. Most of the discussion in this paper focuses on the more negative aspects of such identifications. This is a reflection of the way in which the subject is generally discussed both in the academic literature and in the mass media. Conflict and violence are human and political problems. As such, they become, inevitably, intellectual concerns. The positive functions of the same institutions may therefore be overlooked.

Is religious identification really something else?

For many people, particularly of the 'higher' castes, religious and caste identifies are rooted in the socialisation of early childhood. In this sense, they can be called primordial. For some sociologists and historians, primordiality is in itself a sufficient explanation for mobilisation on a religious basis. For them, religious identity is deeply rooted in the psyche, and in history, and hence is ever watchful in its own defence and glorification, always available and susceptible to manipulation by those hungry for power. An implication of this is that it is only natural for Hindus to support one another in opposition to Muslims. Academics and activists of various persuasions have endorsed or promoted such approaches. These have included British nationalist historians, Indian nationalists of the Bharatiya Janata Party type today and religious studies specialists with their stress on values (see also Smith, 1966; Robinson, 1983; Carroll, 1983; and discussion in Brass, 1991). In social anthropology, Dumont and Gaborieux, among others, have, in practice, endorsed such an approach (Dumont, 1970; Gaborieux, 1985). One of the problems with this so-called primordialist analysis of religious solidarity and conflict is that it does not explain why *one* type of identity, the religious, should overshadow others which are often also primordial, such as sect, caste and language, or even class or gender. Most of these cross-cut religion.

Another problem with this approach has been addressed by those who have argued against the essentialising of religious traditions, against the tendency to impute to them a fixed and unchanging fundamental character with only relatively minor variations. It has been shown very clearly that Islam, like other religions, has taken on a variety of very different forms in the sub-continent (see Ahmad, 1981; Das, 1984). This may be interpreted sociologically as due to adaptation and assimilation, or, theologically, as due to creative interpretation of the basic tenets. Islam has changed over time and varies between groups. Indeed, tensions between different sub-groups may sometimes be greater than those between Muslims and Hindus. Shias and Sunnis have been in violent conflict in Bombay and Lucknow (Ahmad, 1984b:144–155). In Varanasi (Banaras) many Shia Muslims, members of the old elite, were so hostile to upwardly mobile Sunnis, a numerically much larger group, whom they perceived as fanatical and domineering, that instead of favouring Congress in the 1970s, they gave support to the Jan Sangh (Juyal, 1970:190). Similarly among Hindus, sectarian divisions often correspond with status ones. Shaivites, for example, are more commonly found among Brahmins. In south India at the beginning of this century they were in violent conflict with Vaishnavites who tend to draw their members from other castes. The same was true in the Punjab of Satnamis and Arya Samajis. Even where sectarian differences were not involved. Hindu temples have often been plundered or destroyed by Hindu kings from rival states, including the famous Maratha, Sivaji (Ghose, 1973; Ostor, 1984).

The same point can be made even more clearly in the case of Sikhism. In a relatively short space of time, and restricted geographical zone, it has included, and continues to include, vastly different approaches, from the quietistic to the militaristic. Whereas it has usually been easy enough to establish whether a person is a Hindu or Muslim, except for certain minor exceptions like the *Meos* of Rajasthan and major ones like the 'untouchable' castes in general (see Searle-Chatterjee, 1994a), it has often not been at all clear whether an individual was a Sikh or a Hindu. Families included members of both, rituals of both groups were practised within the same household and rituals were performed in both types of place of worship (Nesbitt, 1990; Ballard, 1988). Current political conflicts in the Punjab have led to a hardening of boundaries.

Very often the anti-essentialist critique has proceeded by arguing that religious conflict, so-called, is actually caste or class conflict in disguise, that it has a 'rational' (ie self-interested, non-'primordial') basis. Sometimes this involves a tendency to replace one kind of essentialising with another (Freitag, 1989; Pandey, 1990). Caste groups may be referred to as if they have an enduring identity and consistent self-interest. They do, after all, usually have a smaller range, both geographically and socially, than religions. According to this approach, where caste conflicts happen to coincide with religious divisions (and very often the coincidence is anything but coincidental), the one appears in the form of the other. The so-called 'religious' riots of the south Indian Moplahs which have recurred throughout the last two hundred years, are a well-known example. They were peasant rebellions by impoverished labourers, who happened to be Muslim, against high caste Hindu, *Nayar*, and *Nambudiri* Brahmin, landowners (Saxena, 1984). Similarly, in the 1940s, in the Telengana district of Hyderabad, peasant rebellions against absentee landowners, many of whom were Muslim, were generally interpreted in the national press as being religious in nature.

Religious identification often coincides with local divisions of caste and class precisely because religious conversion, if not a form of cultural or social rebellion, was at least an expression of pre-existing structural difference, particularly among the most exploited groups (Juergensmeyer, 1982). Scheduled castes (the official legal name for 'untouchables') and low status weavers, for example, converted *en masse* to Islam, though mainly to Sunni Islam. East Bengal was an area that fitted the pattern closely. In pre-independence, pre-partition India, its landowners were largely high caste Hindus, its lower classes, Muslim. In India as a whole, today, Muslims are greatly over-represented among the poor, particularly the urban poor (Imam, 1975; Banerjee, 1990:58). Very few are agricultural labourers (Brass, 1974:150). Specific local configurations of caste and religion generally coincide with class ones. In the early 1980s, there was a national uproar when members of certain rural scheduled castes in Tamilnadu converted to Islam. A young and militant group who had been socially mobile led the way. They were experiencing increased pressures from a new capitalist owner-cultivator class. Prospering urban merchant Muslims had been involved in missionary activities. Other scheduled caste government workers in the region noticed the national impact of the conversions and began to threaten to do the same if they were not promoted (Ahmad, 1984a:118).

In the Punjab there are similar close links between religion and caste or class membership. The dominant farming caste, the *Jats*, are all Sikhs: they constitute two thirds of the Sikh population. Urban traders tend to be Hindus (Brass, 1991:222–4). These patterns, however, are far from absolute and there are major caste divisions among Sikhs, as among Hindus. Many castes have a Sikh section as well as a Hindu one and it is more important to marry within the caste than within the 'religion' (Ballard, 1988). So common is the association of 'Muslim' with 'low caste' that caste riots in Gujerat in the early 1980s spilled over into indiscriminate attacks on Muslims. The Government of Gujerat had decided to implement the recommendations of the Mandal Commission advocating an expansion of positive discrimination, of quotas for government jobs and college places. In addition to Scheduled castes and tribes, a much large group known as 'Other Backward Classes' was now to be eligible for reservations. A quarter of these would have been Muslim. This aroused tremendous anger among the high castes who had hitherto dominated higher education and the professions and now faced the prospect of a deterioration in their social position and income. Many of those who initiated the rioting were doctors, lawyers, lecturers and students (Bose, 1981; Desai, 1981; Engineer, 1989; Baxi, 1990; Kelly, 1990). The result was widespread rioting, student suicides and attacks on slum localities. Rivalries of various other types also expressed themselves in the violence. Local Marathi Hindu power loom owners, for example, saw opportunities to destroy the assets of prospering power loom owners who were immigrant Muslims from Uttar Pradesh.

A class analysis is necessary, though not sufficient, in considering aspects of the 'religious' riots which erupted in December 1992 in Bombay. These began with spontaneous outbursts of Muslims attacking buildings in protest at government failure to prevent the destruction of the Baburi Mosque at Ayodhya in North India. This provided the opportunity for a massive attack on Muslims. It was highly organised with marks on houses. Anti-Muslim organisations such as the RSS (the Rashtriya Sevak Sangh, a para-military nationalist group) described this as defensive. Many of those involved in the actual violence were themselves also very poor, including many of scheduled caste (Sebastian, 1993).

A similar situation developed in Surat in nearby Gujerat. Muslims of migrant labour background, in crowded, tension-ridden urban squatter shanty towns, with a dominance of males, began protesting against the Government. The response was something they could not have anticipated. Feeling themselves to be victims, they were yet perceived as dangerous predators, and were attacked with horrendous brutality. Although communalist organisations and a variety of local economic and political interests were involved, many of those physically active in the violence were 'local' Marathi-speaking slum dwellers often belonging to the *Kanbi* caste or other 'backward' castes. They had migrated to the city from nearby villages in Maharashtra. Immigrant Muslim slum dwellers from North India were seen as rivals for jobs and housing, or as encroachers on village lands. The end result was a massive reverse migration and exodus of Muslims. The slums were partially cleared and land made available for profitable urban development by a new powerful elite (Sheth, 1993). Local, long-established urban Muslims were not much affected by the riots. However, the riots cannot be viewed simply in regional terms since 'local' Hindu Marathis were joined in their attacks on Muslim immigrants by other Hindu slum dwellers who were themselves immigrants from North India, including Orissa.[2] They involved, among other conflicts, divisions between two 'fractions' of the 'underclass' which do not appear as a whole to have been economically differentiated prior to the riots. The 'fractions' were defined as such primarily through the operation of cultural categories. In this context religion was the crucial category. Region of origin was a category of secondary importance: it defined which segments of Muslims could be seen as illegitimate residents, as legitimate targets. It did not, in this context, differentiate aggressors. In other contexts, region and religion could have been recombined in different configurations.

The riots occurred in the context of a major recession. They were the result of 'modern' conditions, massive urbanisation and migration of labour. In 1947 there had been no such disturbances in Surat. It has to be said, however, that conflicts among rival groups with differential access to the power of the state were also of major importance. The police, for example, at times functioned as agents of the dominant political group and, at times, as an interest group in their own right.

Religious identities may be mobilised where a change occurs in the material position of a caste of a lower class which happens to be of a different religion. The possibility arises of a 'religious' dimension to any such competition or rivalry. In Varanasi (Banaras) the movement of rising Muslim Weavers into the hitherto Hindu-dominated textile merchant class has been associated with an upsurge of 'religious' tension and communal rioting (Juyal, 1970). Muslim artisans and merchants have made direct contact with middle-eastern buyers and their expanding markets. This has coincided with an expansion of exports and a flow of cash remittances into the pockets of other 'castes' of Muslim from relatives employed as migrant labour in various Arab countries, as well as Malaysia (Searle-Chatterjee, 1994b). Hindu middlemen have turned to the Hindu chauvinist parties. Religious identification is being harnessed 'defensively' by those who fear a reduction of their high income and status. It is also being used 'aggressively' by upwardly mobile *Ahirs* (of the Milkman caste) who compete with the new Muslim merchants for purchase of mansions coming on to the market in the Madanpura neighbourhood.

A more complex example can be seen in Moradabad, a city where Muslims are in the majority. After 1947, Punjabi refugees of trading castes moved into the brass industry as exporters. Most of the producers, the artisans, are Muslims. Since then, Muslims have lost their elite status in the area and have declined relative to Hindus in influence and education. Muslim artisans have recently begun to move up into the merchant class. At the same time, expanding opportunities in the industry have led to Muslims migrating into Moradabad from smaller towns in the district. This means that in terms of sheer numbers they have electoral clout if they choose to vote as a bloc. The police, on the other hand, tend to be Hindu. Punjabi merchants have in recent years aligned themselves with the 'Hindu' parties, like the BJP. On the other side, Congress (I) has backed Muslims on a platform of poor 'locals' against wealthy 'outsiders'. This provided the context for a series of riots in the 1980s. Much property owned by Muslim merchants was destroyed and men at worship in mosques were shot (Saberwal & Hasan, 1984:209).

Although Muslims tend to be disproportionately represented among the poor, the religious identifications of the lower classes cannot simply be understood in terms of horizontal divisions, as is clear from the previous accounts. They have sometimes followed a vertical pattern and corresponded with those of their local landowners. In Uttar Pradesh, Muslim landowners often had Muslim tenants and labourers and Hindu landowners likewise had clients who, if not exactly identical in religious practice, gave no indication of having adopted any marked alternative, even, indeed, sometimes had the same sub-caste name or exogamous marriage divisions as their masters (Crooke, 1896:clxiv, 273–4). Whether the vertical pattern indicated a more harmonious situation, or rather, a more totally oppressed one, is not clear.

In recent decades, the group of Indian and Anglo-American historians associated with the journal *Subaltern Studies* has added its voice to those who attempt to unpackage the notions of 'Hindu' and 'Muslim'. It has focused on local class and caste interests, paying particular attention to the 'view from below' in so far as this can be ascertained from documents. Gyan Pandey's account of conflicts in late nineteenth century East Uttar Pradesh has stressed not so much horizontal dimensions of religious identifications but rather competition between vertical divisions within the dominant landed class. He described how in 1893 in the Azamgarh district at the time of the Baqr-Id festival, large fighting forces composed of members of the chief landowning castes, *Rajputs, Bhumihars* and Brahmins, along with their servants and tenants, attacked villages owned by Muslim landowners. The landowners' dominant status was being eroded by the rising upper tenantry, trading castes and the colonial bureaucracy. They were supported by those with other agendas, like members of the upwardly mobile Milkman caste, 5000 men armed with staffs, who wished to raise their status as Hindus by vigorous support of the cow protection movement. Intra-elite vertical competition of this kind was more common before the weakening of the power of Muslim landowners, partly due to Partition in 1947 and partly due to the land reform acts (*zamindari* abolition) of the 1950s which particularly affected absentee landowners.

On other occasions where there were horizontal cleavages, Muslims had attacked first. Poor Muslim weavers constituted two thirds of the urban population. They had attacked Hindu moneylenders and bankers who, despite the rising price of grain, were spending their gains on large new mansions and temples. Many Hindus argued that the British had added to, or deliberately encouraged, religious tensions. They complained about British permission for a local slaughter house 'to compensate weavers for the high cost of grain', and pointed out that even Muslim kings, in deference to the wishes of the majority, had not permitted cow slaughter. In general, the lower agricultural castes were not much involved in either vertical or horizontal conflict. Gangs of low caste males simply joined in the free-for-all whenever they saw opportunities for looting. The very lowest groups of all, the 'untouchable' castes, the *Chamars* (Leatherworkers), were said to show very little identification with either of the assorted coalitions of 'Hindus' or 'Muslims'. On occasion, they were even attacked by higher 'Hindu' groups for alleged involvement in cow killing and beef consumption. Pandey clearly does not consider that there was any inevitable continuity on religious grounds in these social conflicts. Castes, or local segments of castes, were seen as networks of kin-based interest groups rooted in particular territories which would form fluctuating alliances according to the interests of the moment. In 1921, in the same area, Hindu and Muslim landowners joined together against the *Milkman* caste refusal to give them low cost dairy produce. Large-scale riots resulted, though deaths were not reported (Pandey,1983).

Religious tensions and social identity

It is often argued that communal religious tensions are not great when power lines are clearly drawn. According to Philip Mason, in the British period communalism was less in princely states where there was little possibility of change (1967). Any dislocation in existing power relationship, in the current equilibrium, is said to lead directly to a flowering, or eruption, depending on one's point of view, of rival dominant caste groups into the public domain. Latent groups become manifest (communities become 'communal') and potential caste links activated (see Mitra in this volume). Religious identifications may become involved too, either directly, as above, or, more commonly today, indirectly. This process only operates among groups with land or other assets, though lower castes may be drawn in. The groups concerned may not be of 'high' caste in the Dumontian/ Brahminical sense, but they will be powerful, even though, officially often of *Sudra* caste, for example, *Kammas* in Andhra Pradesh (Elliott, 1970).

Sandra Freitag has argued that in early nineteenth century Banaras (Varanasi) it was, ultimately, destabilisation caused by the British presence, rather than, at that stage, any deliberate attempt to divide and rule, which led to a major local 'communal' ie religious, riot in 1809. Banaras in the eighteenth century was controlled by a triumvirate of *Bhumihars* (large rural landowners), *Gosains*, a religio-communal sect which was the main property owner in the city, and the banker merchants. Unlike other cities in Uttar Pradesh, its elite was Hindu Merchant in style, not Indo-Persian. It had however developed a syncretic culture that was both 'religious' and 'secular', based on *bhakti* (devotional) traditions, in which Muslims Weavers, who constituted a quarter of the city's population, were well integrated, in a manner that corresponded with the close economic integration in the textile industry. In 1809 the acting magistrate Bird said 'the ceremonies of Muhammedans and Hindus are so inseparably blended that any attempt to disunite them would constitute a new arrangement' (1989:206). This culture was upheld by the *Bhumihar* Maharaja and typified in his patronage of integrative festivals. The integration of the 'lower' classes could still be seen much later in the 1890s when there were cow protection riots all over East Uttar Pradesh but not in Banaras. Muslim Weavers who had been impoverished by the effects of protectionist policies in favour of Lancashire textiles even succeeded in persuading Hindu boatmen to call off the highly popular annual river carnival in sympathy (for examples of the survival of this culture today, see Kumar, 1988). However, power lines had gradually become destabilised as a result of Banaras becoming the main inland commercial centre of the British in the late eighteenth century. The new weakening of Banaras's Maharaja and the *status quo* led to a reinvention of 'Hindu' tradition by other groups in an attempt to capture local support, gain power and fill the vacuum. *Rajputs* and *Gosains* were active in encouraging provocation and aggression at the Lat Bhairo site, shared by Hindus and Muslims. This led to a major religious riot in 1809.

In 1810 a much bigger riot occurred than in the year before. This one, however, was a protest against the severity of the British house tax. Shops closed and vast numbers of the populace sat down in silent protest for a month. Twenty thousand people sat in one open space alone (206). The protest was effective and involved a wide range of groups, both Hindu and Muslim. It is interesting and significant that since then popular books on the city have placed far more emphasis on the 'religious' conflict of the previous year than on the secular one of 1810 (Sherring, 1896; Havell, 1933; Sukul, 1977; Eck, 1983).

The destabilisation argument is often used to explain contemporary 'religious' conflicts associated with the destruction of the Baburi Mosque. Congress party dominance based on an alliance of the bourgeoisie, and the poor, has been shaken by the emergence of the middle-caste 'bullock capitalists' in rural areas. The use of religion as a tool in struggles for power has increased (Rudolph and Rudolph, 1987; Alavi, 1989; Noorani, 1989). At the local level, rightwing parties, including nowadays Congress, benefit from Hindu fear and resentment of Muslims (see Juyal, 1970 for an earlier discussion of this). Other parties, or in earlier decades, the Congress, may benefit from a bloc of fearful

Muslims, by presenting themselves as their altruistic protectors. With majority vote democracy there is an automatic potential for destabilisation.

The more general argument that ethnic conflict (whether based on the 'primordial' identities of sect, religion, language or caste) is a product of intra-elite competition, has been put particularly clearly by Paul Brass. He argues that group conflicts remain sporadic and disorderly unless elites are involved and, more specifically, that the critical precipitant for the politicisation of ethnic group conflict is for segments of rival elites to be in alliance with the state. The stakes become raised and the likelihood of widespread violence increased in such situations. Brass demonstrates his argument with descriptions of the several competing elites involved in the Punjab conflicts today and in early twentieth century Tamilnadu (Brass, 1985). Communal massacres in Bihar in 1967 (Ranchi) were linked directly with conflicts between rival groups for control of state power (Brass, 1974:265–9).

An example of a 'negative instance' supporting Brass's approach occurred in Varanasi in 1986. In a weaving locality, mainly Muslim, on the edge of the city in the Bhelupura ward, three Muslim brothers had their throats slit on the 3rd or 4th of November. It was widely believed by Muslim locals that this was the result of a land dispute and that the murder was instigated by a large landowner who had a gang of henchmen at his disposal. For a week the city was extremely tense. On the 5th and 6th the streets were deserted, with only small groups of men talking at street corners. For several days localities with many Muslim inhabitants in the south and centre of the city closed down completely, with all shops and workplaces closed in protest. The police and the local press suggested that an 'illegal love affair' might have been a factor or that there might have been involvement in shady business dealing as one of the murdered men was said to have enjoyed a sudden improvement in financial status. This view was not shared by most locals. On the evening of the 6th, 20,000 were said in the press to have been present at the burial. On Friday the 7th and Saturday the 8th, following Friday afternoon attendance at mosques, crowds said to be of up to 10,000, mainly Muslims, besieged the local police station, burnt police vehicles and closed thoroughfares. Student and opposition party leaders also participated. Muslims claimed that the police must have been bribed into inaction as the perpetrator's identity was obvious. A prominent local Congress party leader was beaten up. The leaders of the opposition parties organised meetings in an attempt to 'mobilise the masses and also to build pressure on the local police. They criticised the present set-up of the Government, the district administration and the local police' (*The Pioneer*, Nov. 7). In fact, the Muslim masses had mobilised themselves before the politicians had entered the scene. It appeared that there was a great opportunity for opposition parties to disturb the government. It was widely believed that there would be major riots and that these would take a religious communal form as Muslims attempted to coerce Hindu shopkeepers into closing in protest. Everyone who could afford to do so began to stock up on food supplies. Only towards the end of the second week in November did the newspaper versions begin to resemble those of the crowds in the streets. This was associated with the fact that on November 9th the ruling Congress party had decided to join in too and an all-party action committee had been formed to protest against police delays. On the 10th they declared a twenty-four hour fast to be followed by a *bandh*, total strike, if no arrests were made. At this point the opposition parties began to lose interest. Within a couple of days the newspapers reported that an arrest had been made. After that, the agitations fizzled out rapidly. Once the ruling party decided to join other political elite groups in 'support' of the protestors, elites in opposition were unable to exploit the situation to their advantage and ethnic mobilisation did not occur. Presumably the murderer, if it was he who was arrested, was not sufficiently influential to influence the outcome.

Religious identifications of the 'lowest' castes

Pandey referred to the fact that in the late nineteenth century conflicts which he studied, 'untouchables' were not only un-involved in ostensibly religious conflict but were even attacked by their supposed co-religionists. This raises interesting questions as to whether it was simply that in this particular case their own interests were not involved, or whether the posited caste/ religion link simply has much less basis amongst the very lowest groups for whom 'primordial' identifications are not attached to 'mainstream' religions. Such a view may be based on empirical observation, but may also be associated with the assumption that the very lowest groups are less likely to suffer from 'false con-sciousness' than castes rather higher up in society. It may be assumed that they are therefore less likely to be drawn into intra-group competition between Hindu and Muslim elites, or between rival dominant 'Hindu' castes or coalitions of castes.

Is there in fact much evidence that Scheduled castes tend to be relatively uninterested in religious communalism, indeed that they can hardly be said to have any religious identifications at all, though of course having religious practices and beliefs? The Gujerati riots referred to earlier make clear that scheduled castes are sometimes involved in 'communal' violence, albeit in a context in which labourers from other regions, not 'sons of the soil', are perceived as economic rivals. In the anti-Sikh massacres in Delhi that occurred after the assassination of Indira Gandhi, 'untouchable' *Chamar* labourers murdered local Sikh slum land-lords and shopkeepers. Class conflicts coincided with regional/lin-guistic ones, as well as with religious divisions. The national political context of public attitudes at that moment made reli-gious hostility legitimate. It was, moreover, actively encouraged and coordinated by those with larger party political interests, by local Congress party workers (Das, 1990:13–4). A whole range of factors, of the type relevant in the analysis of racial and ethnic conflicts in Europe, were important here.

However, although it is clear that the scheduled castes may well be involved in what appears to be religious rioting, this seems to occur only when they perceive themselves to be in a sit-uation of conflict over scarce resources. Is there any reason to think that this is any more true for them than for higher caste groups? There is certainly a long tradition of the 'untouchables' voting with Muslims both at local and national levels (Brass, 1991:155, Jeffery & Jeffery, 1994:552). In both the run-up to Independence in the 1930s and, again today, with the resurgence of 'Hindu' politics, considerable anxiety is expressed among the high castes about the lack of 'loyalty' of the 'lowest' castes. The anxiety is well-founded. It is not simply divisions of class which create this lack of 'reliability': 'untouchables' very often lack any kind of 'primordial' identification as 'Hindus'. Some of their castes have a marked identity as Muslim, Christian or Buddhist: others may belong to break-away sects of Hindu origin. Many do not use any specific marked label to encompass their religious beliefs and practices. Scheduled caste Sweepers in Varanasi do not usually even identify themselves as 'Hindu'. This is because they use the term 'Hindu' very differently from the way the high castes do, in terms of a different set of conceptual oppositions.

The 'clean' castes ie those of the three highest categories of castes, do in some context identify themselves as Hindu. They use the term broadly and inclusively, however, in the sense that it subsumes traditions that would be seen by some, especially foreigners, as being non-Hindu, but which have their origins on Indian soil ie Jainism, Buddhism and Sikhism (though the latter incorporation has recently become problematic). Everyone, then, is *by default* a Hindu, except those who by origin or self-identification, look to some tradition whose geographical origin is outside South Asia ie Christians and Muslims. Parsees appear to be an exception to this. However, they no longer look to any geographical area beyond India, having fled there as a persecuted group. Even so, they are sometimes contrasted with a regional identity ie Marathi. A 'Hindu', then, is not someone with a particular set of beliefs or practices, but rather someone who is not in any way a foreigner. Hinduism is religious activity which has its roots locally. In rural areas, particularly in Bengal, a common conceptual opposition would be a regional one, eg Bengali versus Muslim. In *urban* usage, geographic terms are often replaced by the larger term 'Hindu'. There is no reason to think that this territorial usage is new. It corresponds with that of the various groups of Muslim people who entered India at the beginning of the millennium (Thapar, 1989).

When we examine the categories used by the scheduled castes, however, Sweepers and *Chamar* leatherworkers, for example, we find a different set of conceptual oppositions. For them, 'Hindus' are contrasted not with 'foreigners' but with 'low' or powerless castes. When talking to others of their group, the 'lowest' castes refer to Hindus as though they are people other than themselves eg 'the people who live across the road'. In response to the question 'who are Hindus?' I have often been told 'they are Brahmins and *Thakurs*' (landowning castes). Hindus, then, are people of high status and power, those who are associated with the Brahminical framework of society. A few go further, like the *Raedasis* (or Ravidasis), who give a fresh gloss on the high caste 'myth' of Aryan origin, by claiming that 'Brahmins and *Thakurs* are alien immigrant conquerors, while the untouchables are the true sons of the soil, descendents of the original inhabitants.' Sweeper children, if asked whether they are Hindu or Muslim, are often unable to answer. Adults sometimes expressed their disapproval of my asking about such matters by saying 'its not good to talk like that', or 'we are not like that'. When pressed,

Sweepers will, in the end, reluctantly identify themselves as Hindu or Muslim, often adding some reference to 'us all being mixed up'. However, they show very little positive identification with the label, and do not claim that it is any better than any other. Informants were similarly confused about what were the markers commonly seen as diacritical of the Hindu/Muslim divide. Nor were they easily able to align themselves in terms of these. Most of them eat pork, but are not averse to eating beef either. They do not cremate their dead, like 'Hindus' but either bury or immerse them. They don't usually visit either temples or mosques, only wayside 'Hindu' shrines and 'Muslim' tombs. They consider that it is not good manners to discuss such markers, for the use of the terms 'Hindu' and 'Muslim' is thought to have a divisive intention, not a descriptive one. For these reasons I consider that it is inappropriate to use the term 'Hindu' (though Muslim is sometimes applicable) in relation to the 'lowest' castes (for a fuller discussion of these points see Searle-Chatterjee, 1994a).

Juergensmeyer (1982:24) has argued that lack of attachment to the Hindu label is due to conscious rejection of the caste system. This is undoubtedly sometimes the case and may be more common in the Punjab, the region on which he has focused, where the scheduled castes are unusually politicised because of the demographic parity of the three competing religious groups (Hindu, Muslim, Sikh) in the pre-Independence period. More often, it is, I believe, an indication that the scheduled castes simply do not regard themselves as being of the same category of people as the high castes. The linguistic usage to which I have referred is particularly common amongst the *least* politicised and *least* self-conscious sweepers in Varanasi. It is used inadvertently. Juergensmeyer has suggested that the extended notion of the Hindu as the alien conqueror originated with the anti-Brahmin movement in South India around 1915. The only evidence he can offer to support this genealogy of northern 'low' caste rejection of the label 'Hindu' is the fact that he has not found any reference to it in earlier literature. I suggest that what underlies his interpretation is the assumption that only in modern times could 'untouchables' be capable of thinking of themselves as outside the Hindu category. I suggest, on the contrary, that the ideas may be much older, though only used politically when the possibility of changing the system arose. The 'high' castes have, since ancient times, referred disparagingly to 'untouchables' as descendents of the aboriginal peoples of India (Sharma, 1981). It would be odd if no such tradition had been found amongst the lowest castes themselves. Rather than increasingly differentiating themselves from the high castes, the scheduled castes are now experiencing pressures from above to define themselves as either Hindu or Muslim. Essentialist ideas of religion, partly derived from western Christian concepts, dominant among Religious Studies specialists, may, in practice, function to reinforce high caste endeavours to delineate tighter religious boundaries.

A particular religious identification may, then, have 'primordial' roots only among 'higher' caste groups. Similarly, caste identities may have very different characteristics at different levels of society. Among the scheduled castes they may resemble 'racial' rather than 'ethnic' ones, having been imposed by others (see Shukra in this volume) whereas caste identifies among the higher groups may be more 'ethnic' in nature, being primarily self-ascribed (see Banton, 1983:105).

Tribes and regions

'Religious' solidarities may be related to caste ones in a variety of complex ways, and the same is true of tribal identifications. It is interesting to note that in the nineteenth century many British ethnographers who wrote about India used the terms 'tribe' and 'caste' interchangeably (Crooke, 1896). 'Tribe' may correspond with religion for some of the same reasons as caste may. Tribal groups in Bihar have often adopted Christianity. Working as unskilled labour in the steel towns, they have been drawn into 'religious' rioting where class, region, religion and tribal origins have combined and cross-cut in a complex web of interconnection. The same has been true of Assam (Engineer, 1984:296).

Language and regional origin, as already indicated above in the reference to riots in Gujerat and Bombay, may also underlie or reinforce religious mobilisation. Weiner has shown how 'sons of the soil' movements may emerge among new upwardly mobile middle-class locals in an attempt to restrict competition from well-established educated classes who originate from outside the state. In some cases this is interpreted to exclude people who may have been born in the state, but whose ancestors came from another linguistic region. Agitations in Bombay have attempted to exclude Tamils because of the advantage they had gained from knowledge of English resulting from the fact that the British had established an early base in Madras. In Hyderabad, the 'mulki' movement attempted successfully to exclude not only Tamils but also coastal Andhras who had prospered from modern high input agriculture. In the course of agitations, a new self-conscious stress was placed on cultural traits, often of Islamic origin, that were more common in the city and its immediate hinterland, among both Hindus and Muslims, than among those in other parts of the state of Andhra Pradesh. In these and many other such cases caste was not a major issue. There was certainly no sense of caste solidarity across regional or linguistic lines (Weiner, 1978).

Conclusion

In summary, there are many complex and constantly fluctuating interconnections between a variety of communal identifications. Sect, tribe, caste, class, language and regional origin may each provide a basis for solidarity, and even mobilisation. One could never draw up a state of the art or final list of the fundamental organising identities or principles, for new ones are constantly being invented and will continue to be so. However when the religious label enters the situation, the numbers of deaths in the riots appear far greater, as if religion *is* a crucial differentiating identity. It is difficult to make reliable comparisons with numbers of deaths occurring due to class and caste conflicts for these often taken an endemic rather than epidemic form, what some would refer to as the on-going effects of structural violence embedded in caste relations. However it should be noted that Kodian estimated that from 1977–78 more than a thousand 'untouchables' were killed in caste conflicts (Desai, 1984:12). The media appears to focus more attention on religion than on other identifications: we hear more about conflict *between* religions than *within* them. With modern technology there has been an enormous increase in the speed of transmission of such news. Violence involving local and immigrant labour of the *same* religious background may be less publicised and is certainly not described in such religious terms as 'Hindus murder Hindus'. Why should this be so? We cannot simply argue that religious labels are 'primordial' and rooted in history. So too are caste identifications for many groups, especially powerful ones. However, unlike such identities, religious labels appear to make political statements about the state as a whole. The Hindu label is seen as a vote for the *status quo*, for the state as it is presently constituted, whereas the Muslim one (and others too) are seen as alternative, hence subversive, rather than loyal and patriotic. They are a reminder of the partition of India in 1947. The political unity of India is fragile, for in most of its history, the sub-continent has been divided into a multitude of states. Ironically enough, its unity was largely the creation of a Muslim dynasty, the Moghuls, then continued by the alien British. Linked with the apparent national implications of religious identities today is the fact that religious labels are *pan*-Indian identifications associated with Indian history in a way that tribe and caste are not. Regional identities, although they could potentially be much more threatening to the unity of the state, are perhaps seen as more legitimate because they are associated with a territorial base. One of the 'problems' for Muslim people is that, as with Jewish people in the former Soviet Union, their 'separateness' is seen as illegitimate, indeed becomes a symbol of all threats to the state.

While Muslims are found throughout India, caste identifications are rooted only in local arenas and shared territory. The *varnas* (broad caste categories of the Brahminical/Dumontian model) may, in certain contexts, appear in discourses throughout the sub-continent: the *jatis*, or castes, of 'primordial' identification certainly do not. We do not hear of cases where caste violence in south India, non-Brahmins against Brahmins, or vice versa, for example, leads to reverse revenge conflicts in the north, or even in other linguistic regions of the south. Participation in the pan-Indian ideological category of 'Brahmin' is not seen as having that kind of implication for action. A Brahmin in one place does not act as if his ideological integrity is damaged by violence against a Brahmin elsewhere. Perhaps one can only speak of groups being part of a single holistic ideological system when the notion of substitutability arises as in the vendetta? One Muslim can today in many contexts be substituted for another in a different region. One Brahmin cannot, one 'untouchable' cannot, outside a specific village, or cluster of adjacent villages. Having said this, however, attacks against Muslims usually only occur where substantial numbers are present.

An issue much debated in the sociological literature is whether 'ethnic' conflicts are rooted in class or identity concerns (Tajfel, 1982; Miles,1989; Rex, 1991; Macdonald, 1993). Do they originate in self-interest, or in concerns with self-identification in terms of cultural socialisation and historical perceptions? I would argue that the study of interest groups and cultural identities in India shows clearly that it is mistaken to attempt to reduce one to the other. Each has a reality in its own right and an independent influence which cannot be reduced to something else. In Britain, outsiders ('offcomers' in Yorkshire, 'lodgers' in Cheshire) who are generally richer, urban people, buy holiday homes in beautiful rural villages, outpricing the offspring of local people. In the Lake District this leads to ill feeling but no visible conflict, even though separate traditions rooted in regional and class cultures do exist. In Wales, where a greater reservoir of linguistic, historical and cultural resources can be drawn on, house burning results. A sense of communal affiliation, a 'sub-national' identity is sufficiently great in this case to provide the cognitive base for a greater level of mobilisation. Similarly, in India, too, mutual support activities or aggressive social mobilisation are more likely to occur where self-interest coincides with emotive social identifications such as caste and religion.

Notes

1 See introduction, note 4.
2 Personal communication from P. Patel, Professor of Sociology, University of Baroda.

References

Ahmad, I., (1984a), 'The Tamilnadu Conversions, Conversion Threats and the Anti-Reservation Campaigns: Some Hypotheses', in A.A. Engineer, (ed.), *Communal Riots in Post-Independence India*, London: Sangam.

Ahmad, I., (1984b), 'Perspectives on the Communal Problem', in A.A. Engineer, (ed.), as above.

Alavi, H., (1989), 'Politics of Ethnicity in India & Pakistan', in H. Alavi & J. Harriss, (eds), *South Asia*, London: Macmillan.

Ballard, R., (1988), 'Disunity and Disjunctions among Sikhs in Britain', in G. Barrier & V. Dusenberry, (eds.), *The Sikh Diaspora*, Delhi: Chandakya.

Banerjee, A., (1992), 'Comparative Curfew: Changing Dimensions of Communal Politics in India', in V. Das, (ed.), *Mirrors of Violence: Communities, Riots and Survivors in South Asia*. Delhi: Oxford University Press.

Banton, M., (1983), *Ethnic and Racial Competition*, Cambridge: Cambridge University Press.

Baxi, U., (1992), 'Reflections on the Reservation Crisis in Gujerat', in V. Das, (ed.), *Mirrors of Violence: Communities, Riots and Survivors in South Asia*. Delhi: Oxford University Press.

Bose, P.K., (1981), 'Social Mobility & Caste Violence: a study of the Gujerati Riots', *Economic and Political Weekly*, 16:713–16.

Brass, P., (1974), *Language, Religion and Politics in North India*, Cambridge: Cambridge University Press.

Brass, P., (1991), *Ethnicity and Nationalism*, New Delhi: Sage.

Carroll, L., (1983), 'The Muslim Family in India: Law, Custom and Empirical Research', *Contributions*, 17:205–22.

Crooke, W., (1986), *Tribes and Castes of the North West Provinces and Oudh*, Vol. 1, Calcutta: Thacker.

Das, V., (1984), 'For a folk theology and theoretical interpretation of Islam', *Contributions*, 18:293–300.

Das, V. (ed.), 1992, *Mirrors of Violence: Communities, Riots and Survivors in South Asia*. Delhi: Oxford University Press.

Desai, I.P., (1981), 'Anti-reservation Agitations and the Structure of Gujerati Society', *Economic and Political Weekly*, 818–23.

Dumont, L., (1970), *Religion, Politics and History in India*, Paris: Mouton.

Eck, D., (1983), *Banaras City of Light*, London: Routledge.

Elliott, C.M., (1970), 'Caste and Faction among the Dominant Caste: the Reddis and Kammas of Andhra Pradesh', in R. Kothari, (ed.), *Caste in Indian Politics*, Bombay: Orient Longman.

Engineer, A.A., (1982), Gujerat: Communal Violence in Ahmedabad', *Economic and Political Weekly*, 17:100.

Engineer, A.A., (ed.), (1984), *Communal Riots in Post-Independence India*, London: Sangam.

Engineer, A.A., (1989), 'Bombay-Bhiwandi Riots in National Political Perspective', in H. Alavi & J. Harriss, (eds), *South Asia*, London: Macmillan.

Fox, R., (1990), 'Hindu Nationalism in the Making or the Rise of the Hindian', in R. Fox, (ed.), *Nationalist Ideologies in the Production of National Culture*, Washington DC: American Anthropological Association.

Freitag, B.S., (ed.), (1989), *Culture and Power in Banaras*, California: University of California.

Gaboriau, M., (1985), 'From Al-Beruni to Jinnah: Ideas, Ritual and Ideology of the Hindu-Muslim Confrontation in S. Asia', *Anthropology Today*, 3:7–14.

Ghouse, M., (1973), *Secularism, Society and Law in India*, Delhi: Vikas.

Havell, E.B., (1933), *Benares*, Calcutta: Thacker Spink.

Imam, Z., (1975), *Muslims in India*, New Delhi: Orient Longman.

Jeffery, R. & P., (1994), 'The Bijnor Riots: Collapse of a Mythical Special Relationship', *Economic and Political Weekly*, Vol. xxix, No. 10:551–558.

Juergensmeyer, M., (1982), *Religion as Social Vision*, California: California University Press.

Juyal, B.N., (1970), 'Communal Riot and Communal Politics: Case Study of a Town', in M. Rafiq-Khan, (ed.), *National Integration: its Meaning and Relevance*, Varanasi Navachetna Prakashan for the Gandhian Institute of Studies.

Kelly, E., (1990), 'Transcontinental Families – Gujerat and Lancashire: a Comparative Study', in C. Clarke, C. Peach & S. Vertovec, (eds), *South Asians Overseas*, Cambridge: Cambridge University Press.

Kumar, N., (1988), *The Artisans of Banaras: Popular Culture and Identity 1880–1896*, Princeton: Princeton University Press.

Mason, P., (1967), *India and Ceylon: Unity and Diversity*, Oxford: Oxford University Press.

Macdonald, S., (ed.), (1993), *Inside European Identities: Ethnography in Western Europe*, Oxford: Berg.

Miles, R., (1989), *Racism*, London: Routledge.

Nesbitt, E., (1990), 'Pitfalls in Religious Taxonomy – Hindus, Sikhs, Ravidasis and Valmikis', *Religion Today*, Spring.

Noorani, A.G., (1989), 'The Babri-Masjid – Ram Janma bhoomi Question', *Economic and Political Weekly*, November: 2461–2466.

Ostor, A., (1984), *Culture and Power: Legend Ritual, Bazaar and Rebellion in Bengali Society*, New Delhi: Sage.

Pandey, G., (1983), 'Rallying round the cow', in R. Guha, (ed.), *Subaltern Studies*, 2.

Rex, J., (1991), *Ethnic Identity and Mobilisation in Britain*, Coventry: Centre for Research in Ethnic Relations.

Robinson, F., (1974), *Separatism Among Indian Muslims*, Cambridge: Cambridge University Press.

Robinson, F., (1983), 'Islam and Muslim Society in South Asia', *Contributions to Indian Sociology*, 17:185–203.

Rudolph, L. & Rudolph, S., (1987), *In Pursuit of Lakshmi: the Political Economy of the Indian State*, Chicago: University of Chicago Press.

Saberwal, S. & Hasan, M., (1984), 'Moradabad Riots 1980: Causes and Meanings', in A.A. Engineer (ed.), *Communal Riots in Post-Independence India*, London: Sangam.

Saxena, N.C., (1984), 'The Nature and Origin of Communal Riots in India', in A.A. Engineer, (ed.), as above.

Searle-Chatterjee, M., (1994a), 'Urban Untouchables and Hindu Nationalism', *Immigrants and Minorities*, Vol. 13, No. 1.

Searle-Chatterjee, M., (1994b), 'Wahabi Sectarianism among Muslims of Banaras', *Contemporary South Asia*, forthcoming.

Sebastian, P.A., (1993), 'Peoples' Commission Report on Bombay Riots', *Economic and Political Weekly*, Vol. XXVIII, No. 42:2256–57.

Sharma, R.S., (1958), *Sudras in Ancient India*, Delhi: Banarsidass.

Sheth, P., (1993), 'Degeneration of a City', *Economic and Political Weekly*, XXVIII, No. 5.

Sherring, M., (1896), repr. 1975, *Benares the Sacred City*, Delhi: B.R. Publishing.

Smith, D.E., (ed.), (1966), *South Asian Politics and Religion*, Princeton: Princeton University Press.

Sukul, K.N., (1977), *Varanasi Vaibhav*, Patna: Rashtra bhasha Parishad.

Tajfel, H., (ed.), (1982), *Social Identity and Inter-Group Relations*, Cambridge: Cambridge University Press.

Tharpar, R., (1989), 'Imagined Religious Communities, Ancient History and the Search for a Hindu Identity', *Modern Asian Studies*, 23:2.

Weiner, M., (1978), *Sons of the Soil*, Princeton: Princeton University Press.

Newspapers

The Pioneer, 1986 November 7–19, Lucknow.

Caste – a personal perspective

A. Shukra (pseudonym)

Abstract

The author, a member of the Dalit caste of Chamars, describes and analyses his own experience of caste. He recalls that a sense of his own low caste identity was impressed upon him at a very early age, especially at school. Yet the practice of the high castes was not always consistent and inflexible – a low caste person who has influence or whose skills are sought after might be offered hypocritical respect. In any case the high caste view of the low castes is not internalised by the latter, especially those who have been influenced by the modern Dalit movement. Caste consciousness and behaviour pervades all communities in India in some form; it is not a monopoly of Hindus.

When the author came to Britain at an early age he was initially more concerned by the effects of racism, but soon found that castism was as strong among Indians living in Britain as in India. This is not always made explicit, but most Asian organisations are in fact caste-based. If anything, this castism is stronger than it was in the early days of Indian settlement in Britain when migrants were more inclined to share facilities with each other. Even those who did not practise caste openly effectively support the institution by marginalising the issue of caste intellectually and politically. The only explanatory model which can make sense of the contradictions in Indian society is a model of groups with conflicting interests which however survives because of the capacity of the thin cement of Brahminism to hide the rifts in the structure.

A personal perspective

Caste is a complex phenomenon; this much is agreed by students of the caste system. There are many tools available for analysing caste; economic, social, political, religious, anthropological, etc.

or a combination of any of these. The writer lacks formal qualifications in any of the above fields. However my interest in the
caste system goes back some twenty odd years. Having had a
personal involvement in the debate raging about the caste system;
I feel I have something to contribute to understanding of some
aspects of the caste system. But first some details of my background.

I hail from the *Ravidasi* community, commonly referred to by
the so called high caste Hindus and Sikhs as *Chamars.*[1] I say 'so
called' since no *Dalit*[2] I have met, and I have met them from all
corners of India, remotely thinks that the others are superior to
them. They may envy others their wealth, education etc. but I
have yet to come across a *Dalit* who thinks that people are born
superior and inferior. Many of them may believe in the karma
theory but not in the Brahminical sense. It is not the *Dalits* who
have a belief in the concept of untouchability, it is the high castes
who have this problem.

For me it is a question of identity. We *Dalits* are an 'invisible'
community, not only in India but also in the UK. The non-*Dalits*
tend to be dominant here also and these are the people who tend
to monopolise all the jobs that require interfacing with the host
English community. Hence a plethora of books have been produced dealing with the Hindus, the Sikhs and the Muslims. But
on *Dalits*, both here and in India, there is painfully little.
Everything in books both here and in India tends to deny the
existence of the identity of *Dalit* people. Most scholars dealing
with caste issues also tend to take the explanations offered by the
other Indians at their face value, ie there is no caste system
amongst the Sikhs or the Muslims, caste does not exist in the
UK, etc. To my knowledge very few anthropologists have really
taken up the question of how the thinking section of the *Dalit*
community perceives itself.

The earliest I had to deal with the identity question was at the
village high school at the age of 11. The declaration of religion
on the school's paperwork led the Brahmin teacher to ask if *Adi
Dharam*[3] meant *Adharam* (meaning no religion) or *Adi Dharam*
(meaning Ancient Religion). The Brahmin teacher more than
anyone else must have known and appreciated what *Adi Dharam*
meant. After all Brahminism is only a veneer, at times a fairly
thin one at that, on top of the ancient beliefs and practices. In
the village school this amounted to castist baiting. I found his
chiding very offensive. Even at this early age I could have

answered back but decided that it would be too risky. It was at this point that not being able to answer back and out of frustration I lost my native Indian absolute faith in teachers. I consider this a lucky co-incidence. If it had not happened I might never have lost my naive belief in teachers in general and thus acquired a belief in myself.

From a very early age I began to realise that the rules of caste, untouchability etc. were not static but pliable. It was dependent on who was applying it in what situation. For example both my father and one of my uncles faced the untouchability problem at school. Both had to sit separately from the class, often outside the classroom. However once they obtained their qualifications and obtained jobs their high caste contemporaries started to treat them as normal. The justification was that their house was very clean. This I felt was only an excuse for many people to get my father's services as someone who not only could read and write three Indian languages but also English. I was also to find out that the rules of untouchability were complex and hypocritical. There were wells in my own village and in other villages where, as a *Dalit* you could not get water to drink. I still remember one household, one of whose members had refused to let me drink water from their water-pot in the field during the harvest season. However a few years later the same family sought my help in tutoring one of their sons with his studies. On that occasion I was fed like an honoured guest. Lest there is some doubt in the reader's mind about the way the high castes try to justify the practice of untouchability let me provide a further example. One of our distant relatives was a wandering minstrel, a professional singer. I was allowed to accompany him on one of his tours of the adjoining villages. What stuck in my mind was that we, members of one of the most polluting castes around, were treated as if we were royalty. Our presence brought prestige to the household we were staying at. Indeed my 'uncle' had to be very diplomatic in turning down the invitations, as he was unwittingly put in a situation where he could decide who the most prestigious family in the village was.

Many such incidents made me realise that most of what the high castes said about the practice of untouchability and the caste system was untrue. I never believed that the *Jats*,[4] one of the land owning castes, were any better fighters or braver than the *Chamars* as the *Jats* had often asserted. It was only a question of time and place. My subsequent experiences were to prove that I was right. I was to find much later the part played by *Dalits* in the development of such militant religions as Sikhism and the *Satnami* movement. I found it difficult to believe that the high castes could be genetically or otherwise educationally superior to us as I was the brightest in my class. As for their supposed intellectual superiority, I find it rather amusing. It is no co-incidence that Hindu society did not produce a Voltaire-like figure.

Lest I create an impression that I somehow developed these ideas on my own, I have to confess that both my maternal grandfather and my maternal uncle helped me to see things in a certain way. Both of these men were very radical for their day. Without their support I doubt if I could ever have become the person I am. They had the experience of *Adi Dharam* and Ambedkar's[5] movement behind them. One of the things that I noticed later on in my life was that both of these movements, very important in the North Indian setting, were more or less completely ignored by the western scholars. This is not surprising as these writers hardly ever address the future of India in serious terms. The future of India and the future of the *Dalits* is inter-linked.

My second recollection of identity formation is the time my family moved to Bootan Mandi, a *Dalit* suburb of Jalandhar city. I did not grasp the significance of Bootan Mandi till I came to the UK and studied the history of the Ravidasi community. In the early 1930s and '40s this was the centre of the *Adi Dharam* movement and later, in the '60s and '70s, of Ambedkarism in the Punjab. People whose business mainly involved leather work[6], were nevertheless, comparatively speaking, fairly well off. Not only that but I found that in the city environment it was difficult for people to subject you to overt castism. Furthermore in the village school I was exposed to Sikhism but in the city where the Hindus predominated I had the chance to learn about their religion. There were people in Bootan Mandi who belonged to the *Radha Soami*[7] sect and there were other suburbs where Muslims predominated. I was lucky enough to be exposed to all these places, otherwise I feel that like most people brought up in India I too would have developed a tunnel vision of convenience and hypocrisy. But more than anything, *Ambedkarism* taught me to question everything. I have sometimes pondered on the question of why did not more people in my community turn out like me. The answer, it seems to me, is a combination of factors. My maternal grandfather's family was comfortably well off. The family, although untouchables, owned a village shop! In fact my maternal grandfather owned a number of shops. We would be mildly amused at times at my mother's recollections of how the high caste customers would leave the money at the door and take the goods left there.

On my father's side, he and one of his brothers did manage to go as far as the tenth grade. This was something of an achievement for them, as they had to sit outside the classroom. My father's best friend of life, whilst recounting old times, would not spare even the Muslims. 'They would invite me to their weddings etc. because I could sing the *Koran* beautifully, but I would be told to sit away from the others, when it came to eating' was his frequent lament. He could forgive the Hindus, and the Sikhs, who were after all ex-Hindus, but the Muslims became the object of his pity. He should not have felt like this. Caste is not a unique Hindu phenomenon, it is part of Indian society, Hindu, Muslim or Christian. In this sense it acts like a class cutting across religious boundaries. Besides, most of the Indian Muslims are ex-Hindu converts anyway.

I was born in Poona, in Maharashtra state, but of Punjabi parents. Having been born in Poona is a good talking point when meeting educated Indians. I was given a Sikh name by my father who perhaps felt that it would be advantageous not to be openly known as a *Dalit*. In this he was absolutely right. When young I also had *OM*[8] tattooed on my right hand for a bet, without realising that this too could unwittingly allow me to pass off as a so called high caste Hindu. These factors in themselves are minor. A keen knowledge of both Hindu and Sikh folklore has proved indispensable to gain confidence in a number of situations. The knowledge of the former I acquired from a number of sources, from my maternal uncle's town, where the Hindus were in the majority, and from another large town where novels and books could be hired for the day, which I could afford since my father was in England. From the stay in my father's village and attending a Sikh high school I was exposed to Sikhism which I found very attractive, since by this time both my father and my older brother had left for the UK and this created a vacuum in my life. Not having a mentor, I found that I could indulge myself in acquiring as much knowledge as possible. But the problem of knowledge also created another problem. How was I able to explain the internal fantastic contradictions of Hinduism and the day-to-day behaviour of the 'caste free' *Jat* Sikhs? While I was living in a large town, which was the centre of activities of the Republican Party of India, two aspects must have had a significant influence on me. One was the campaign by the Republic Party of India, in which both my mother and I attended demonstrations where people willingly courted arrests. This exposed me to Ambedkarism. Secondly I came across a holy man named Lal Bawa who was to undertake a fast unto death which was later called off, by the request of the RPI leadership. In my later experiences I came to realise that there was no artificial Chinese wall between caste, politics and religion in India.

In the school in the UK I found no real castist behaviour. We were all too busy defending ourselves against the racist taunts of the white boys. Things are actually worse these days, I am informed by the *Dalit* children. Born and brought up in the UK, many of them find castist insults very emotionally disturbing. In the UK I undertook an engineering apprenticeship in the foundries of the West Midlands. This proved to be another eye opener. Caste feelings were very strong with the best jobs being zealously monopolised by the Punjabi *Jats*. Being a technical apprentice I was an outsider, presumed a *Jat* by other *Jats*. This gave me a chance to study the caste conflict in the British climate. In and out of the factory the castes are separated, each caste having its own place of worship. This was not always so. In the '50s and '60s people of different castes shared houses, cooked for each other, even shared the same bed under a rota system. This however changed when the womenfolk started to arrive from India and the system reproduced itself with some interesting variations, tailored to British conditions.

It is a truism that an outsider cannot really know the inside story. However the outsider does possess some degree of objectivity although this itself may be conditioned by his or her background. In this the non-Indian sociologists and anthropologists are better than their counterparts. There is no substitute for firsthand experience, however. An English friend of mine, who was doing his PhD thesis in India, unwittingly found himself 'excommunicated' and treated like an untouchable, after attending a 'low caste' wedding. He confided to me that after that incident he began to look at his own work in a different light. Many thousands of miles away, ten years later, I found that the wife of a *Gujerati* friend of mine will not drink water or eat food at my house. My friend himself had in the past asked me *not* to declare my caste to his son or daughter either, both of whom are graduates of British universities. I had known about the practice of untouchability and caste taboos in the UK but this experience brought home to me the depth of these feelings, even in the second generation. It is a well known fact that nearly every caste-grouping has its own organisation or temple and strict caste divisions are observed when arranging marriages.

Most Asian organisations are caste based. The control exists even in community organisations up to and beyond the local council level. The degree of control exercised by these caste groups did not become clear to me till I, together with some English friends, tried to persuade the local library to stock books by Dr B.R. Ambedkar. The types of excuses used by the 'high caste' officials to justify refusal would be laughed at if it was a race question. Six years later we have given up the effort. That this can happen in a borough which has declared anti-racist policies is more of a revelation. Even more shocking was the revelation that a very respected journal on race did not want to know about this. It is not only the people in power who behave like this. In a research group that I belong to I have found very strong tendencies to marginalise the caste issue and sometimes to deny it altogether. Interestingly enough my English colleagues have always been very sympathetic whilst the greatest hostility has come from the supposedly caste-free Sikhs. Again my personal experience, and that of my white English friends, of the Indian political left in the UK is that it is so riddled with castism that it merits a study in its own right as to the reason for the enduring power of the caste system.

All this is not really surprising at the end of the day. There is no liberal tradition in India. If there are supposedly groups of people who suffer from a guilt complex, then Indian society forces people to be the polar opposite. Keen observers of Indian society may have noticed the *degree* of prevailing hypocrisy. They are not mistaken in this. Even writers critical of the caste system, writing for the western audience, try to portray the image of a well lubricated, co-operative and harmonious society providing peace and contentment all around. The Indian caste system is viewed by the *Dalits* as the largest Apartheid system in the world. Indian intellectuals both in India and the UK have found that the best policy of defence is attack. Hence, silence, denial, justification and many times downright dishonesty are resorted to. Four years ago, I had a chance to talk to the cast of a famous drama group who had performed a play about the untouchables in ancient India. It came as somewhat of a shock to me that they saw the play in terms of anti racist work, to illustrate racism in British society. They did not think that there was any caste problem in the UK or indeed in India. This group has credentials as *the Indian left* drama group in this country.

In the UK I was to realise that most of the things that I had read about caste did not seem to fit with the reality as I had experienced it. Secular countries such as UK ought not to be able to sustain caste, but here it was in some ways stronger than in India. This is the feeling of many visitors that I have come across from India.

Much later I was to find out that it was not what the books told you that was important. It was the contradictions in the arguments that were more important. There was a whole range of subjects which did not make sense if one went by the Brahminical or sociological explanation of things. The low caste people appeared not to have any history at all. Yet there was no need to invent one. It was there all right, and there was no need to throw away everything and start from scratch. In some instances it merely needed a critical approach but in others the truth had to be stood on its head. A functional, or a structural approach was the least effective way of approaching the issue. A model of groups with conflicting interests is the only model I know which can explain all the peculiarities of the caste system. The caste system is supposedly an *Aryan* invention, and yet the *Aryans* went to other countries[9] without reproducing this system there. The cause must therefore be uniquely Indian. Race, discredited as a concept in anthropology, is another red herring that is sometimes used to explain the caste system. Black Brahmins and fair skinned untouchables are not uncommon. What is more important is that the history of Brahmins is only a fraction of the history of India and at times it is distorted history. What they call history is a veneer on top of the development of the Indian history and culture. What is underneath is the real thing.

The best way to view the caste system is to view Indian society as a flexible matrix, a sort of invisible ether in which the economic, social, religious, and increasingly political forces can influence the society without causing rupture of the basic fabric of society. That is not to say that minor ruptures and scars are not there. These have been repaired so skilfully that it is difficult to say if there has been any damage to the mosaic. Only a close critical viewing will reveal the thin cement known as Brahminism and this too has changed over the years!

Will I stop 'passing' myself and one day declare what I am, for example in my office? The answer must be a definitive *no*. From my bitter experience and that of my friends I know what happens when people find out about your caste. I know it is the society which is to blame, but for me I have only one life to live. I must choose my own battleground for struggle and it is not the workplace, at least not in the UK. Besides passing myself off as someone else allows me to be a 'fly on the wall' in the Asian community and understand it much better than any other 'outsider'.

I look to the future with apprehension for my two year old son. In this I am perhaps no different from other Asians in the UK who face similar problems. But there is a crucial difference. My community, according to the socialists and sociologists alike, does not even exist. There are Hindus, Sikhs, Jains but no *Dalits*. There are no text books on the history, tradition, culture etc. of my community. People have neither time nor education to write books that require such Herculean effort. From my personal experiences I know that my son will face a similar if not worse kind of castism, more confusing and hence psychologically more insidious. He may decide to drop out of the Indian culture altogether if he gets disgusted with it beyond limits. That would be a pity as above the stinking Indian society lies the lotus flower of an alternative tradition which is comparable with the best in the world. My next main project will have to be to write the history of the *Dalit* people for the ordinary public.

Notes

1 A pan-North Indian caste of leather workers. The word Chamar is about as offensive as the word 'nigger'.
2 Literally means 'oppressed' – a word most so-called low-caste people like to use to describe themselves as it conveys a more universal and defiant meaning.
3 A Punjabi socio-political self respect movement of this century whose basic purpose was to fight for the human rights of the so-called untouchable groups.
4 Mostly Sikh landlords or rich peasants – the major dominant caste in the Punjab countryside.
5 Dr B.R. Ambedkar, the first law minister of independent India and the best known twentieth century *Dalit* leader. Ambedkarism is the core of the pan-Indian *Dalit* philosophy.
6 Considered ritually highly polluting by Hindu tradition.

7 A sect whose members profess to follow the teachings of North Indian Bhaktas and the Sikh Gurus. The members are keen on vegetarianism and are theoretically anti-caste. The reality is somewhat different as the sect in reality is a Rotary club for the upwardly mobile people of all castes.

8 A sacred Hindu utterance.

9 For example the Romans, Greeks, Slavs, Teutons and the Hittites all have Aryan roots.

Notes on contributors

Robert Deliège, after a Diploma and M. Litt in social anthropology at Oxford University, did two years of fieldwork in South India and was later awarded a doctorate at the University of Louvain. His main publications include a monograph of a South Indian village, *Les Paraiyars du Tamil Nadu* (Studia Instituti Anthropos Nr 42, Nettetal, Steyler Verlag, 1988) and a *'Que sais-je?'* book on caste, *Le système des castes* (Paris, Presses Universitaires de France, 1993). He has just completed a general study of Indian 'untouchables'. He teaches social anthropology at the University of Louvain, Louvain-La-Neuve, Belgium.

Subrata Mitra is currently visiting Professor to the Chair in Indian Studies, University of California, Berkeley, and was a Senior Lecturer in Politics and Director of the Centre for Indian Studies at the University of Hull. His main interests are: India and comparative politics, rational choice and local elites. His most recent book is *Power, Protest and Participation* (Routledge, 1992). He has been appointed to the Chair of Political Science at the South Asia Institute, University of Heidelberg.

Declan Quigley is Lecturer in Social Anthropology at the Queen's University of Belfast. He is author of *The Interpretation of Caste* (Oxford: Clarendon Press, 1993) and co-editor of the forthcoming ethnography *Newar Society: Caste and the Social Order in the Kathmandu Valley* (also Clarendon Press). He has spent four years carrying out fieldwork among Hindu communities in Nepal. After completing his PhD at the London School of Economics, he held a Leverhulme Study Abroad Scholarship while affiliated to the Centre for Nepal and Asian Studies at Tribhuvan University, Kathmandu. This was followed by a British Academy postdoctoral fellowship and a subsequent two year lectureship at the University of Cambridge. He is currently working on a book on monarchies.

Mary Searle-Chatterjee is Senior Lecturer in Applied Community Studies at Manchester Metropolitan University. After reading English and philosophy at Nottingham University, she was awarded a Commonwealth Scholarship to study philosophy at Banaras (Varanasi). Subsequently, she studied social anthropology at Manchester University, then was awarded a PhD in Sociology by the University of Banaras, where she lectured for four years. She has also lectured at the University of Bristol in the Theology Department and the University of Manchester in the History Department. She is the author of *Reversible Sex Roles: the special case of the Banaras Sweepers* (Pergamon, 1981) and has published more than a dozen papers, mainly on urban 'untouchables' and low status Muslims.

Ursula Sharma is Reader in Sociology and Social Anthropology at Keele University. She has carried out fieldwork in various parts of North West India, mainly on Hindu ritual and on gender divisions of labour. She has published two monographs on the basis of this work: *Women, Work and Property in North West India* (1980) and *Women's Work, Class and the Urban Household* (1985) (both published by Tavistock). Her most recent work concerns medical anthropology.

A. Shukra was born in Poona, Maharashtra, of Punjabi parents. He spent much of his childhood in the Punjab before emigrating to Britain at the age of fourteen. He is an activist in the Dalit movement and has written polemical articles in various magazines and newspapers. Some of these have been translated into other South Asian and South East Asian languages. He holds a professional post in the UK. (A. Shukra is a pseudonym).

Maya Unnithan received her doctoral degree in social anthropology from the University of Cambridge in 1991. Currently she is a Lecturer in Social Anthropology at the School of African and Asian Studies, University of Sussex. Her research interests include kinship, family and gender relations in India, economic anthropology and popular religion.

Index

Adi Dharam movement, 45, 170, 172
Adi Dravida movement, 45
Alavi, H., 21
All India Depressed Classes Federation, 45
Ambedkar, B.R., 37, 172, 175
Ambedkarism, 172, 174
Andhra Pradesh, 156, 163
Anop Mandal, 116
Appadurai, A., 2
Ardener, S., 86

Baden Powell, B.H., 112, 113
Baechler, J., 35
Bahujan Samaj Party, 61
Bailey, F.G., 76, 94
Banfield, E.C., 12
Baykan, A., 10, 11
Becker, H., 79
beliefs, 58–9
Benedict, Ruth, 81
Berreman, G., 11, 31, 51, 57, 72–89, 125
Béteille, A., 1, 17, 18, 31, 36, 37, 44, 57, 94, 124
Bharat Seva Sangh, 148
Bharatiya Janara Party, 148, 154
Bhil tribe, 94, 95, 106
  and Rajputs, 108–17
Bihar, 158, 163
Boddy, Janice, 14
Bombay, 152, 163
Bootan Mandi, 172
Brahmans, 7, 30, 65, 87, 127, 165
  caste identity of, 18–19, 31–2
  Dumont on, 33, 78, 79
  as priests, 27–8, 33, 59
Brass, P., 158
Brundavana Nagara Socio-Economic and Cultural Development Trust, 65–6

Buddhism, 37, 39, 160
Burakamin, 76
Burghart, R., 1, 79, 89n.

caste, 170, 175–6
  Dumont on, 2, 3–6, 32–5, 98
  language of, 7, 8
  theories of, 26–43
  and tribes, 7–8, 93–4
caste associations, 61, 65–6, 67
centralisation, territorial, 39, 40, 42
chamars, 64, 155, 161, 170, 177n.
Chambers, E., 51
Chauhan, B.R., 94
Chettiars, 127
Chhachhi, A., 115
Chinoy, E., 26
Christians, 56, 131, 132, 161, 163
Civil Rights Act, 63
class, 13–14, 17–20, 53–4
Cohen, B., 112
colonialism, 60, 69, 112–13
community formation, 66–7, 68
comparison, 76, 81–5
conflict, 150–1, 152, 153–60, 164
Congress Party of India, 45, 154, 157
Constitution of India, 62–3, 69
Coomarswamy, Ananda, 70n.
Copland, I., 113
Cox, O.C., 75
cultures, 81–8

Dalits, 9, 170, 172
Dave, P.C., 114
deference, 74–5, 77, 85
Delhi, 160
Deliège, R., 14, 43, 44, 87, 110
democracy, 16–17, 52, 61, 69, 124
Den Ouden, J., 139
Derrett, D., 59, 70n.

Index

Deschamps, J.C., 16
Dirks, N., 43, 44, 45
Donnan, H., 84
Douglas, Mary, 82
Dumont, L., 2, 3–6, 7, 9, 21n., 33–5,
    42, 44, 117n., 125
  and Berreman, 78–81
  Homo Hierarchicus, 2, 28, 29, 123
  and tribes, 97–9

Eck, D., 157
egalitarianism, 14, 93, 124
Epstein, S., 143
essentialism, 51–8

family, 17–20, 36
Fox, R., 54, 110
Frankel, F., 57
Freeman, J., 16
Freitag, S., 156
Fuller, C.J., 45, 117n.

Gaborieux, M., 149
Gandhi, M.K., 53
Gawa, 83
Gellner, D.N., 39, 83, 108, 125
gender, and kinship, 95, 101–8
Ghanyari, 18–19
Giddens, A., 11, 26, 27
Girasias, 101–17
Goffman, E., 74, 75
Good, A., 45
Goody, J., 81, 82
Gosains, 156, 157
Gough, K., 140
Gould, H., 58
Gujerat, 151–2, 163

Hall, J.A., 35
Hamilton, M., 42n.
Harijans, 122, 138–9
Havell, E.B., 157
hierarchy, 3, 7, 14, 55, 93, 122, 123
  and democracy, 61–2
  low castes and, 15–16
Hinduism, 35, 36, 51, 52–3, 132,
    173
  caste unique to, 3, 35, 36, 51, 52
  and Muslims, 152–65
  sectarian divisions in, 150
  and Sikhs, 151
Hirszowicz, M., 42n.
Hocart, A.M., 25, 36, 42, 98, 99
Hutton, J.H., 51
Hyderabad, 151, 163
Hymes, D., 88

Inden, R., 5, 6, 9, 45, 55, 56, 67, 124–5
India, 4, 8, 75, 76–7, 175, 176
  caste and community in, 18–19, 50,
    51–70
  shared culture in, 85, 86
  intercaste relations, 126–9, 130–1
  izzat (honour), 14

Jamia Salfia, 148
Jan Sangh, 148, 150
Japanese, 5
jath lineage, 102–4, 105
jatis, 3–4, 27, 28, 50, 65, 69, 93, 148,
    165
Jats, 151, 171, 174
Jeffrey, P. and R., 84
Juergensmeyer, M., 44, 162

Kallars, 127–9
Kanda Devi festival, 128–9
Kangra, 110–11
Kathmandu Valley, 38–9
kingship, 25, 34, 42, 59, 98
kinship, 92–3, 94–5, 96, 101
  and affinity, 133–7
  of Girasias, 101–17
Klass, M., 35
Kolenda, P., 45
Kothari, R., 115, 124
Kroeber, A.L., 51
Kuper, A., 124

Lal Bawa, 174
Leach, E.R., 32, 76, 80
Leibniz, G.W., 4
Levi-Strauss, C., 3, 96–7, 98, 100,
    117n., 118n.
Levinson, S.C., 85
Levy, R., 28
Lewis, O., 12
lineages, 39, 41
  in Girasia kinship, 102–5, 110–11
Lingayat, 65
Lok Dal, 61
Lyon, A., 84

Macfarlane, Alan, 44
Mahabrahmans, 33
Mandal Commission, 17, 151–2
market transactions, 64–6
marriage, 17, 97, 110–11, 118n.
  and gender roles, 104–8
  Tamil, 135–7
Marriott, M., 117n.
Mason, P., 156
Meherda, B.I., 114

182

Index